Rhetorical Poetics

RHETORICAL POETICS

Theory and Practice of Figural and Symbolic
Reading in Modern French Literature

DONALD RICE
and
PETER SCHOFER

THE UNIVERSITY OF WISCONSIN PRESS

Published 1983

The University of Wisconsin Press
114 North Murray Street
Madison, Wisconsin 53715

The University of Wisconsin Press, Ltd.
1 Gower Street
London WC1E 6HA, England

First Printing

Printed in the United States of America

For LC CIP information see the colophon

ISBN 0–299–09440–5

Permission to excerpt from *Circus* by Maurice Roche has been given by the
author.

To Yvonne and Mary,
who endured the long and the short
of tropes and figures

Contents

vii

Contents   ix

Preface

From the time of the ancient Greeks, rhetoric and poetics have been tightly intertwined. For Aristotle, poetry was a counterpart (antistrophe) of rhetoric. Horace believed that poetry and rhetoric had a common end, didacticism (persuasion). Both Cicero and his follower Quintilian made liberal use of poetic examples to illustrate their principles of rhetoric. Renaissance poetics mingled Aristotle's poetic terminology with Ciceronian rhetorical vocabulary, a mix which one finds again today in the works of Northrop Frye.[1]

If rhetoric has continued to play a central role in literary theory, the nature of that role has changed over the centuries. Gérard Genette has admirably described the evolution of rhetoric from a full description of elocution to what he has termed "la rhétorique restreinte" [limited rhetoric] found in contemporary literary studies.[2] Ancient rhetoric sought to teach the arts of invention, arrangement, style, memory, and delivery. As deliberative oratory declined in importance, the major emphasis switched to *elocutio* (style), and specifically to figural language. The two major rhetorical treatises in French, Dumarsais's *Des Tropes* (1730) and Fontanier's *Traité général des figures du discours* (1821), deal exclusively with the figures of discourse. More important, at the heart of their discussions are tropes: eighteen varieties in Dumarsais, reduced to only three in Fontanier. The tendency to limit more and more the scope of rhetoric, in general, and the

---

1. *Princeton Encyclopedia of Poetry and Poetics*, ed. Alex Preminger (Princeton: Princeton University Press, 1965), pp. 702–5.
2. Gérard Genette, *Figures III* (Paris: Editions du Seuil, 1972), pp. 21–41.

xi

number of tropes, in particular, has continued; as Genette points out, for many modern theorists, there exists only one basic trope: "the secular movement of rhetorical reduction seems thus to lead to an absolute valorization of metaphor, linked to the idea of an essential metaphoricity of poetic language—and of language in general."[3] This ultimate reduction is reflected in the many discussions of metaphors, or even more loosely of images, which, from the time of the Romantics and on into this century, reveal little or no knowledge of the origins of the terms and of their relationship to ancient rhetoric.

In the past fifteen years, however, French scholars and critics have shown a renewed interest in the ancient rhetoric, a conscious desire to reintegrate it into modern theories of literature, and a concomitant rediscovery of some of the "lost tropes." Part of the impetus for this revival can be attributed to the republication in 1968 of Fontanier's *Les Figures du discours.*[4] This "classical manual for the study of tropes" was used during the nineteenth century in French *lycées* to help students in the humanities read and appreciate written classical texts. More generally, it was also considered to be "indispensable for knowledge of the mind [*esprit*] and the artifices of language" (p. 31). Fontanier assumed that the artifices of language could be fully understood and that tropes and figures could be "translated" into perfectly comprehensible terms. In other words, his work appealed to the students' "raison" and gave them the tools for decoding literary language, which, when understood as figures and tropes, presented no ambiguities or obstacles to meaning. For students of French literature today his work represents one of the first modern attempts to understand how rhetoric works.[5] It is also an

3. Genette, *Figures III*, p. 36.
4. Pierre Fontanier, *Les Figures du discours* (Paris: Editions Flammarion, 1968).
5. Of course Fontanier was not alone nor without predecessors, such as Dumarsais (*Les Tropes*, 1730), d'Alembert (*Mélanges de littérature, d'histoire, et de philosophie*, 1767), and Beauzée (*Dictionnaire de grammaire et de littérature*, 1782) in France; Vico (*La Scienza nuova*, 1725) in Italy; and Dugald Stewart (*Philosophical Essays*, 1810) in England. In our own generation, research along the lines of a more classical definition of rhetoric continues at almost all major universities.

invaluable catalogue of rhetorical terms as they were inherited from antiquity and used in nineteenth century France.

The reedition of *Les Figures du discours* also threw new light on another landmark in the development of modern rhetorical poetics—Roman Jakobson's "Two Aspects of Language and Two Types of Aphasia," first published in 1956.[6] More than one hundred years after Fontanier this article recast the ancient rhetoric into a new model for language, where rhetorical operations could be studied within a binary system of either the metaphorical (similarity) or the metonymic (contiguity). His seminal work displaced tropes and figures from being mere "artifices" of literary language to being at the very center of language functions, as the primary axes of language. At the same time, because of the vastness of his enterprise and its scientific orientation, literature became subordinate to a larger linguistic model, and the "reader" was objectified into a scientific point of view. Generally, studies on rhetorical poetics since Jakobson have retained the pose of scientific objectivity and have looked at rhetoric from the perspective of the writer and the text.

While it is possible to see a continuity and evolution between Fontanier's *Les Figures du discours* and Jakobson's article on aphasia, a relationship underlined by the retrospective glance that the reedition of the Fontanier text offered, during this span of time the practice of writing underwent drastic changes with far-reaching implications for the rhetoric of the text and the role of the reader. At approximately the same moment as Fontanier catalogued encoded figures and tropes, French writers appeared to

---

See, for example, Eugene E. White's collection of essays, *Rhetoric in Transition: Studies in the Nature and Uses of Rhetoric* (University Park: Pennsylvania State University Press, 1980) and *La Nouvelle Rhétorique: Traité de l'argumentation* by Charles Perleman and L. Olbrecht-Tyteca (Paris: Presses universitaires de France, 1958). H. P. Grice's work, such as "Logic and Conversation," in *Syntax and Semantics* (ed. P. Cole and J. L. Morgan, New York: Academic Press, 1975), falls between the classical and the contemporary literary approaches to rhetoric, but his findings open up the possibility of bridging the gap between the two.

6. Roman Jakobson, "Two Aspects of Language and Two Types of Aphasic Disturbance" in Roman Jakobson and M. Hall, *Fundamentals of Language* (The Hague: Mouton, 1956).

discard classical Euclidian rhetoric.[7] But Hugo's famous declaration that he had put his "bonnet rouge" on the "vieux dictionnaire" and had chased rhetoric from the printed page did not
really mark an end to rhetoric; rather it announced rhetoric's
transformation from a highly encoded part of literary language
to the individual pursuit of what Francis Ponge has called "personal rhetoric." It has become a commonplace in recent years to
write that French literature since 1850 has introduced ambiguity,
polysemia, open texts, and writing on writing. But little study
has been devoted to the place of rhetoric in this transformation
of literature. If, as Jakobson asserted, rhetorical processes are at
the center of language processes, it follows that the changes in
literary writing came about because of a new consciousness of
what Baudelaire termed "la rhétorique profonde" of the text. As
Hugo perceived, this new rhetoric cast into the shadows the notion of a universal rhetoric easily learned and decoded by educated readers. The growing complexity and difficulty of literary
texts demanded new approaches by readers and, eventually, a
new interest in the role of the reader. Whereas ancient rhetoric
taught speakers the rules of public address, modern rhetorical
practice has created a new literature which asks the reader to
participate constantly in the construction of texts, and to discover in the texts themselves the rules for reading and understanding.

It is not surprising that modern literature would engender
a new movement in criticism which also looks closely at the act
of reading with the aim of formulating new conventions for
reading. The plethora of works in both Europe and the United
States attests to the importance of examining literature from the
point of view of the reading process. It is surprising, however,
that very few of these works consider rhetorical processes as an
integral part of reading. For example, in those sections of *The
Role of the Reader* which treat directly the question of reading,
Umberto Eco devotes a mere three lines to rhetoric, as "stylistic

7. See John Mowitt's "Towards a Non-Euclidean Rhetoric: Lautréamont
and Ponge," *Sub-Stance* 30 (1981), where Ponge is quoted as distinguishing between an old rhetoric based on "figures of the old geometry, of Euclidean geometry" and a new rhetoric freed of the Euclidean model (p. 64).

overcoding."[8] In his ten-box model for reading there is no mention of rhetoric, figures, or tropes. At the most, American critics such as Stanley Fish, Norman Holland, and E. D. Hirsch give only passing mention to tropes and figures.[9]

Other theoreticians and critics, while not consciously and explicitly adopting a rhetorical approach, might be said to read rhetorically without knowing it. For example, much of Wolfgang Iser's theory of reading is synecdochal and metonymic.[10] The first chapter of *The Act of Reading* is entitled "Partial Art—Total Interpretation," suggesting strongly that Iser's theory is based on the relationship of part to whole. He argues that readers are confronted by "blanks" in a text which must be filled in.[11] The partiality of reading leads Iser to question seriously the objectivity of reading and to shift emphasis from meaning to effect. In rhetorical terms, he proposes a metonymical relationship of cause and effect between text and reader.

At the opposite theoretical pole from Iser's theories of "consistency building," deconstructionist critics are among the few who have most clearly insisted on the importance of rhetorical reading. Derrida has devoted his career to the study and deconstruction of metaphors in philosophical texts, and rhetoric is a keystone in Paul de Man's deconstructive readings. De Man has also made invaluable contributions to situating the work of rhetoric within the general study of semiotics, separating rhetoric

8. Umberto Eco, *The Role of the Reader* (Bloomington: Indiana University Press, 1979), p. 19

9. See, for example, Stanley Fish, *Is There a Text in this Classroom?* (Cambridge: Harvard University Press, 1980); Norman Holland, *The Dynamics of Literary Response* (New York: Oxford University Press, 1968); and E. D. Hirsch, *Validity of Interpretation* (New Haven: Yale University Press, 1967). Hirsch does write of the "metaphorical assimilation" of the author (*Validity*, p. 105), but in *Aims of Interpretation* (Chicago: University of Chicago Press, 1976) he devotes several pages to warning of the dangers of rhetoric in literary criticism (pp. 153–54).

10. These terms are used in the redefined meanings we attribute to them: synecdoche—a relationship of inclusion (part-whole for example), metonymy—a relationship of causality. See Chapter 1 for a complete discussion of tropes.

11. Wolfgang Iser, *The Act of Reading* (Baltimore: Johns Hopkins University Press, 1978), pp. 182–87.

from grammar and the study of grammatical forms.[12] Within the
American schools of criticism which have been influenced by the
French, Harold Bloom's theory of poetry stands out, for example, by its notion of the reader "troping" the text, or "misreading" it.[13] Four of his "revisionary ratios" of reading are the
tropes of metaphor, metonymy, synecdoche, and irony. While it
can be argued that deconstruction (and related approaches such
as Bloom's) represents but a limited theory of reading among
many other theories, there is no question that in its various forms
deconstructive criticism has demonstrated the urgent need to in-
corporate figures and tropes into literary theory and theories of
reading.

　　While not pretending to be deconstructive, *Rhetorical Poetics*
shares the view, expressed by de Man, equating "the rhetorical,
figural potentiality of language with literature itself."[14] The starting
point of this book is that limited rhetoric of which Genette speaks,
the rhetoric of tropes and figures. But whereas ancient and modern rhetoric, both in the restricted and general senses of the term,
have concerned themselves with the speaker and the writer, this
book operates a reversal on the traditional perspective by con-
ducting its analyses from the point of view of the reader. Reading is thus treated here as a fundamentally rhetorical activity: the
reader constructs a text by establishing *figural* and *symbolic traces*,
based on *metaphorical, metonymical, synecdochal,* and *ironic relationships*.

　　In arguing for this approach to reading, *Rhetorical Poetics*
redefines key rhetorical and poetical terms (including those italicized in the preceding sentence). At the same time, the book
argues, implicitly, that the reading of literature reveals most fully
rhetoric at work—not just as a potential, but as the primary force
of the text. In literary texts above all others, language is continually displaced, condensed, twisted, and deformed. In literature
we can see most clearly the effects of figurations and symboli-

---

12. Paul de Man, "Semiology and Rhetoric," *Diacritics* 3 (1973): 27–33.
　　13. Harold Bloom, "The Breaking of Form," in *Deconstruction and Criticism*
(New York: Seabury Press, 1979).
　　14. De Man, "Semiology and Rhetoric," p. 30.

zations, where rhetorical language becomes a second sign system working on and against conventional written language. The reader of literary texts seeks out symbolic levels of meaning more than in reading other texts and comes to expect the literary text to communicate much more than a simple, straightforward message. In fact, a rhetoric of reading is founded on an initial theory of noncommunication. Whereas linguistics sets as a primary goal the study of communication and communication acts, rhetoric looks first at what is not directly communicated in a text. A theory of rhetorical reading accepts the fact that in all texts there are moments of incompatibility, where the reader either does not understand or does not accept what he is reading. In seeking to resolve the incompatibility, the reader comes to interpret the text, to arrive at a plausible meaning.

Rhetorical reading is also what the reader brings to the text. A text by itself, without a reader, is somewhat like the noise created by a tree falling in a forest with no one to hear the sound. The noise, some say, does not exist without a listener. A text does not exist without a reader. At the most, it is a dead, inanimate object which is reactivated and animated by the reader. Without a reader, the text is incomplete, and it is completed only by the intervention of the reader's mind and imagination. A theory of rhetoric, thus, means that texts, with the letters present on the page, are incomplete artifacts. They achieve completion only when the reader provides what is absent. The reader carries to the text a knowledge, a psyche, a culture, which fill in the gaps and the incomplete meanings. Reading implies interpretation, or giving a meaning to the text. The rhetorical process is the gift or the addition of the reader to the incomplete text. The process of addition, or interpretation, can become an endless one. American deconstructionists, in their continual "troping of tropes," illustrate the layers of interpretive gestures which can be added to a text, as readings spiral from the metonymical to the metaphorical and the synecdochal, and finally to the ironies of the ironical. In reading, the question often is to know when to stop adding.

Finally, this book argues that *all* acts of reading literature—whether structuralist, deconstructionist, phenomenological, existential, biographical, New Critical, or historical, and no matter what the genre of the text—are governed by the rhetorical operations of figuration and symbolization. Just as a writer constructs a literary text, the reader constructs a second text by means of metaphor, metonymy, synecdoche, and irony. This construction of an interpretation takes place at all levels of reading. As a reader establishes traces between words, sentences, paragraphs, and larger units of a text, he creates figurations in his mind. Likewise, symbolization inevitably determines the reader's formation of the plot, story, themes, and myths.

Rhetorical Poetics is divided into two parts. Part One represents a theory of rhetorical reading. After an Introduction which reviews and evaluates Jakobson's binary system of metaphor and metonymy, Chapter 1 proposes a redefinition and a reclassification of tropes, arguing that there are four fundamental relationships: metaphorical (similarity), metonymical (causality), synecdochal (inclusion), and ironical (opposition). In Chapter 2 we expand these relationships beyond one-word tropes to include larger and more diverse textual elements: figures, sentences, paragraphs, chapters; characters, setting, story; etc. The first two chapters might be given the general title "How Readers Read Rhetorically without Really Knowing It." The processes described in the two chapters are grounded on a hypothetical reader and present highly encoded figurations and symbolizations which a reasonably competent reader could—and in most cases should—perceive in a text. Chapters 3 and 4, on the other hand, seek to demonstrate how the reading process might be expanded by reading rhetorically on the level of the signifier and by taking into account the powers of condensation and displacement. Chapter 5 concludes the first part by resituating the rhetoric of reading among current discussions of poetics and psychoanalysis and by addressing the questions of truth and pleasure in reading. Chapters 3 through 5 might be entitled "Toward a New Rhetorical Reader."

Part Two is devoted to our own readings of four nineteenth- and twentieth-century French literary texts: two prose works (Balzac's *La Duchesse de Langeais* and Claude Simon's *Leçon de choses*) and two poems (Baudelaire's *Les Bijoux* and Mallarmé's *Le Pitre châtié*). Although the four essays vary in their approach and format, they are unified by the thesis that conscious rhetorical reading can reinvigorate interpretation. They are also unified by arguments which seek to question past conventions of reading while proposing new interpretive strategies.

Most of the examples and texts are drawn from modern French literature. We hope, however, that the theory of reading figurally and symbolically as outlined in this book will be of value to readers of literature from other periods and other languages. This hope is based on the theory that all reading is governed by the four rhetorical operations developed in the following pages.

Acknowledgments

We are grateful for permission to reprint sections of this book which originally appeared in journals. The Introduction and Chapter 1 first appeared as "Metaphor, Metonymy, and Synecdoche Revis(it)ed" in *Semiotica* 21, nos. 1/2 (1977): 122–49. Chapters 2 and 6 are extensive revisions of "Tropes and Figures: Symbolization and Figuration," published in *Semiotica* 35, nos. 1/2 (1981): 93–124. Chapter 4 appeared in a modified form in *Pre/Text* 3, no. 1 (1982), as "The Rhetoric of Displacement and Condensation."

This book would not have been possible without the help of several institutions. Summer support from the Graduate School of the University of Wisconsin, Madison, for Peter Schofer and a sabbatical from Hamline University and support from the Camargo Foundation for Donald Rice provided much needed time for research and writing. Staff at the University of Wisconsin Press deserve special thanks: Carolyn Moser for her patient and judicious editing of inconsistencies and *maladresses*, and particularly Peter Givler, whose kindness and encouragement cannot be fully repaid.

As is normal, this project would never have reached print without the support of many friends, colleagues, and students. Christian Metz's seminar in Paris and personal advice helped clarify many of our ideas. Jim Bailey's enthusiasm in the early stages overcame initial doubts and discouragement. Bill Berg, Sydney Lévy, Tom Conley, Donna Kuizenga, and Lou Rossi acted as invaluable catalysts and goads along the way. Thanks are also extended to the graduate students at Madison, who suffered through various forms of rhetoric in seminars. Of special note is Jeff Hixson's work on Mallarmé, which is echoed in some of our writing on sound in Chapter 8.

Rhetorical Poetics

INTRODUCTION:

JAKOBSON'S NEW RHETORIC

The rebirth of interest in rhetoric in France during the past twenty-five years has in no way been limited to linguistics and literary studies. Rhetorical terms and concepts have come to permeate the discourse of numerous fields making up the social and human sciences. For example, readers interested in anthropology find in Levi-Strauss's *La Pensée sauvage* the following categorization of animal names:

> If, therefore, birds are *metaphorical human beings* and dogs, *metonymical human beings*, cattle may be thought of as *metonymical inhuman beings* and racehorses as *metaphorical inhuman beings*. Cattle are contiguous only for want of similarity, racehorses similar only for want of contiguity. Each of these two categories offers the converse image of one of the two other categories, which themselves stand in the relation of inverted symmetry.[1]

Students of psychoanalysis can examine Lacan's discussion of metaphor and metonymy as the "two slopes of the effective field of signification in the constitution of meaning." They can see the terms further enlarged as Lacan attaches them to symptom and condensation (metaphor) on one axis and to desire and displacement (metonymy) on another axis:

> The *Verdichtung*, or condensation, is the structure of the superimposition of signifiers which is the field of metaphor, and its very name condensing in itself the word *Dichtung* shows how the process is connatural with the mechanism of poetry to the point that it actually envelops its properly traditional function.
>
> In the case of *Verschiebung*, displacement, the German term is closer to the idea of that veering off to meaning that we see in metonymy, and which from its first appearance in Freud is described as the main method by which the unconscious gets around censorship.[2]

Those interested in semiotics can follow Barthes as he studies the several subsystems which interact to form the "system of fashion." The final metasystem he describes is the rhetorical:

> When its signified is explicit, the vestimentary code cuts the world up into semantic units that rhetoric will take over in order to dress them, order them, and build out of them a veritable worldview: *evening, weekend, walk, Springtime*, are erratic units, coming from the world but implying no particular "world," no definite ideology, which explains why, on the level of the vestimentary code, they have been refused classification. This rhetorical structuring of a world, which could be compared to a veritable cosmogony, occurs via two principal paths: metaphor and parataxis.[3]

As diverse and wide-ranging as these nonliterary, nonlinguistic applications may be, they share a common feature: a tendency to polarize their use of rhetoric around two terms, to reduce rhetorical concepts to the binary opposition of metaphor and metonymy.[4]

THE SCIENCE OF ASSOCIATIVE LISTS

If someone were to trace the recent history of the polarization of metaphor and metonymy, that person might well start with the seminal article by Roman Jakobson on aphasia.[5] While defining the two terms and extending their conceptual force into all realms of the arts, Jakobson also aided in establishing linguistics as the

"master science," as the model for the other "sciences."[6] To be
sure, the supremacy of linguistics as a model did not come exclusively from his work on metaphor and metonymy, but this
article stands as a classical example of the predominance of linguistics in the human sciences. By its very suggestiveness, it also
provided the necessary links between linguistics, literature, cinema, the plastic arts, psychoanalysis, and anthropology and helped
to legitimize these various disciplines as "sciences." Thus, while
Jakobson suggested the lines for a general science centered on
metaphor and metonymy, his article also initiated a chain of associations linked to the two words. Associations and science were
to create a strange and contradictory constellation with metaphor and metonymy as the key stars.

This mixture of science and associations can be explained in
a number of ways. One explanation is outlined by Barthes: "Let
us note, following a remark by Jakobson, that the analyst (in the
present instance, the semiologist) is better equipped to speak about
metaphor than about metonymy, because the metalanguage in
which he must conduct his analysis is itself metaphorical, and
consequently homogeneous with the metaphor which is its object: indeed there is an abundant literature on metaphor, but next
to nothing on metonymy."[7] This observation reminds us that the
analyst can never escape the metaphorical, but it also implies
that the "science" of associations circulating around metaphor
and metonymy was based on metaphors, and, as there "is an
abundant literature on metaphor," there is also an abundance of
metaphorical thinking behind the "science" of sign systems. The
metaphoricity of the science resided in binary paradigms outside
any texts and independent of them. The lists, based on similarity
and opposition, continued the contradictory play between science and association which might be termed "paradigms of
metaphors" or "metaphorized paradigms."

An initial list abstracted from Jakobson's article would read:

Metaphor	Metonymy
selection	combination
substitution	contexture
in absentia	in praesentia

internal relationship of   external relationship of
   similarity   contiguity

The list could be expanded on the basis of suggestions made by
Jakobson at the end of the article:

Russian lyric poetry   Epic poetry
Romanticism and   Realism
   Symbolism
Surrealism   Cubism
Charlie Chaplin films   D. W. Griffith films

Recent works in the field of humanities and social science have
elaborated on the binary divisions. For example, Anika Lemaire,
using selection and combination as the two poles, proposes the
following paradigms:[8]

Selection   *Combination*
substitution   context
paradigm   syntagm
oppositions   contrasts
similarity   contiguity
metaphor   metonymy
language   speech

Anthony Wilden provides another variation:[9]

Metaphor   *Metonymy*
synchronic axis of si-   diachronic   axis   of
   multaneity   succession
symptom   desire
condensation   displacement
substitution   combination
paradigm   syntagm
code, text   context
similarity   contiguity

David Lodge, building on Jakobson's expanded list, offers the
following breakdown:[10]

Metaphor	Metonymy
paradigm	syntagm
similarity	contiguity
selection	combination
substitution	(deletion) contexture
contiguity disorder	similarity disorder
contexture deficiency	selection deficiency
drama	film
montage	close-up
dream symbolism	condensation & displacement in dreams
surrealism	cubism
imitative magic	contagious magic
poetry	prose
lyric	epic
romanticism & symbolism	realism

These key words have thus permitted readers to slide smoothly from one discipline to another, from one conceptual realm to another, without hesitation or serious questioning. Because the lists are constructed like a scientific model, and because the "metaphorical paradigms" act in turn as metaphors to one another (all of the lists share certain key words), they can serve as giant grids of knowledge from which sentences and theories of the text can be generated in those moments when the reader becomes writer and perpetuates the metaphorical play between metaphor and metonymy. But this movement from one list to another, from one conceptual realm to another, from one discipline to another, results not in a deliberate scientific movement toward knowledge, but rather in a confusion rivaling that of the Tower of Babel. This passage from science to delirium can be traced in a composite of quotations from various texts:

> What interests us here is the relationship between the paradigmatic (metaphor) and the syntagmatic (metonymy) in communicational and linguistic processes. . . . One notes that Marcuse's analyses in *One Dimensional Man* (1964) pick up many striking examples of metonymic disavowal.[11]

In the metalanguage of criticism, metonymy ultimately yields to metaphor—or is converted to it.[12]

There may be some theoretical value in seeking an overall preference for metaphor in neurosis and metonymy in schizophrenia.[13]

If we understand that metaphor is, above all, substitution and mediation, this study as a metaphor wants to be a form of passage which all psychoanalytic practice should be: from metaphor to the phallus and to the missing object.[14]

The most striking thing is that this double metonymic structure is found in a text that also contains highly seductive metaphors . . . and that explicitly asserts the superiority of metaphor over metonymy in terms of metaphysical categories. . . . The narrator who tells us about the impossibility of metaphor is himself, or itself, a metaphor, the metaphor of a grammatical syntagm whose meaning is the denial of metaphor stated, by antiphrasis, as its priority.[15]

By itself, each statement might appear coherent; taken as a group, they defy classification and comprehension.

There have been, of course, those who did not accept this binary division. For the most part, however, attempts to question the central role assigned to metaphor and metonymy have led to privileging one of the two or to subordinating them both to a third rhetorical category. Albert Henry, Umberto Eco, and Gérard Genette have sought to underline the metonymical basis of all metaphors, while the Groupe de Liège and Tzvetan Todorov have tried to promote synecdoche to the position of master trope on which both metaphor and metonymy depend.[16]

TWO ASPECTS OF LANGUAGE: JAKOBSON ON METAPHOR AND
METONYMY

In his seminal article, "Two Aspects of Language and Two Kinds of Aphasia" (published in 1956), Jakobson shows convincingly that rhetoric stands at the very core of our verbal processes, whether in literary works or in everyday speech. He does so by studying the language difficulties experienced by aphasics and by distinguishing two fundamental forms of their disorder. One type involves a problem with word selection and substitution; the other, with word combination and connection. The first, which Jakobson calls similarity trouble, manifests itself in aphasics who, although capable of stringing words together in a syntactically satisfactory manner, cannot define words or recognize synonyms or, in particularly severe cases, name objects. The second, which Jakobson calls contiguity trouble, is found in aphasics who, although possessing a rich vocabulary, cannot link words together to form a grammatical sentence; in the severest cases, each "sentence" consists of a single one-word utterance. These two forms of aphasia stand in direct opposition one to the other. In cases of similarity trouble, all linguistic relations tend to be based on contiguity. When asked to enumerate some names of animals, the aphasic gives them in the order in which he saw them at the zoo. In cases of contiguity trouble, linguistic relations tend to depend on similarity. Such an aphasic confuses grammatical forms of the same words (cases or tenses) and often strings together sets of synonyms. In other words, the blockage of one kind of verbal process leads to the exclusive reliance on the other, a phenomenon which can be seen in the aphasics' use of figurative language. Whereas aphasics of the second type (those whose problems reside in the domain of word combination) make identifications which are "metaphoric in nature" (ex., *fire* for *gas light*), those of the first type make "metonymical identification" (ex., *fork* for *knife*, *smoke* for *pipe*, *glass* for *window*.)

Jakobson sees this reliance on relations of similarity (metaphors) or contiguity (metonymies) by aphasics as an extreme example of a basic predilection among "normal" speakers to favor one of these two modes of verbal activity:

> The development of a discourse can take place along two different semantic lines: one topic leads to another either by similarity or by contiguity. It would be best to speak of metaphorical process in the first situation and metonymical process in the second, since they find their most condensed expression, the one in metaphor, the other in metonymy. In aphasics one or the other of these two procedures is reduced or totally blocked. . . . In normal verbal activity, the two procedures are continually in operation, but close observation shows that, under the influence of cultural models, personality and style, sometimes one, sometimes the other takes preference. (76)

In a word association test, the stimulus *hut* can evoke both "metaphorical" answers, such as *is a poor little house*; *cabin*; *hovel*, and "metonymical" responses, such as *thatch*; *straw*; *poverty*. For Jakobson, the manipulation of similarity and contiguity reveals the personal style of each individual speaker. To his thinking, it is a logical step to extend the discussion of these two linguistic poles to literature and to processes that extend beyond the verbal—painting, cinema, and "human behavior in general" (79). The lists cited above as well as the tendency to see rhetoric in binary terms stem, either directly or indirectly, from this initial investigation into a language disorder.

Although Jakobson has contributed enormously to bringing rhetoric out from the obscure backwaters of literary history, problems do arise with his theories. These problems are of two sorts: some derive from the manner in which his article has been read and interpreted; others result from Jakobson's own blurring of important distinctions between the linguistic and the nonlinguistic and his overextension of the meaning of key words.

MISREADINGS, BLURRINGS, AND OVEREXTENSIONS

Given the binary nature of Jakobson's theory, the temptation is strong to organize his categories into convenient lists of opposing items (just as we did above). It is significant, however, that Jakobson himself performs no such reduction. He takes care in his writing to place his generalizations "*between* the two poles metaphor and metonymy" (our italics), not at the poles themselves, where they can be frozen into lists. In addition, he writes of the "*primacy* of the metaphoric process," of the "*predominance* of metonymy," of the "metonymical *orientation* of cubism" (70; italics ours). These qualifiers help to attenuate to some degree the absolutism of a binary system, permitting gradations between poles rather than fixed grids. Moreover, in a later article dealing with poetics, Jakobson stresses the interrelationship of the two poles: "In poetry, where similarity is projected onto contiguity, every metonymy is slightly metaphoric, every metaphor has a metonymic tinge."[17] But what Jakobson saw as gradations and interactions were subsequently polarized by others into noncommutative opposites, such as paradigm and syntagm, symptom and desire, drama and film.

A second source of misreading derives from the fact that Jakobson sees metaphors and metonymies as the condensed forms of symbolic processes. As a result, it is necessary to consider the question of point of view: in whom are the processes at work? An example of confusion arising from the failure to ask this question can be seen in the frequent association of metaphor with similarity and the paradigmatic, and of metonymy with contiguity and the syntagmatic (see, for example, the lists of Lemaire, Wilden, and Lodge).[18] At first glance, such associations appear perfectly reasonable, given that similarity troubles involve an inability to select within the code of language (a paradigmatic operation) and contiguity troubles involve an inability to combine words syntactically (a syntagmatic operation). Jakobson is studying the question from the perspective of the aphasic who is speaking, however, and for this speaker relations of contiguity also exist within a paradigm. For example, Jakobson explains the tendency of contiguity-troubled aphasics to use the nominative form of a pronoun even when the objective or possessive cases are required and to drop prefixes and suffixes from words of the same family by pointing out that words such as *he-him-his* and *grant-grantor-grantee* are contiguous in the grammatical or semantic paradigms to which they belong. Thus, the opposition syntagmatic/paradigmatic does not cover perfectly the opposition similarity/contiguity.

In fact, careful study of Jakobson's examples reveals that, especially when considered from the perspective not only of the speaker but also of the listener or reader, both metaphor and metonymy have paradigmatic *and* syntagmatic forms. For example, when an aphasic says *fire* instead of *gas light*, this is clearly a case of a paradigmatic substitution based on similarity. Yet when a child on a psychological association test responds to the stimulus *hut* by the phrase *is a poor little house*, the relationship, although based on similarity, is syntagmatic in form: the words are contiguous in a signifying chain. In the same way, when Jakobson cites a question from *Alice's Adventures in Wonderland* ("Did you say *pig* for *fig*?," 52), he does so as a case where the speaker tries to determine which word the partner in the dialogue has selected (a paradigmatic operation); however, for a reader of the book, the play between the words *pig* and *fig* is a syntagmatic play of rhymes on the page. Similar reversals occur in the examples chosen to illustrate the concept of contiguity. When an aphasic states "I have a good apartment, entrance hall, bedroom, kitchen" (58), thus recreating in the syntax the referential contiguity he experiences, the form of the example is clearly syntagmatic. But when other aphasics substitute *smoke* for *fire*, *dead* for *black*, and *to eat* for *toaster*, the relationships, although based on contiguity (elements in a causal chain), are paradigmatic in form. Only one of the terms appears in the signifying chain; the other is absent, and the listener must guess its identity.

One can thus understand why Jakobson himself does not identify the paradigmatic exclusively with metaphor and the syntagmatic exclusively with metonymy. That others do make such a connection stems in part at least from Jakobson's over-extended use of the terms *similarity* and *contiguity*. In his attempt to globalize the implications of his theories concerning aphasia, Jakobson chooses examples which range from the linguistic (syntax, semantics, phonetics) to the literary (rhymes, parallel verse forms, descriptive details) to the referential (the world as perceived by the speaker). The vastness of the system invites application to specific disciplines such as literature without transformations and without accounting for the specificity of the individual disciplines. This danger is the greatest in the two key words just discussed because neither of them is specific to linguistics.

Similarity in linguistics is not necessarily equivalent to similarity in real life or in a literary text. The statement "Linda looks like Linus" may be correct, but its truth does not have any value to a linguist (or for that matter to a literary critic). For a social scientist the similarity might be significant in a number of ways: the two people might be from the same family; they could belong to the same social club which dictates similar dress; one of them might be under the influence of the other and thus would make an effort to look similar. For a linguist the statement might serve in a study of similarity of phonemes: *Linda, Linus, like*. A poetician could find metaphorical relationships in the repetitions of the /i/, /s/, and /n/, which create similarities and ties between the words. In Jakobson's own system of thought, the words are part of the "poetic function." In each of these examples, the so-called "metaphorical" is concentrated on different parts of the statement, and the definitions of similarity are grounded on different concepts: the phenomenologist seeks common traits in the persons to verify the similarities, the phonetician studies the individual sounds in relationship to larger sound patterns, the poetician "uses" the similar sounds to establish similarities between the words. Jakobson does in fact associate linguistic similarity with literary metaphor, but he is often careful to note a difference between similarity of meaning and metaphorical similarity, in rhetorical or poetic metaphors, where there is "deliberate transfer of meaning" (64). In the examples that he cites, there are very few poetic metaphors showing transfer of meaning, and Jakobson clearly marks true metaphors as such. For example, he defines as metaphors *den* and *burrow* when they are substituted for *hut*. But often he leads the reader to associate linguistic similarity with metaphorical process, in other words, to subsume the rhetorical into the linguistic, as in the following statement: "The patient confined to the substitution set (once contexture is deficient) deals with similarities, and his approximate identifications are of a metaphoric nature" (64). If synonyms and metaphors do share in the same "metaphorical nature," they do not have the same value for the literary critic.

The association of metonymy with contiguity has suffered a worse fate by the suppression of distinctions. Just as the metaphorical in literature is a restricted type of similarity, metonymy is a particular variation of contiguity. The absorption of metonymy into the very general concept of contiguity has resulted in labeling almost any relationship "metonymy" if two signs can be perceived in any way as being "next to" and "near" one another. In this overextended definition of metonymy the statement "Linus lives next to Linda" illustrates a variety of contiguities which can be defined according to the reader's perspective.

The social scientist may examine the statement from the point of view of similarity and ascertain that the two people not only live next to one another but also have similar tastes, incomes, and social aspirations. He could also see in the statement a synecdochal relationship if both individuals proved to be part of a larger group—such as the same class or institution. The contiguity might also be based on a causal relationship if one of the persons had persuaded the other to live next door. For the linguist, the statement might serve as an example of syntactic reversal to see if there is appreciable change in meaning when the proximate names are reversed (Linus lives next to Linda/Linda lives next to Linus). The literary critic would see little or no rhetorical significance in the statement from the point of view of contiguity. The statement would take on some meaning only in relation to other parts of the text. The five words are "next to one another," are "part" of the same sentence, and express proximity (contiguity) without having any literary metonymic value.

Coupled with this blurring of differences between disciplines is a tendency to blur important distinctions *within* the notions of similarity and contiguity. Thus, *similarity*, limited at first to relationships of resemblance (partial identity), comes at one point in the article to include *contrast* or *opposition*. Certainly one can discover a link between the notions of similarity and opposition. However, to then include the latter within the former obscures some very important differences. Replacing *hut* by its opposite, *palace*, in an association test neither denotes nor connotes the same things as responding *is a poor little house* or *cabin*. As for *contiguity*, the examples offered by Jakobson include, in addition to simple juxtaposition of lexical items such as sail + boat, associations based on spatial proximities such as *thatch* for *hut*, *sky* for *God*, as well as connections dependent on causal links, as in *smoke* for *fire*, *grant-grantor-grantee*, *death* for *black*. Although one may well accept a physical theory of causality based on the notion of temporal contiguity, one needs also to recognize the fundamental distinction between a provisional contiguity limited to a specific moment or event, as in *smoke/fire*, and a permanent or semipermanent contiguity, as in *thatch/hut*.[19]

REVISING AND EXPANDING JAKOBSON

Jakobson's contribution to the reawakened interest in rhetoric is undeniable. In particular, his emphasis on metaphor and metonymy as processes (rather than just examples of figurative language) has made possible the application of rhetoric to a wide variety of fields. Nevertheless, the oversimplification inherent in the binary character of his system makes it important to reexamine the rhetorical base of language and literature in order to retain important distinctions blurred by Jakobson and his epigones. Rather than accepting the Jakobsonian binary system or a further reduction to a single master rhetorical category, we will argue that there are (at least) four distinct rhetorical operations: metaphor, metonymy, synecdoche, and irony (or opposition). A system centered on the perspective of the reader and based on the four tropes of metaphor, metonymy, synecdoche, and irony can revitalize and expand Jakobson's pioneering work. In such a system, the four basic tropes become part of larger, interrelated processes of symbolization and figuration grounded on the relationships of similarity, causality, inclusion, and opposition.[20] Tzvetan Todorov's argument that debates over the taxonomy of tropes are of little theoretical value only underlines the fact that the ambiguity and oversimplification of classifications have prevented readers from seeing the central part played by rhetoric in the process of reading literature. The redefinition of the four tropes that follows in the first chapter is but a starting point for a more elaborate presentation of readings grounded on rhetorical processes.

Part One

Rhetorical Theories

1

THE FOUR TROPES

Definition of a Trope

A trope is a semantic transposition from a sign in praesentia *to a sign or signs in* absentia *and (1) based on the perception of a relationship between one or more semantic features of each signified, (2) marked by the semantic incompatibility of microcontext and the macrocontext, (3) motivated by a referential relationship of resemblance or causality or inclusion or opposition.*
The term *semantic feature* designates a unit of meaning; a word, or more precisely, a signified, consists therefore of a group of semantic features. Since these features enter into the composition of both the denotative and connotative values of the signified, the semantic group is subjective because different readers can attribute different semantic features to the signified. It is also variable because new connotations can add to or modify the meanings of the word.[1] The terms *microcontext* and *macrocontext*, borrowed from Michael Riffaterre, have a somewhat different definition here. The microcontext is the segment of the signifying chain which the trope occupies; in the case of one-word tropes, it would be the sign *in praesentia* itself. The macrocontext includes those parts of the signifying chain necessary for the determination of the sign *in absentia*.[2] Much more difficult to deal with is the term *referential*, a source of great confusion and controversy. The problem becomes even more complex when one is dealing with literary texts, for what is designated by the sign can be both contextual, other linguistic ele-

19

ments of the text, and extratextual, the fictional world created
by the text and the real world known by the reader. The referent
of a literary sign can be real or imaginary, physical or conceptual
or verbal; it can be known directly by the reader through experience or indirectly through more general culture experiences
such as schooling, reading, and word-of-mouth. Recognition of
the importance of the referent demands substituting for the
Saussurian bar a quasitriangular definition of the sign:[3]

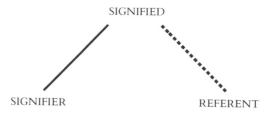

SIGNIFIED

SIGNIFIER   REFERENT

In this schema, although the sign (signifier + signified) remains
distinct from the referent, the referent, in its contextual and extratextual functions, plays a key role. Such a theory of the sign
reflects the complexity of contemporary semantic research. For
Georges Mounin, the debate between logical, contextual, and
situational theories of meaning can only be resolved by means
of the notion of complementarity—i.e., a signified is definable
by "pertinent 'logical' features . . . then by pertinent 'contextual' features . . . and by pertinent situational and connotative
features."[4] In similar fashion, the tropic process is based on the
interaction of semantic features, contexts, and referents. Such a
notion resembles that of Ricoeur's "discourse event." For him,
"the essential part of metaphorical attribution consists in the
constructing of the network of interactions which make a particular context real and unique."[5]

Reading a trope involves a series of operations which occur
almost simultaneously. Confronted with a sign (S^1) in a text in
the form of a signifier whose signified(s) is (are) incompatible
with the signifieds immediately surrounding it, the reader, using

the textual and extratextual information at his disposal, seeks a second sign (S^2) whose signified can resolve the incompatibility. Whether they are lexical, contextual or cultural in origin, these semantic features form the intermediary (I) which permit the association between S^1 and S^2. The intermediary varies in nature according to the kind of trope involved. Unless he is analyzing the trope, rather than just reading it, the reader often does not consciously produce the signifier of S^2, for the tropic process involves a relationship between signifieds.

RECLASSIFICATION OF TROPES

Metaphor

Metaphor is characterized by a semantic and referential relationship of resemblance made possible by the possession of one or more common semantic features. Figure 1—in which S^1 = the sign in praesentia, S^2 = the sign in absentia, x = semantic feature, and I = the intermediary—summarizes the process. The metaphorical process involves a transfer of meaning, with some of the nonidentical semantic features of S^1 becoming part of the intermediary and modifying the meaning of S^2. This definition of metaphor, based on resemblance or similarity, does not then differ appreciably from traditional and modern notions of the term.[6]

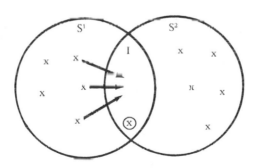

Figure 1

To illustrate how one reads a metaphor, let us take the first
verses of *Chanson d'automne* by Verlaine:

> Les sanglots longs
> Des violons
> De l'automne
> Blessent mon coeur
> D'une langueur
> Monotone.

[The long sobs / Of the violins / Of autumn / Wound my heart /
With monotonous languor.]

The first two lines confront the reader with a semantic and referential incompatibility between the microcontext (*sanglots*) and
the macrocontext (*Les . . . longs des violons*): sobs emanate from
people, not from inanimate objects such as violins. The reader
can resolve the incompatibility by proposing the signified *sons*
[sounds]. The two signifieds—S^1 (*sanglots*) and S^2 (*sons*)—share
the common semantic feature "auditory sensation." However,
the metaphor does not involve just this identity of a semantic
feature; other semantic features of *sanglots*—for example, "pain,"
"suffering," "tears," "unhappiness"—transfer to help characterize more precisely the sound of the violins. On the other hand,
sanglots does not substitute entirely for *sons*: certain semantic features of both S^1 and S^2 are eliminated. For example, "contrac-
tion of the diaphragm," "heavy breathing," "noise," do not play
a role in the metaphor and are "bracketed," to use Ricoeur's term.
It is quite possible that the reader may not articulate the actual
signifier of S^2 (*sons*). Nonetheless, the associative process described here links the signifieds to produce a new meaning. The
importance of referential (i.e., nonlexical) information in reading the metaphor cannot be overlooked. As Ricoeur states, "There
are no metaphors in the dictionary."[7] For someone who knew
only the dictionary definitions of *sanglot* and *violon*, the metaphor would prove difficult to understand, especially in terms of
the transfer of semantic features such as "unhappiness" and "suffering." Once this meaning is assured, the reader continues along
the signifying chain—in this case to run immediately into another incompatibility (*violons de l'automne*) which forces the metaphoric reading process to start again.

One difficulty in metaphor arises when dealing with the question of presence and absence. A "pure" metaphor, which is perhaps rarer than is often realized, would demand that neither the intermediary nor S^2 be present in the syntagmatic segment immediately in contact with the trope. The microcontext would contain only S^1. As Genette very clearly demonstrates, however, the metaphorical process is often found in *figures d'analogie*,[8] where, to varying degrees, all three terms can be present. An abbreviated and slightly modified list of Genette's categories illustrates how the metaphorical process works in comparisons, identifications, and metaphors:

S^1
My flame   metaphor

I S^1
My ardent flame   motivated identification

S^2 I S^1
My love, ardent flame   motivated identification

S^2 S^1
My love, flame. . .   unmotivated identification

S^2 S^1
My love is like a flame   unmotivated comparison

S^2 I S^1
My love burns like a flame   motivated comparison

In the first example—a "pure metaphor" where I and S^2 are both missing—the reader would have a multitude of choices to make in order to understand the metaphor. In practice, of course, the macrocontext would to varying degrees limit the possible choices and, consequently, the degree of ambiguity in the trope. Because of the macrocontext, all metaphors are more or less unmotivated, but motivated nonetheless. When Genette uses the term *motivation*, he is referring to figures which include the intermediary in

the microcontext, but even in these cases, some ambiguity can
still persist. For example, in the sentence "My love burns like a
flame," the intermediary *burns* contains a variety of semantic features, some positive, others negative: "illuminates," "warms,"
"destroys." It is only by referring to the macrocontext that the
reader limits his own interpretation.

A second problem with metaphor also concerns the ambiguity of the intermediary. While the uncertainty in "My love
burns like a flame" involves the exact choice of semantic features, the intermediary *burns* is clearly present in the text. Some
metaphors, however, pose serious difficulties for the reader when
he attempts to discover the intermediary. In fact, one can see
metaphors as organized along a continuum based on the specificity or lack of specificity of the intermediary. At one end, one
finds what Fontanier calls catachresis: "Catachresis, in general,
consists of a sign already attached to one idea being attached to
a new idea which either had no sign or no longer has one all to
itself."[9] In other words, what was originally a trope (and very
often a metaphor) becomes encoded in the language as the only
sign designating a particular referent. For example, *head of a pin,*
arm of a chair, a soft voice, no longer present any incompatibility
and are immediately understood. At the other extreme, one finds
surrealist metaphors for which multiple intermediaries are possible. For example, in Breton's "Ma femme aux épaules de
champagne" [My woman with champagne shoulders], does one
look for the intermediary in terms of color? shape (of the bub-
bles)? feel? all of these? none? The difficulty, intended by the
poet, is compounded by the failure of the macrocontext to limit
the possibilities.

Metonymy
Metonymy is characterized by a semantic and referential relationship of
causality made possible by the presence of the category of semantic fea-
ture cause. Our notion represents a radical limitation of traditional concepts of metonymy. The tendency has been either to
combine metonymy with synecdoche using the notion of contiguity or, in the case of Fontanier, to divide metonymy into two
subgroups—causal and spatial. On the other hand, if one follows the lead of Nietzsche, who suggested that metonymy is

causal,[10] and removes the notion of spatiality from metonymy, it is possible to arrive at a much clearer concept of both metonymy and synecdoche. To do so, however, requires that we define in detail the area covered by cause-effect relationships fitting the model shown in Figure 2. Each of the paired relationships can motivate a metonymy, with either term of the pair acting as S^1.

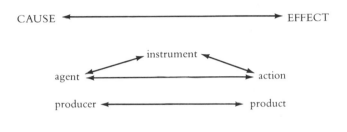

Figure 2

Although the general process (S^1 I S^2) resembles that of metaphor, there are two fundamental differences. First, whereas the two signs in a metaphor are joined initially by a common semantic feature or features, the two signs in a metonymy remain separate and distinct; the presence within S^1 of a semantic feature belonging to the general category of causality permits the relationship. This can be either an active or a passive form of the feature, depending on whether S^1 is cause or effect. Thus one finds the following possibilities:

to cause or to be caused   (cause-effect)

to produce or to be produced   (producer-product)

to use or to be used   (agent-instrument)

to perform or to be performed   (agent-action)

to use or to be performed   (instrument-action)

Second, unlike the movement in metaphor, which also involves the transfer of additional semantic features from S^1 to S^2, in metonymy the two signifieds remain intact. It is for this reason that both Le Guern and Ricoeur, while willing to speak of "substitution" of terms in regard to metonymy and synecdoche, prefer to treat metaphor as a "modification" of meaning.[11] The metonymical process can be schematically represented as shown in Figure 3. To illustrate, let us take Fontanier's example of a metonymy of action for instrument: "Je l'ai vu cette nuit, ce malheureux Sévère, / La *vengeance* à la main, l'œil ardent de colère" [I saw him that night, this unfortunate Severus, / Vengeance in his hand, his eyes burning with anger]. The macrocontext (in particular, *à la main*) suggests that S^2 is a sword. The intermediary would thus be the semantic feature *to be performed* (the act of avenging). Yet the signified of *vengeance* and *sword* retain their usual meanings. This particular metonymy illustrates clearly the importance of the referential in the reading of tropes. Because the reader can situate S^1 in a particular text (a seventeenth-century play), the reader can make the association to *sword*. The same trope, in a different literary and cultural context, could well demand another S^2, such as *gun*.

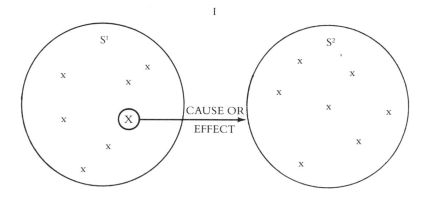

Figure 3

All metonymies work on the same model. The following list illustrates possibilities for each subcategory:

Cause for effect	"Je reconnus *Vénus* et ses redoutables effets." [I recognized Venus and her fearful effects.]	The goddess for the emotion she controls.
Effect for cause	"O mon fils! O ma *joie!* O l'honneur de mes jours!" [O my son! O my joy! O honor of my days!]	The emotion for its source.
Instrument for agent	"The *clarinets* forgot to come in."	The musical instruments for the people playing them.
Instrument for action	"Il a le *pinceau* délicat." [He has a delicate brush.]	The painter's brush for his manner of painting.
Action for instrument	"La *vengeance* à la main." [Vengeance in his hand.]	*Vengeance* for *épée*.
Agent for action	"He pulled a *Houdini*."	The magician for the disappearing act he performed.
Action for agent	"Voilà la belle Hélène, *l'infamie* des Grecs." [There is the beautiful Helen, the infamy of the Greeks.]	The crime for the criminal.
Producer for produced	"Prenez votre *César*." [Take out your Caesar.]	The author for his work.

| Produced for pro-
ducer | "*Computers* lose ten
points on Wall
Street." | The product for
the company
that produces it. |

Synecdoche

Synecdoche is characterized by a semantic or referential relationship of inclusion made possible by the fact that one of the signifieds is also a semantic feature of the other signified. Whereas all but causal relationships are eliminated from metonymy, synecdoche is expanded to include not only the part for the whole but also the container for the contained. Care must be taken, however, in relying on these traditional categories—particularly the part for the whole. In the past, this notion has been interpreted mainly in terms of the real world, but one must take into account the interaction between semantic and referential factors. For example, a person might refuse to classify *iron* as a synecdoche for *sword* because iron is not a part of the whole, since a sword can be made entirely of iron. But semantically iron is a feature of *sword*, and referentially the sword is *made* of iron. Similarly, one could reject *glass* for *wine* in the expression *boire un verre*, or *crown* for *king*, on the basis that the glass and the wine, the king and the crown, are separate entities. Nevertheless, both referentially—through personal experience and cultural knowledge— and semantically—the lexical codings of the terms—the pairs form an entity. It is encoded in the language that one drinks a glass of wine, and that crowns are worn by kings.

Whereas metonymy is exclusive (cause *and* effect) and metaphor is analogical (the resemblance of two distinct elements), synecdoche is inclusive; consequently, the absence of a separate intermediary somewhat alters the basic tropic model. Because one of the signifieds is also a semantic feature of the other, the intermediary is simply that signified as semantic feature. Semantic features are not only coded lexically, as part of a dictionary definition, but also contextually and extratextually. In the examples given above, *iron*, *crown*, and *wine* are semantic features of *sword*, *king*, and *glass* both on the basis of the lexicon and of general culture. But in the sentence "This is the glass that will kill him," without any textual reference a reader could read *glass* as a metonymy of instrument for agent, as in a sharp piece of glass used as a dagger. If, however, the macrocontext alluded to cyanide, then the semantic feature "poison" would become a connotation of the sign *glass*, and the trope would function as a synecdoche (*glass* for *poison*). It is important to realize that the notion of inclusion on the physical (extratextual) level and on the semantic level is reversed. Physically, the crown is part of a totality of the king sitting on a throne, wearing a crown, holding a scepter, etc. The trope is possible on the level of semantic features because of the presence, in the signified *crown*, of the semantic feature "monarch" or "king." The synecdochal process, with its "absent" intermediary, can be schematized as shown in Figure 4. To illustrate more fully, let us take the classic example of *sail* for *boat*, such as in Voltaire: "Comme à Londres, à Bordeaux, de cent *voiles* suivie" [As in London, in Bordeaux by one hundred sails followed]. The macrocontext, as usual, plays a double function: (1) It marks the trope by a logical (in this case, referential) incongruity. A *voile* by itself cannot follow. (2) It forces the reader to discard the signified *veil* in favor of *sail*. The reader has no difficulty recognizing and understanding the trope because *sail* is encoded lexically by the close association of *bateau* and *voile*, because Voltaire's context is trade, and because the reader's general knowledge includes the fact that a sail is part of a boat.

For the reader, the problem with synecdoche is the opposite

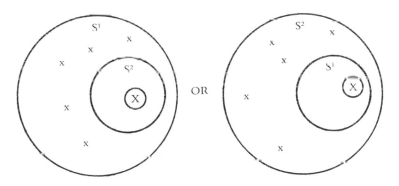

Figure 4

of that with metaphor. Confronted by a metaphor, the reader
can discern the motivation, even reconstruct the intermediary
and S^2 from the context, and still find that the trope is ambiguous, since there can be a number of valid intermediaries (recall,
for example, the metaphor of love as a flame where the flame
could be beneficial or destructive). Synecdoche, on the other hand,
is easily understood because of the identity of the intermediary
and one of the signifieds. What can sometimes prove difficult is
discovering the absent signified. The Groupe de Liège illustrates
this problem by giving the two examples "Le fer mieux em-
ployé cultivera la terre" [Iron better used will cultivate the earth]
and "L'or tombe sous le fer" [The gold falls under the iron]. In
neither case does *iron* replace *sword* (as in our previous examples
of metonymy). In the first example, S^2 is *plow*; in the second, S^2
is *scythe*. Moreover, given the complexity of the second example, where *or* for *blé* is a second synecdoche, the line would
be totally meaningless if the context and the cultural background
did not complete the pairing of *gold-wheat* and *iron-scythe*.

The traditional subcategories of synecdoche can be classified as part of the general definition of inclusion under the following rubrics:

Physical (or Spatial) Synecdoches
physical part for the whole (*head* for *body*)
physical attribute for the whole (*black* for *Negro*)
object or physical attribute for possessor (*crown* for *king*)
material or physical attribute for object (*steel* for *sword*)
container for contained (*stein* for *beer*, *Paris* for *Parisians*)

Conceptual (or Abstract) Synecdoches
attribute for possessor (*youth* for *young* people)
singular for plural (*man* for *men*)
species for genus (*lion* for all *animals*)
genus for species (*animal* for *bear*)
common name for proper name (the *Trojan* for *Aeneas*)

Irony
A victim of the reduction discussed in Chapter 1, irony has disappeared from most of the works of neorhetoric. In those cases
where it has remained, it has been relegated to a secondary sta-

tus. Fontanier deals with it under the category of "tropes en plusieurs mots, ou improprement dits" [multiple word tropes, or
those incorrectly named], while the Groupe de Liège treats it as
a "métalogisme," a figure modifying not the grouping of sèmes
but rather the logical value of the sentence. More traditional
rhetorics do offer, however, a precedent for the inclusion of irony
among the major tropes. In *Des Tropes* (1730), Dumarsais suggested a reorganization of tropes based on the principles of similarity, liaison or contiguity, and opposition. Moreover, both
Vossius and Vico proposed a quadrumvirate of major tropes—
metaphor, metonymy, synecdoche, and irony.[12] Any theory of
literature and reading would be inadequate without a place for
oppositions and irony.

   *Irony is characterized by a semantic and referential relationship of
opposition made possible by the possession of one or more contrary semantic features.* Unlike the other three tropes, irony is not semantically marked, because there is no incompatibility between
the microcontext and the *immediate* macrocontext. By reference
to the complete macrocontext, however, the reader knows that
one word is in fact incompatible with the macrocontext and thus
functions as a trope. For example, if one reads the sentence "His
answer was perfect," there is no violation of the semantic code;
however, if, upon further consulting the macrocontext, the reader
discovers that the answer showed a definite lack of intelligence
or good sense or tact, he will recognize the trope and substitute
for the signified *perfect* a contradictory signified, such as *imperfect*
or *terrible* or *ridiculous*. The substitution is possible on the semantic level because the two signifieds possess one or more common
semantic features *and* one or more semantic features which are
contrary or antagonistic. The intermediary thus consists of both
similarity and opposition. (If the two signifieds did not share at
least one semantic feature, there would be difference rather than
opposition—for example, *perfect* and *empty*.) Figure 5 shows the
close relationship between irony and metaphor. Both involve a
transfer of semantic features; in the case of irony, however, the
transfer is so great as to obliterate almost totally S^1. It is only
the presence of the latter signifier in the text which reminds the
reader of S^1 and of the irony at work.

   Let us take as an example of irony this sentence from Sten-

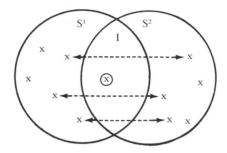

Figure 5

dhal's *La Chartreuse de Parme*: "A ce moment, l'escorte allait ventre
à terre et notre héros comprit que c'étaient des boules qui fai-
saient voler la terre de toutes parts" [At that moment the escort
was going like the wind, and our hero realized that those were
cannonballs making the ground fly in every direction]. The reader
may suspect that the sentence is not a conventional description
of a hero in the face of the enemy, since the "hero" appears a bit
slow in understanding that he is under fire, but there exists no
marked incompatibility between the word *héros* and the immediate macrocontext, the rest of the sentence. The extended macrocontext, however, which contains other descriptions, signals
to the reader that the word does not fit with the activities of
Fabrice, the "hero." Semantic features of S^1, *héros*, are transformed into semantic features marked by opposition: for example, "bravery" → "cowardice"; "purposefulness" → "aimless-
ness"; "alertness" → "confusion"; "exceptional" → "common."
The result is S^2, "nonhero" or "coward," which nevertheless retains at least one semantic feature in common with S^1—quality
of conduct.

Very often, irony, in both everyday conversation and literature, exceeds the limits of a one-word trope. However, the following two examples involve an irony dependent on the change
of meaning of a single word. The first is taken from Corneille's
Horace: "Viens voir mourir ta soeur dans les bras de ton père; /

Viens repaître tes yeux d'un spectacle si *doux*" [Come see your sister dying in her father's arms; / Come feast your eyes on such a lovely sight]. The reader, aware that Horace has just fatally wounded his own sister, understands Sabine's use of the word *doux* ironically. For the character and the reader, the sight of the dying sister is not "lovely," but rather, "horrible." In a lighter vein, the extended macrocontext of the following passage from Voltaire's *Candide* causes the reader to understand the gestures of two about-to-be-lovers as not at all innocent and naïve: "Cunégonde laissa tomber son mouchoir, Candide le ramassa; elle lui prit *innocemment* la main; le jeune homme baisa *innocemment* la main de la jeune demoiselle . . . leurs bouches se rencontrèrent, leurs yeux s'enflammèrent, leurs genoux tremblèrent" [Cunegonde dropped her handkerchief, Candide picked it up; she innocently took his hand; the young man innocently kissed the young lady's hand , . . their mouths met, their eyes flashed, their knees shook].

RELATIVITY OF TROPES

On several occasions we have pointed out the overlap between metaphor, metonymy, and synecdoche. At times, the inability to define precisely a trope was attributed to the particular definition in question; however, at other times, the confusion arose from the very relativity of tropes. Depending upon the historical period in which a text is read, the cultural background and even the psychology of the reader, some tropes change their nature and consequently their meaning. A person in the fourteenth century reading *St.-Denis*, the name of the cathedral north of Paris, would in all likelihood interpret the sign as a metonymy and would be fully aware of the causal relationship between the patron saint and the church in his name. For the twentieth-century reader the metonymy would be more elusive and the term *St.-Denis* might be either a synecdoche (the name being considered an attribute of the building) or a nontrope. A certain amount of cultural background is often necessary for the reader of any period to identify and understand a trope. For example, a foreign ornithologist, totally unfamiliar with Britain in the 1960s, would be rather surprised were he to order the book *Birds of Britain*, having seen only the title and having missed the metaphor *girls* and *birds*. On the psychological level, a reader of Baudelaire who believed that the spleen does in fact produce ill temper and low spirits would interpret the word *spleen* as a metonymy, placing more emphasis on physicality in his interpretation of the *Spleen* poems. Another reader might well see the word as a metaphor, consequently playing down the aspect of physical causality in Baudelaire's works. In a recent issue of *Littérature* (vol. 18 [1975]) devoted to rhetoric, repeated attacks are made against the over-categorization of rhetorical devices. These critiques are reminders that if individual words can be isolated and identified out of context, the process of reading symbolically is neither a fixed nor an absolute categorization of fragments of a text. Similarity, causality, inclusion, and irony interact to create shifting and allusive meanings for the reader.

2

SYMBOLIZATION AND

FIGURATION

Emile Benveniste suggested the need for an expanded rhetoric, based on tropes, which would involve two types of operations or, as he called them, "dynamic structures."[1] First, he would extend the operation of replacement beyond the single word to include larger statements such as euphemisms, allusions, antiphrases, preteritions, and understatement. Second, he suggested that tropes can be treated as "discursive stylistic operations" [procédés stylistiques de discours], as combinations in the syntagm, and, consequently, as parts of the linearity of the text. In a rhetoric of reading, the replacement of one-word tropes would be extended to the process of symbolization across the text to groups of words, paragraphs, and the entire text. Combination in the syntagm or figurations, opens tropic operations to relationships between syntagmatic units of various lengths dispersed throughout the text.

EXTENSION AND TRANSFORMATION: TROPES AND FIGURES
Since tropes by definition demand a transposition from a single word in the microcontext to a sign which is absent from both the micro- and the macrocontexts, they are necessarily paradig-

matic. Yet there are relatively few "pure" tropes. Although the second sign may be absent from the microcontext and the immediate macrocontext, the larger macrocontext (which could include the rest of the text) often provides either the intermediary or the second sign. The processes which govern tropes can pass into the syntagm itself, and an extension of rhetorical analysis beyond the word implies a shift to the syntagm both as the juxtaposition of signs along the signifying chain and as the linking of two or more signs present, but separate from one another in the text.

Traditional rhetoric accounted in part for this shift by distinguishing between tropes and figures. While tropes are included in the general catalogue of figures and are part of a figuration, most figures, according to Fontanier are not tropes, because they include groups of words and because they do not involve a paradigmatic operation.[2] As tropes are absorbed by the syntagm, the paradigmatic and syntagmatic operations meld, and there no longer exists a clear demarcation between terms present and terms absent. For example, the word *temple*, referring to Nature, by itself is a pure trope, since both S^1 and I are missing. The clause "La Nature est un temple" contains both S^1 (*temple*) and S^2 (*Nature*) but lacks an intermediary. "La Nature est un temple où de vivants piliers" [Nature is a temple where living pillars] contains the two signs plus an intermediary (the *vivants piliers*, a metaphor for trees), thus marking a progression from a pure trope to a figural operation in the syntagm. Similarly, the words "ma joie," used to designate a child, are pure metonymy. But in "Mon fils, ma joie" part of the tropic process has become explicit in the signifying chain, thanks to the copresence of S^1 and S^2; the reader need only supply the missing intermediary, "source of."[3] The examples involving syntagmatic relationships where S^1 and S^2 are present in the texts correspond to Benveniste's notion of combination; pure tropes (where one sign is absent) correspond to replacement. But it is preferable to call the paradigmatic relationships, where the reader deals with present and absent signs, symbolic operations or symbolization. Likewise, syntagmatic relationships, where two or more signs are present, are more accurately described as figures or figuration.

Recasting Benveniste's terms reminds us that both kinds of operations involve the combination of signs; that in paradigmatic operations, one sign does not "replace" the other, but combines with it in various ways to form a new entity. The difference lies mainly in the location of the second sign. In this sense, the use of *symbolic* reflects the etymology of the word—*symbolum*, a token for identification through comparison with its counterpart, and *sumballein*, to throw together. This use of *symbolic* is therefore parallel to that of Todorov: "The *two* associated terms are present in (ordinary) discourse, whereas *only one* of them is present in symbolic evocation." Todorov differs sharply in the role played by symbolic operations, however; for him, interpretation involves primarily the realm of symbolization ("I want in fact to posit the solidarity of the symbolic and of interpretation").[4] For us, figuration—"the determination of a certain form" (*OED*)—describes the act of reading the signs present in a text and, through their combination, the creation by the reader of a form, outline, or representation of the work. The construction of these forms is part of the interpretive act, as the reader selects and combines parts of the text to form his mental text. In a sense one can say that figuration also implies replacement because parts of the text are given precedent over others, and the text formed in the reader's mind replaces that of the original graphic text. Extended over an entire text, the act of reading and interpretation is a complex interplay between symbolization and figuration. Although figures and tropes can be isolated for analysis, in reading there can be no figuration without symbolization and no symbolization without figuration.

INCOMPATIBILITY AND INCOMPLETENESS

Metaphors, metonymies, synecdoches, and ironies which become figural retain several important characteristics of pure tropes, particularly incompatibility. In Chapter 1 a trope was defined as a transposition marked by a semantic incompatibility of the microcontext (S^1) and the immediate macrocontext. In the case of figuration, there remains a semantic incompatibility between the microcontext and the immediate macrocontext also; the difference lies in the fact that the latter includes S^2 (and in some cases, I). Thus the simile "La Nature est un temple" is marked by incompatibility of *La Nature*, belonging to the biological world, and of *temple*, an inanimate, man-made construction. Likewise, in the metonymy "Mon fils, ma joie," *son* indicates a relationship and *joy* communicates an emotion.

Nevertheless, there are operations, both paradigmatic and syntagmatic, where there is no incompatibility between microcontext and macrocontext and yet where the reader decodes the text symbolically or figurally. Such cases are marked only by incompleteness, an incompleteness which the macrocontext may suggest, which conventions of the genre may dictate, or which the reader may seek and find in the text.[5] A line from *Phèdre* will illustrate a symbolic process where there is incompleteness without incompatibility: "Sa main sur ses chevaux laissait flotter les rênes" [His hand on the horses allowed the reins to hang loose (float)]. The line is part of Théramène's *récit*, when he describes Hippolyte riding to meet Aricie; it refers to the moment before Hippolyte is attacked by the monster. The line can be read purely denotatively: Hippolyte was holding the reins loosely with one hand. The alert reader also understands, however, that this uncharacteristic casualness is indicative of Hippolyte's distraction and worry. Even though there is no incompatibility with the macrocontext—"A peine nous sortions des portes de Trézène / Il était sur son char; ses gardes affligés / Imitaient son silence, autour de lui rangés / Il suivait tout pensif le chemin de Mycènes" [Scarcely had we left the gates of Troezen / He was in his chariot; his grief-stricken guards / Imitated his silence, gathered around him / He went pensively along the road to Mycenia]—and even though the microcontext involves an entire statement rather than a single word, the process of symbolization functions exactly as for a trope:[6]

S^1 (present): *Sa main sur ses chevaux laissait flotter les rênes*
I (absent): relationship of cause-effect
S^2 (absent): distraction, worry

Set in motion by the desire to complete the statement when the reader asks what the function of this detail is, the process is directed by the referent—the macrocontext as well as the reader's extratextual knowledge. From the immediate macrocontext the reader picks up additional clues to the characters' mental state: the suffering of the guards, Hippolyte's silence and pensiveness. At the same time, experience "reading" gestural languages further suggests a meaning for the loose reins. Moreover, to understand completely Hippolyte's mental state, the reader must consider the expanded macrocontext. This includes not only the other lines of the récit, where repetition of the same metonymic device reinforces the incompleteness, but also other passages in the play which the reader reconstructs metonymically in order to arrive at the ambiguity of Hippolyte's distracted condition: pursued by his stepmother, hated and unjustly rejected by his father, he is also in love with a woman whom his father has exiled. The incompleteness may eventually encourage the reader to extend the extratextual information further, which will expose an extended metonymic chain leading from Hippolyte's hand to the monster, the instrument of Neptune's wrath, to the gods themselves and Greek mythology. Thus, a movement which started as a relatively simple symbolic operation (the metonymy of the original line) can develop into a complex interplay of figural associations between various passages in the text and the symbolic use of extratextual knowledge in order to complete the line in the fullest sense of the word.

A second example shows how the operation also works when there is no initial symbolization but only a figuration marked by incompleteness with no initial incompatibility. The opening sentences of François Mauriac's *Thérèse Desqueyroux* cause the reader to start elucidating the story by relating several details and seeking to interpret them.

> L'avocat ouvrit une porte. Thérèse Desqueyroux, dans ce couloir dérobé du Palais de Justice, sentit sur sa face la brume et, profondément, l'aspira. Elle avait peur d'être attendue, hésitait à sortir. Un homme, dont le col était relevé, se détacha d'un platane; elle reconnut son père. L'avocat cria: "Non-Lieu" et, se retournant vers Thérèse:
>
> "Vous pouvez sortir: il n'y a personne."[7]

[The lawyer opened the door. Thérèse Desqueyroux, in this
hidden corridor of the Courthouse, felt the mist on her face and
breathed it in deeply. She was afraid someone would be waiting
for her, was hesitating to go out. A man, with his collar turned
up, moved away from a plane tree; she recognized her father. The
lawyer shouted: "All charges dismissed" and, turning back toward
Thérèse:

"You can come out: no one's here."]

Without being told directly, the reader assumes that the lawyer
is Thérèse's, that she is near him (he opens the door for her), and
that the lawyer calls "Non-Lieu" to the father. Further, the text
is replete with details that suggest that the reader decode the
passage metonymically. Read as metonymies of effects, the details lead the reader to establish causes and to conclude that
Thérèse's imprisonment was long and that the trial was scandal-
ous: Thérèse breathes in the foggy air as one who has been confined over a long period; the presence of a hidden corridor, her
hesitation and fear at being seen, her father's partially concealed
appearance outside by or behind a tree, with his collar up, suggest a desire to conceal the entire affair. These metonymies, initially symbolic, are then gradually integrated figurally into the
narration. For example, several pages later, the father declares
emphatically that only he knows how to smother scandals such
as Thérèse's.

The notion of incompleteness obviously carries with it considerable freedom for the reader. Although the incompleteness
may be marked, for example, by the need to fill in a gap in order
to understand the story or to grasp the motivation of a character,
in other instances the reader may "attack" and "force" the text
by assuming incompleteness at every moment. Such an extension of the notion should cause no problem, provided that the
relationships established as a result of the "forcing" share other
points of contact with the text and thus do not result in an interpretation based on a few isolated elements of the text. On the
other hand, incompleteness does not necessarily imply that one
must "complete" the text by means of a unified reading which
reassembles every element of the text into a coherent whole.
Todorov talks of modern literary criticism founded on "roman-

tic aesthetics, and above all on that of organic form. . . . Everything in a work fits together, everything contributes to a same 'figure in the carpet' and the best interpretation is the one which allows the integration of the greatest number of textual elements. We are, from the start, badly prepared for reading the discontinuous, the incoherent, the non-integratable."[8] The notion of incompleteness can be perfectly consistent with the open, plural, and discontinuous readings suggested by Todorov.

THE FOUR BASIC RHETORICAL CATEGORIES

Table 1, a theoretical table based on the four tropic processes—the operations of symbolization and figuration, and the principles of incompatibility and incompleteness—reveals four different categories of rhetorical functions. For simplicity, the four categories may be designated as Symbolization I, Symbolization II, Figuration I, and Figuration II. The Roman numeral I identifies a process marked by both incompleteness and incompatibility; Roman numeral II, one marked by incompleteness only. The examples cited earlier fall into the categories in the following manner:

Symbolization I: un temple; paradigmatic metaphor, in which S^2 is absent and where there is incompatibility between the micro- and macrocontexts.

Symbolization II: Sa main . . . les rênes; paradigmatic metonymic relationship, in which the statement is read as incomplete but where there is no incompatibility between the micro- and macrocontexts.

Figuration I: La Nature est un temple; Mon fils, ma joie; syntagmatic metaphor and metonymy, in which S^1 and S^2 are both present and where there is semantic incompatibility.

Figuration II: the opening lines of *Thérèse Desqueyroux*; syntagmatic metonymic relationships, where there is no initial incompatibility but in which the reader attempts to supply causal links between signs present in the text.

Like all charts, Table 1 oversimplifies and distorts the processes it seeks to describe. In particular, it fails to account for the

TABLE 1

	SYMBOLIZATION I (Incomplete and Incompatible)	SYMBOLIZATION II (Incomplete)
	TROPE: ONE WORD	ONE OR MORE WORDS
PARADIGMATIC S¹ PRESENT AND S² ABSENT	Metaphor Metonymy Synecdoche Irony	Paradigmatic metaphorical relationship Paradigmatic metonymical relationship Paradigmatic synecdochal relationship Paradigmatic ironical relationship
	FIGURATION I (Incomplete and Incompatible)	FIGURATION II (Incomplete)
	FIGURE: TWO OR MORE WORDS	TWO OR MORE WORDS
SYNTAGMATIC S¹ PRESENT AND S² PRESENT	Syntagmatic metaphor (simile) Syntagmatic metonymy Syntagmatic opposition	Syntagmatic metaphorical relationship Syntagmatic metonymical relationship Syntagmatic synecdochal relationship Syntagmatic relationship of opposition

close interaction between the operations. The sections that follow describe in greater detail the precise manner in which metaphor, metonymy, synecdoche, and irony individually work on the syntagm and suggest some ways in which the processes interact.

Metonymy

We have defined metonymy as a relationship of causality made possible by the presence within S^1 of the semantic feature "cause" or "effect" extended to include "producer" or "produced" as well as "agent" or "instrument" or "action." In symbolization, S^2 is absent from the microcontext; in figuration, both S^1 and S^2 are present.

Symbolization I. The previously discussed example from Corneille illustrates metonymy as a simple trope:

> "Je l'ai vu cette nuit, ce malheureux Sévère,
> La vengeance à la main, l'oeil ardent de colère."

[I saw him that night, this unfortunate Severus, / Vengeance in his hand, his eyes burning with anger.]

Here, S^1 = *vengeance*; S^2 = *épée* [sword]; and I = "to be performed" (the act of avenging).

Symbolization II. The previous discussion of the line from *Phèdre* demonstrates how the metonymic process can function in the absence of incompatibility. Such an operation is not limited, however, to a single statement or detail, as the example from *Thérèse Desqueyroux* illustrated. Nor is Symbolization II limited to the movement from effect back to cause. The famous final words of Balzac's *Le Père Goriot*—"A nous deux" [Now it's the two of us]—suggest a double metonymic operation: on one hand, the reader treats these words as the effects of events narrated in the novel and reconstructs the causal chain which has produced the conclusion. As such, the words remain on the figural level and complete one causal chain running through the novel. On the other hand, the reader can see the words as the possible cause

of future events. For the person who follows Rastignac's saga in
other volumes of the *Comédie humaine*, the symbolic meaning of
the words (Rastignac's conscious effort to conquer Paris) is spelled
out, as the symbol becomes, once again, part of a larger figuration.

Figuration I. In the statement "Voilà la belle Hélène, l'infamie des Grecs" [There is the beautiful Helen, the infamy of the
Greeks] the two signs (*Hélène* and *infamie*) figure in the syntagm
and are linked by a causal relation of action and agent. If the
reader is unaware of this intermediary and unable to provide it,
the statement is meaningless.

Figuration II. The juxtaposition of two passages in a text
often encourages the reader to seek a relationship between them.
S^1 and S^2 need not, however, be immediately juxtaposed along
the syntagmatic chain in order for such metonymic relationships
to come into play; in fact, frequently S^2 and S^1 are separated by
other parts of the text. For example, a passage from Flaubert's
Un Coeur simple narrates a trip taken by Félicité, Madame Au-
bain, Paul, and Virginie to Trouville. As they pass through the
center of Toucques, Monsieur Liébard, who accompanies them,
comments "avec un haussement d'épaules:—'En voilà une Mme
Lehoussais qui au lieu de prendre un jeune homme . . .' Félicité
n'entendait pas le reste; les chevaux trottaient, l'âne galopait; tous
enfilèrent un sentier, une barrière tourna, deux garçons parurent,
et l'on descendit devant le purin, sur le seuil même de la porte."
[With a shrug of his shoulders:—'There's a Mme Lehoussais who
lives here and who instead of taking a young man . . . ' Félicité
did not hear the rest; the horses were trotting, the donkey was
galloping; they all turned into a bridle-path, a gate opened, two
boys appeared, and everyone got off in front of the manure-
heap, right outside the door.] It is possible that the reader will
not question why Félicité did not hear the rest of Liébard's statement and will simply continue the story. But the suspension
marks, not previously used in the story, indicate that the reader
should seek to complete the sentence by reference to an earlier
passage which describes Félicité's loss of her only suitor:

Le moment arriva, elle courut vers l'amoureux.
A sa place, elle trouva un de ses amis.
Il lui apprit qu'elle ne devait plus le revoir. Pour se garantir de
la conscription, Théodore avait épousé une vieille femme très riche,
Mme Lehoussais, de Toucques.

[The time came, she hurried to meet her sweetheart.
Instead of him she found one of his friends.
He informed her that she would not see him (the suitor) again.
In order to make sure of avoiding the draft, Theodore had married
a rich old woman, Mme Lehoussais from Toucques.]

The association of the two passages establishes a metonymic link
and explains the cause for Félicité's failure to hear: her desire to
avoid a painful memory. Moreover, the reader can discover a
series of metonymical and metaphorical associations which are
among the main structuring devices of the narrative: the loss of
a lover causes Félicité to lavish affection on Virginie; the departure and eventual death of Virginie causes Félicité to transfer her
love to her nephew Victor; the death of Victor causes Félicité to
transfer her love to the parrot; the parrot shares certain features
with various objects and events of the story (the map of Victor's
travels, Virginie on her deathbed) and ultimately resembles the
Holy Spirit.

Synecdoche

Synecdoche has been characterized as a relationship of inclusion
made possible by the fact that one of the signifieds is also a semantic feature of the other signified. In symbolization, S^2 is absent from the microcontext; in figuration, both S^1 and S^2 are
present. Synecdoche poses a unique problem compared to the
other processes because it does not normally show an incompatibility between the micro- and the macrocontext, even in some
tropes. While there is incompatibility in the statement "The crown
has spoken," there is none if the word *animal* replaces *lion*. In a
sense all descriptions and namings—whether in literature or
everyday conversation—are synecdochal because an object or a
person cannot be fully described. Thus we are accustomed continually to fill in bits of information, going from the part to the

whole, in order to communicate. In literature, the synecdochal process tends to be associated with description, where several details serve to represent an entity (for example, a chair, a table, and a lamp suggest a whole room) or where one general word suffices to imply the presence of numerous elements (for example, the word *room* implies a door, window, floors, etc.). The nature of the description usually determines to what degree the reader makes use of synecdoche. Because of this association with description, synecdoche most often appears as groups of words. In addition, it frequently works in concert with metaphor, metonymy, and irony. The examples that follow stress this alliance between synecdoche and the other processes.

Symbolization I. The often-quoted example from Voltaire illustrates synecdoche as a trope: "Comme à Londres, à Bordeaux, de cent voiles suivie" [As in London, in Bordeaux by one hundred sails followed.] Here, S^1 = *voiles*; S^2 = *bateau* [ships]; S^1 is a semantic feature of S^2.

Symbolization II. In the passage cited from Mauriac, the exterior world is indicated by only three words—*porte* [door], *brume* [mist], *platane* [plane tree]—on which the reader constructs an imaginary décor outside the courthouse. In other situations, such as a Balzacian description, the reader is guided through a minute reconstruction of the whole, because the synecdoches serve as a base for a metonymic operation. Prévert's poem *Le Message* illustrates the complex interplay possible between synecdochal and metonymic operations. The first lines force the reader to create from very few details a room, which is never directly mentioned (the S^2), and a series of movements which must be completed:

> La porte que quelqu'un a ouverte
> La porte que quelqu'un a fermée
> La chaise où quelqu'un s'est assis
> Le chat que quelqu'un a caressé.[9]

> [The door that someone opened / The door that someone closed /
> The chair on which someone sat / The cat that someone petted.]

While creation of the room in the reader's mind is definitely synecdochal and relies on just two words, "door" and "chair," the movements take on a metonymical meaning as the poem progresses:

> Le fruit que quelqu'un a mordu
> La lettre que quelqu'un a lue
> La chaise que quelqu'un a renversée
> La porte que quelqu'un a ouverte
> La route où quelqu'un court encore
> Le bois que quelqu'un traverse
> La rivière où quelqu'un se jette
> L'hôpital où quelqu'un est mort.

[The fruit into which someone bit / The letter that someone read / The chair that someone knocked over / The door that someone opened / The road on which someone is running / The woods that someone goes through / The river into which someone throws him(her)self / The hospital where someone has died.]

The actions which lead to death function as a series of paradigmatic metonymies created by reading a letter and culminating in a suicide metonymically described through the instrument—throwing oneself into the river. The letter also works synecdochally in the poem because the reader is given no information of what it contains. Having inferred by metonymy that the letter is the cause of a suicide, one then can construct a second sign as desired: the absent contents of the letter. Taking the poem in its entirety, the reader has considerable latitude to create, through metonymy and synecdoche, the whole of the person's life and death.

Figuration I. Because incompatibility does not play a role in synecdoches, there are no syntagmatic synecdoches here.

Figuration II. The opening lines of Hugo's *A Villequier* establish a syntagmatic synecdochal relationship of the whole and the part. Paris (S^1) is described by four details (S^2) which come to represent the city in general: "Maintenant que Paris, ses pavés et ses marbres, / Et sa brume et ses toits sont bien loin de mes yeux" [Now that Paris, its pavements and its marbles, / And its mist and its roofs are far from my eyes]. From the details, the reader constructs a Paris of hardness (*pavé* and *toits*), of obscureness (*brume*), and of undefined, impersonal buildings (*see toits*). The description of Paris composed of four details takes on its full significance when contrasted with nature, defined synecdochally as trees and sky: "Maintenant que je suis sous les branches des arbres, / Et que je puis songer à la beauté des cieux" [Now that I am beneath the branches of the trees, / And that I can dream about the beauty of the heavens]. The two lines provide a macrocontext which permits the reader to interpret the smog as effects of the industrial revolution and a part of nineteenth-century metropolitan life, and the roofs as impediments to daydreaming (*songer*) and symbols of ugliness which are in direct contrast with nature (the roofs versus the trees; the smog versus the beauty of the skies). To arrive at this "whole" vision of Paris, Hugo has suppressed many other features of the city—the façades of buildings, the parks and the river, the beauty of the monuments—and has depersonalized the city by suppressing any mention of human activity. The synecdochal operation here imposes a selected number of details which replace and suppress other features of the whole. In other terms, a limited number of features occupy the entire field. This expansiveness is not a peculiarity of syntagmatic synecdochal relationships, but rather a general trait of the part standing for the whole.

Irony

Irony has been characterized as a relationship of opposition made possible by the identity of one or more semantic features *and* the presence of one or more contrary semantic features. As soon as one goes beyond the level of one-word tropes, however, it is evident that all oppositions are not ironic, and also that both irony and opposition play major roles in reading literary texts. Consequently, it is necessary within the general category of the relationship opposition, to make distinctions between irony, paradox (or contradiction), and antithesis (or simple opposition). Although each of these oppositional varieties has its own modality, they are joined by the fact that they all can be explained by the basic model of opposition: a combination of common and opposed semantic features.[10]

Symbolization I. This category involves what is normally called irony, which can be defined as a paradigmatic relationship (S^2 is not explicitly stated in the text) based on a resolved incompatibility. In the tropic example from *Horace* cited in Chapter 1,

> Viens voir mourir ta soeur dans les bras de son père;
> Viens repaître tes yeux d'un spectacle si *doux*.

[Come see your sister dying in her father's arms; / Come feast your eyes on such a lovely sight.]

there is obvious incompatibility between the adjective *doux* and the nature of the *spectacle* until the reader understands "horrible" or "terrible" in place of *doux*.

In most cases, irony involves much larger textual segments; however, the mechanism functions in the same manner. In the following passage from Voltaire's *Candide* the protagonist witnesses the horrors of war for the first time:

> Rien n'était si beau, si leste, si brillant, si bien ordonné que les deux armées. Les trompettes, les fifres, les hautbois, les tambours, les canons, formaient une harmonie telle qu'il n'y eut jamais en enfer. Les canons renversèrent d'abord à peu près six mille hommes de chaque côté; ensuite la mousqueterie ôta du meilleur des mondes environ neuf à dix mille coquins qui en infectaient la surface. La baïonnette fut aussi la raison suffisante de la mort de quelques milliers d'hommes. Le tout pouvait bien se monter à une trentaine de mille âmes. Candide, qui tremblait comme un philosophe, se cacha du mieux qu'il put pendant cette boucherie héroïque.

> [Nothing was as beautiful, as active, as brilliant, as well-trained as the two armies. Bugles, fifes, oboes, drums, cannons, formed a harmony such as Hell itself had never had. First the cannons destroyed about six thousand men on each side; next rifle-fire removed from the best of worlds about nine to ten thousand rogues who were infecting its surface. Bayonets proved to be the "sufficient reason" for the death of several thousand men. The total could well have reached thirty thousand souls. Candide, who was shaking like a philosopher, hid as best he could during this heroic slaughter.

Nowhere does the text indicate directly that war is bad; everything seems the best of possible worlds: the armies are characterized as brilliant and beautiful; the narrator gives statistics as

evidence of great success; the slaughter is qualified as heroic. But
within this apparent tribute to war appear certain incongruities
or incompatibilities—the cannons sounding with the musical instruments, the allusion to hell, the recognition that the statistics
refer to people—which can only be resolved by concluding that
the narrator considers war, not *beau* and *héroique*, but rather, "ugly
and stupid." We would stress two points: first, S^2 (here, "ugly
and stupid," or whatever other adjectives the reader can oppose
to *beau et héroique*) does not appear directly in the text; second,
when the reader substitutes S^1 in order to resolve the incompatibility, S^1 does not totally disappear but remains to mark the
passage as ironic.

   Symbolization II. This category, which requires a paradigmatic relationship of incompleteness, without incompatibility,
is the most problematic of the four groups under opposition.
Irony requires incompatibility; paradox and antithesis involve
syntagmatic relationships. What is needed here is a text which,
although offering no internal incompatibilities, nonetheless can
be read as meaning the opposite of what it apparently says. One
might conceive of a situation where extratextual information—
such as the author's biography and the cultural and intellectual
context—could encourage the reader to read the text ironically.
Clandestine literature or literature written in captivity might offer examples of texts which the reader, provided he were aware
of the circumstances surrounding the writing of the text, would
choose to interpret as ironic despite the absence of internal
markers.

   Figuration I. This category involves what is often called paradox or contradiction, which can be defined as a syntagmatic
relationship of unresolved incompatibility. At the tropic level,
this figure takes the form of an oxymoron, as illustrated by this
line from Corneille: "Cette *obscure clarté* qui tombe des étoiles"
[This dim brightness which falls from the stars]. Here, both S^1
(*clarté*) and S^2 (*obscure*) are present in the signifying chain; the
two share a common semantic feature (dealing with light), but
one indicates the presence of light, the other, its absence—a contradiction which the text does nothing to resolve. Except in the

case of the relatively infrequent oxymoron, whenever one normally encounters paradoxical or contradictory elements in a text
the opposition is ultimately cleared up: one version proves to be
correct or an explanation appears that renders the contradiction
only apparent. Modern literature, however, often leaves the reader
in the uncomfortable situation of being unable to resolve the
incompatibility.

For example, the reader of Robbe-Grillet's *Dans le labyrinthe*
is unsure of the setting after reading the first paragraph:

> Je suis seul ici, maintenant, bien à l'abri. Dehors il pleut, dehors
> on marche sous la pluie en courbant la tête, s'abritant les yeux
> d'une main tout en regardant quand même devant soi, à quelques
> mètres devant soi, quelques mètres d'asphalte mouillé; dehors il
> fait froid, le vent souffle entre les branches noires dénudées; le vent
> souffle dans les feuilles, entrînant les rameaux entiers dans un ba-
> lancement, dans un balancement, balancement, qui projette son
> ombre sur le crépi blanc des murs. Dehors il y a du soleil, il n'y a
> pas un arbre, ni un arbuste, pour donner de l'ombre, et l'on marche
> en plein soleil, s'abritant les yeux d'une main tout en regardant
> devant soi, à quelques mètres seulement devant soi, quelques mètres
> d'asphalte poussiéreux où le vent dessine des parallèles, des fourches,
> des spirales.[11]

> [I am alone here now, under cover. Outside it is raining, outside
> you walk through the rain with your head down, shielding your
> eyes with one hand while you stare ahead nevertheless, a few yards
> ahead, at a few yards of wet asphalt; outside it is cold, the wind
> blows between the bare black branches; the wind blows through
> the leaves, rocking the boughs, rocking them, rocking their shad-
> ows across the white roughcast walls. Outside the sun is shining,
> there is no tree, no bush to cast a shadow, and you walk under the
> sun shielding your eyes with one hand while you stare ahead, only
> a few yards in front of you, at a few yards of dusty asphalt where
> the wind makes patterns of parallel lines, forks, and spirals.]

The contradiction, the incompatibility between rain and sun-
shine, cannot be resolved, but only interpreted through a second-
level rhetorical operation, a metonymical reading of the paragraph (effect) as illustration of the arbitrariness of all writing
(cause).

Figuration II. This category includes antithesis or simple opposition, which can be defined as a syntagmatic relationship involving opposition without incompatibility. It is a favored and well-known technique of poets, such as Lamartine, who in *Le Papillon* restricts the two parts of the antithesis to the two hemistiches "Naître avec le printemps, mourir avec les roses" [To be born with springtime, to die with the roses]. The *stances* of Rodrique from Corneille's *Le Cid* offer an example of a longer passage constructed around a series of antitheses:

> Que je sens de rudes combats!
> Contre mon propre honneur mon amour s'intéresse:
> Il faut venger un père, et perdre une maîtresse:
> L'une m'anime le coeur, l'autre retient mon bras.
> Réduit au triste choix ou de trahir ma flamme,
>   Ou de vivre en infâme,
> Des deux côtés mon mal est infini.
>   O Dieu, l'étrange peine!
> Faut-il laisser un affront impuni?
> Faut-il punir le père de Chimène?

[What harsh struggles I feel! / Against my own honor my love has an interest: / I must avenge a father and lose a sweetheart: / The one pushes my heart to act, the other holds back my arm. / Reduced to the sad choice of either betraying my passion / Or of living as an ignominious wretch, / On both sides my trouble is infinite. / O God, what a strange difficulty! / Should I leave an insult unpunished? / Should I punish the father of Chimene?]

Rodrigue, caught between the conflicting claims of his father and his beloved, his honor and his passion, his glory and his pleasure, finally resolves the conflict by choosing one of the two terms of the opposition: his duty to his father. In terms of larger textual elements, when the reader of Zola's *Germinal* arrives at the opening chapter of Part II, he can read the description of morning at the home of the Grégoires, owners of the mine, in relation to the earlier chapter dealing with morning in the Maheu household, a family of miners. A radical opposition develops between the warmth and comfort of bourgeois existence and the cold and misery of proletarian life. Each detail reinforces the contrasts. For example, the Grégoire daughter remains luxuri-

ously in bed well into the morning, while all six Maheu children
awaken at four after a restless night crowded two to a bed; the
Grégoire breakfast of brioches and hot chocolate contrasts with
the meager Maheu breakfast of stale bread, cheese, and watery
coffee.

Metaphor

Metaphor is characterized by a relationship of similarity made
possible by the copossession of one or more semantic features.
In symbolization, S^2 is absent from the microcontext; in figuration, S^1 and S^2 are both present.

Symbolization I. The opening lines from Verlaine's *Chanson
d'automne* illustrate metaphor as a trope: "Les sanglots longs /
Des violons" [The long sobs / of the violins]

S^1 = *sanglots*; S^2 (absent) = *sons* (sound or music);

I = auditory sensations (by transfer, sadness) By association with S^1, "sobs," the sounds or music of the violins now
carry the connotation of human suffering or pain.

Symbolization II. When one considers paradigmatic metaphorical relationships, where there is incompleteness without
incompatibility, one again discovers that metaphor differs from
the other rhetorical operations. Metonymy, synecdoche, and irony
depend on processes which are quite highly deterministic and
limiting in the choices offered to the reader: logic (cause-effect,
classification, negation), quantitative and spatial relationship (part
and whole), cultural codes (mythology, social and political insti
tutions). In addition, as already suggested, metonymy and synecdoche are linked in a fundamental way to two basic elements
of literature—narration and description. But metaphor is based
on association and needs only one shared semantic feature among
many found in two words in order to establish a relationship.
Thus it allows the reader much more freedom of selection. This
is particularly true when, in the absence of incompatibility, the
metaphorical relationship is not marked in the text, when there
is only incompleteness, a feeling on the part of the reader of a
lack which moves the reader to activate the metaphorical pro-

cess. An obvious illustration of this sometimes dangerous liberty is found in simplified Freudian searches for sexual symbolism. For example, in the following lines of Corneille's *Horace* one might identify the sword as a penis: "Ce crime quoique grand, énorme, inexcusable, / Vient de la même épée et part du même bras" (lines 1740–41) [This crime, although huge, enormous, inexcusable / Comes from the same sword and issues forth from the same arm]. Even though the word *sword* is perfectly compatible with the context and the text offers no direct support for such a reading, the reader could use other metaphorical readings of the text emphasizing virility and sexual metaphors to justify the symbolic meaning assigned to *sword*. At this point rhetorical decoding becomes part of interpretation, an activity which takes place when the reader does not just consider the signs of the text at face value but also exploits the associations that a word or a group of words provide. Despite the difficulties inherent in this freedom, to refuse the possibility of applying this model of metaphorical symbolization is tantamount to condemning the reader to accepting the expressed intentions of the author.

Figuration I. "Quand le ciel bas et lourd pèse comme un couvercle" [When the low, heavy sky weighs like a lid]. $S^1 =$ *couvercle*; $S^2 =$ *ciel*; $I =$ *pèse* (by transfer, "enclosure," "heaviness," "pressing down"). By association with S^1 ("cover"), the sky, here present in the syntagm, does not just occupy the space above the poet's head but takes on the idea of enclosure.

Figuration II. Because syntagmatic metaphorical relationships, where there is incompleteness but no incompatibility, require the reader to locate S^2 within the text, they create fewer problems of judging the validity of the interpretation than does Symbolization II. The first line of Ronsard's sonnet "Quand vous serez bien vieille, au soir, à la chandelle" [When you are very old, in the evening, by candlelight] contains no marked metaphors; yet the reader can begin the metaphorical process by examining the juxtaposition of *au soir* and *vieille*. Even though there is no semantic incompatibility, the reader may search for a common link between the two terms. Since the macrocontext is still quite limited, the reader has recourse to extratextual information to identify the intermediary *end*. One then integrates this result into the macrocontext and repeats the operation. With further reading of the poem, a chain of metaphorical relationships develops having as intermediaries *death*, *weakness*, and *monotony*. As is almost always the case, figuration and symbolization work together as complementary processes in the act of reading.

BEYOND THE WORD: TRACES IN THE TEXT

In expanding the four tropes beyond one word, we are no longer dealing with metaphors, metonymies, synecdoches, ironies per se, as identities or elements, but with metaphorical, metonymical, synecdochal, and ironic processes tied together by the four basic relationships of similarity, causality, inclusion, opposition. One reads these relationships in the same way, be it a question of one word or many, of paradigmatic or syntagmatic links, of incompatibility or just incompleteness.

The importance of this extension comes from the place rhetoric occupies in the reading process. The rhetoric of tropes plays a very small part in the reading of most texts, for the number of "pure" tropes in a text is quite limited. If the rhetorical processes are extended to include various kinds of symbolization and figuration, the domain of rhetoric can include the entire text. Rhetorical operations can thus be seen as the basis of such traditional literary analyses as those of character, plot, and setting: similar ties and oppositions between characters (or between characters and settings), causal chains linking plot events or relating a character's acts to the setting, and so forth. In addition, the general interpretive approach reflects the type of rhetorical process employed by the reader. A metaphorical reading seeks parallels between the structures in the text and those of other systems, for example, sociological or psychoanalytical modes and theories. A metonymical reading attempts to link the text with those facts that have determined it, as in biography and historical studies. A reading based on synecdoche treats the text, or elements of it, as part of a larger "text," such as the writer's words, a literary style or movement, an historical or ideological moment. An ironical reading opposes the text to other texts by the same or different writers. In short, reading is essentially a rhetorical operation.

But in the actual process of reading there is a huge gap between confronting specific configurations and symbolizations and making statements about entire literary works. Individual operations can be isolated for the sake of definition and analysis, but the complexity of literary texts and the multiple possibilities of the rhetorical operations contained in even one word prevents the reader from retaining and combining all the processes offered by a text, even a highly encoded and conventional one. Wolfgang Iser has renewed the eighteenth-century metaphor of the reader likened to a traveler in a stagecoach, "who has to a make the often difficult journey through [a] novel gazing from his moving viewpoint."[12] Although a ride through a poem may not be the same as one through a play or novel, movement through the time and space of the text brings about the same result: "At no time can [we] have a total view of the journey" (p. 16). The problem of reading is further complicated because at almost any given moment we are called upon to look at more than one element of the landscape. Even isolated words will have more than one meaning and point in more than one direction. We are continually making choices as we read, as we retain some meanings and discard others. But the problem extends far beyond semantic and lexical selection and combination to rhetorical strategies. Just as rhetoric is different from one century to another and from one culture to another, it is multiple within a text. The short title of Valery's *Les Pas* can by itself stimulate all four of the rhetorical processes to enter into different interpretations of the poem. Footsteps generate synecdochally the person walking and lead the reader to imagine that a "full" person is realized in the body of the text. They also are part of metonymic chains of creation and cause and effect, suggesting to the reader a motivation or force creating the steps and the walk. In Valery's poetry, with its emphasis on the creative act, a reader could immediately associate the steps metaphorically to the creative act itself. The final line of the poem, "Et mon cœur n'était que vos pas" [And my heart was just your footsteps] suggests an ironical relationship between the heart and the mere footsteps of the other person. In the corpus of the poem, *traces* can be found to fill out the image of the other person, to create the source of the moving feet, to generate a metaphorical interpretation of poetic creativity, and to read the irony of poetic desire. Traveling through a text is a continual pursuit of traces in individual words, in the relationship of words in one paragraph and another, in one chapter and another, one stanza and another. Yet a reader cannot possibly retain all the traces which accumulate from the beginning to the end of a text as more rhetorical choices present themselves and more figurations and symbolizations come to him. Thus, as the reader travels through the text, he retains some traces and represses others; parts of the text stay clearly in mind while others are forgotten, transformed in his memory, or relegated to his unconscious. It is out of this action of remembering and forgetting that traces are constructed to lead to a reading or interpretation.

In *S/Z* Roland Barthes described the act of reading as the creation of *tresses* or braids which are eventually bound together.[13] Although similar to Barthes's *tresses*, "traces" more accurately suggests the complexity of the literary text and the act of reading. As in Freud's mystical writing pad, on one level of reading, such as "relaxed reading," the text appears as a set of clear-cut lines depicting a neat image. Such readings often are at the level of the plot or the literal meaning. But for the alert reader there lie, underneath the multiple traces of previous fragments of the text, previous readings and previous rhetorical constructions.[14] The act of reading demands choosing among the apparent chaos which the traces can create. From this necessary selection and repression readers find satisfaction and fulfillment.[15]

3

THE RHETORIC

OF THE SIGNIFIER

In *Le Signifiant imaginaire*, Christian Metz maintains that tropes and figures are purely "referential operations" and do not involve the signifiers: "There hardly exists any concept of metaphor or metonymy in which these figures would involve the phonetic or graphic aspect of words."[1] Although traditional rhetoric dealt with figures such as alliteration, assonance, paranomasis, and antanclasis which involve the signifier, Metz points out that such figures are the most difficult to connect with metaphor or metonymy: "Moreover, defenders of the binary concept, in the contemporary period, have not tried to link them together; they have been content to no longer speak of these figures. And in fact, the link was impossible, not due to any secondary or late-appearing difficulty, but because these figures are from the start indifferent to the referent, while metaphor and metonymy are defined in relation to it" (359). Metz is correct in that previous studies of tropes and figures, of symbolization and figuration, have depended on referentially based connections between signifieds.

If one examines carefully the activity of the reader, however, rhetorical operations of the four basic types come into play on the level of the signifier as well as on that of the signified. The most elementary acts practiced by traditional readers of poems require these basic rhetorical operations. Recognizing rhyme schemes and rhythmic patterns, pointing out sound frequencies, describing formal structures (such as sonnet, ballad, ode) are all part of rhetoric. Certainly such schemes, patterns, and structures are not metaphors, metonymies, synecdoches, or ironies. Nonetheless, they depend on associations of similarity, opposition, inclusion, and causality; and they are the result of metaphoric, ironic, synecdochal, and metonymic symbolizations and figurations.

The study of the phonetic aspects of the signifier presents nothing new in literary criticism. Very little, however, has been done with graphemes. Yet, in many languages graphemes and phonemes can differ radically, making possible situations where they can play against each other as well as work together. While Derrida has dramatically shown the differences between speech and writing, he does not stress that the graphic (the written) is, for the most part, typographic, a fact that numerous writers, especially since Mallarmé, have tried to exploit. The typography includes:

1. The place a word occupies in the signifying chain: for example, before or after a verb, at the beginning or end of a work.
2. The location on the page: at the top, bottom, in the margin, to the left or right, or in columns.
3. The size and shape of the typeface.

Some readers, notably Ricardou, Kristeva, and Finas, have at times explored these aspects of the signifier.[2] They have not seen, however, the relationship between the processes they use in analyzing the signifiers and the readings that they and others do primarily on the level of the signified. The insistence on the "play of the signifier" (*jeu du signifiant*) in contemporary criticism does not represent a radical new way of reading, but rather a *displacement of basic rhetorical reading processes to a different aspect of the text*. The signifying chain is regarded not just as a vehicle for transporting signifieds, but as a disposition of signifiers susceptible of analysis in their own right.

Resemblance (Metaphorical Operations)

In Chapter 1 metaphor was described as a semantic and referential relationship of resemblance made possible by the co-presence of one or more semantic features. When dealing with signifiers, this definition reads as "a relationship of resemblance made possible by the copossession of one or more phonetic, graphic, or typographic features." The minimal degree of resemblance necessary to establish a link or trace remains constant, requiring at least one common element, whether it is a question of signifieds or signifiers. But whereas on the level of the signified the subjective and variable nature of semantic features makes total synonymy impossible and thus establishes an upper limit on the degree of resemblance, with signifiers one can have a perfect resemblance: the same combination of graphemes and phonemes presented in the same order and printed in the same typeface, as in *phare* [far] / *phare* [far].[3] Consequently, the most basic example of metaphorical linking of signifiers involves recognizing the repetition of a word, of a group of words, of a sentence, and so on. Resemblance can be inscribed on a continuum between the poles of identity and difference, as illustrated in Figure 6. The variations in the degree of resemblance depend on relationships and interrelationships between phonemes, graphemes, typographemes, and, eventually, even signifieds. The words *sein* [breast] and *saint* [saint] share a phonetic identity [sẽ] but differ graphically, typographically, and semantically. The play of signifiers can range from individual words to a fairly extensive textual sequence.

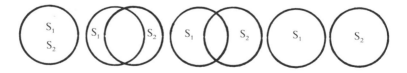

Figure 6

Individual Words

Rhyme, alliteration, and assonance all require the reader to act on metaphorical figurations. Each act depends on the identification of at least one common element such as the final sound, initial consonant, or final vowel. The intermediary can be either purely phonemic (*automne / monotone* [otɔn] / [mɔnɔtɔn]; *ces serpents* [se sɛrpɑ̃]; *pleut / veux* [plø] / [vø] or both phonemic and graphic (*trêve / grêve* [trɛv] / [grɛv]; *siffler ses serpents* [sifle se sɛrpɑ̃]; *chat / rat* [ʃa] / [ra]). The search for similarity can lead also to connections which permit recombination of some or all of the elements of the signifiers. The reader who sees in the word *abeilles* the anagram of *Isabelle* does so on the basis of a "strong" metaphorical figuration: the common elements are all eight graphemes; the only obstacle to identity is the order in which they appear. The relationship between *train* and *rient*, on the other hand, represents a "weaker" metaphorical figuration, with only four of five common graphemes. The reader may find it much easier to establish such relationships when they are overdetermined, for example signifiers such as *rouge* [ruʒ] and *joue* [ʒu] which share both graphemes (*o, u, e*) and phonemes ([ʒ], [u]).[4] Typographical considerations can also lead the reader to make connections based on similarity. These traces can be purely typographical. For example, in the final sentence of Ricardou's *La Prise / Prose de Constantinople* the capitalization of JE SUIS and LE LIVRE invites the reader to connect the four words: "Certaine lecture consciencieuse suffit maintenant pour que l'irradiation de toute figure élabore qui JE SUIS, et par un phénomène réflexif point trop imprévu, en un éclair, me LE LIVRE" [A certain conscientious reading is now enough so that the irradiation of any figure works out who I AM, and by a not totally unexpected reflexive phenomenon, in a flash, BETRAYS IT to me]. Traces may also involve the interaction of typography and graphemes or phonemes, as in *dures* [dyr] and *architectures* [arʃitektyr], the first and last words of Valéry's poem *Les Grenades*.

The trace-work need not remain only on the level of the signifier. Most readings tend to use the relationship of signifiers as a bridge to thematic interpretation. Readers of Mallarmé's *Le vierge, le vivace et le bel aujourd'hui* establish a metaphorical trace based on the vowel [i] ("*vivace*," "aujourd'hu*i*," "*il*," "déch*i*rer," "*i*vre," "fu*i*," "*cygne*," "lu*i*" . . .), which so dominates the poem that the "sonnet du cygne" has also been called the "sonnet de symphonie en i majeur." Critics searching for a link between the sound pattern and the symbolic meaning of the poem (the sterile agony of the swan-poet) usually then propose a metaphorical interpretation: the efforts required to articulate the [i], the most spread, the tensest vowel sound in French, resemble the efforts of the swan to free itself from the ice. Whereas in the Mallarmé sonnet the metaphorical link includes a series of signifiers, in Baudelaire's *Le Balcon* the rhetorical process involves at first a single word. The reader of the final stanza

> Ces serments, ces parfums, ces baisers infinis
> Renaîtront-ils d'un gouffre interdit à nos sondes
> Comme montent au ciel les soleils rajeunis
> Après s'être lavés au fond des mers profondes?
> —O sermènts! ô parfums! ô baisers infinis!!

[Those vows, those perfumes, those infinite kisses / Will they be reborn from a gulf forbidden to our soundings / As rejuvenated suns rise up to heaven / After having bathed in the depths of deep seas? / —O vows! o perfumes! o infinite kisses!!]

may well be tempted to read *mers* as *mères* (common elements: the phonemes [mɛr]). Such an association, motivated by traces involving the poem's signifieds, could lead to a metaphorical interpretation of the poem as a fantasy of repression and rebirth: *maîtresse* [mistress] → *mère* [mother], the intermediaries, from earlier stanzas, including *seins* [breasts], *genoux* [knees], *corps* [body], *coeur* [heart]; *maîtresse* → *nuit* [night], the intermediaries being *cloison* [wall], *noir* [black], *gouffre* [abyss], *interdit* [forbidden].

Some contemporary readings remain completely on the level of the signifier. Ricardou uses metaphorical figuration to analyze processes of text generation in his own novels where, for example, *Isabelle* gives rise anagramatically to *abeilles*, *Silab Lee*, Dr. *Baseille*, la *belle Isa*, *Bel Asile*, *Ile de Sable*. Nevertheless, most often readings that begin only with signifiers slide toward the level of the signified. In a generative series from Robbe-Grillet's

Projet pour une révolution à New York, Ricardou reads the generator *rouge* as producing not only *jour, joue, roue, roux*, all of which
appear as signifiers in the text, but also *rogue* [arrogant] ("c'est
impossible et tu nous embêtes" [It's impossible and you are a
nuisance to us]), *goure* [*se gourer*: to make a mistake] ("j'ai dû
commettre une grave erreur" [I must have made a serious er-
ror]), and *roué* [a rake] ("je l'ai giflée plusieurs fois" [I slapped
her several times]), where the link depends on the signified of
the second sign.[5] In an analogous fashion, he associates two apparently disconnected sequences, one of two boys walking in the
country and another of a couple in town, in Claude Simon's
Triptyque:

> L'un des garçons chuchote à l'autre de ne pas bouger et qu'elle va
> bientôt ressortir. Deux *papillons* blancs se poursuivent, voletant,
> se croisant. . . .
>   Le couple enlacé contre le mur de briques est apparemment im-
> mobile. . . . L'homme est vêtu d'un costume noir. Il s'écarte par-
> fois légèrement et l'on entrevoit alors le plastron blanc de sa che-
> mise qui luit dans l'ombre et le noeud *papillon* noir qui ferme le
> col. (Pp. 15, 19; our italics)

> [One of the boys whispers to the other not to move and that it
> (the fish) will soon come out again. Two white *butterflies* chase
> each other, wings fluttering as they pass one another. . . .
>   The couple caught in an embrace against the brick wall is ap-
> parently immobile. . . . The man is wearing a black suit. Occa-
> sionally he steps back slightly and one then catches a glimpse of
> his white shirt-front glowing in the shadows and of the black bow-
> tie closing the collar.]

Here the metaphorical figuration links the two appearances of
papillon, and the same signifier serves as a vehicle for two signifieds of *insect/bow-tie*.[6] This and numerous other examples allow Ricardou to show how Simon produces his text. The lengths
to which Ricardou goes in his search for anagrammatical and
other metaphorical relationships suggest the great freedom the
reader enjoys in playing with the signifier. Freed from the dictates of the intentional fallacy, the reader can discover rhetorical
relationships on all levels, not just that of the signifier, which the

writer may not be aware of, and use these relationships in the traces he establishes in the process of reading.

A final example will show how typographical features can enter into the metaphorical interplay between reading signifiers and signifieds. When confronted with the following passage from the beginning of Butor's *Mobile*, the reader is forced to make metaphorical links based on typography and the repetition of signifiers:

> nuit déjà moins noire à
> FLORENCE, temps central
> *Bleu nuit.*
> Les monts Ozarks, —passée la frontière du Sud-Ouest,
> FLORENCE.
> GEORGETOWN, comté de White ou comté Blanc.
> *Les monts la nuit.*
> Sur la route une Buick (vitesse limitée à 60 miles).
> GEORGETOWN, chef-lieu de Williamson, —en continuant vers l'ouest
> GEORGETOWN, NEW MEXICO, —la réserve des Indiens Zunis.
> LA GRANGE, comté de Lee, ARKANSAS.
> *Le réveil sonne.*
>
> [already not so dark in
> FLORENCE, Central Time.
> *Blue night.*
> The Ozark Mountains, —across the southwest state line,
> FLORENCE.
> GEORGETOWN, White County.
> *The mountains at night.*
> A Buick on the highway (speed limit 60 miles).
> GEORGETOWN, county seat of Williamson County, — continuing west,
> GEORGETOWN, NEW MEXICO, —the Zuni Indian Reservation.
> LA GRANGE, Lee County, ARKANSAS.
> *The alarm clock goes off.*][7]

The names of towns, initially linked by type size and homonymy, can be differentiated by their location on the page: no two names with the same signifier appear in the same column. Consequently, the GEORGETOWN and FLORENCE of the first

column can be linked to one state eventually marked as Arkan-
sas, the GEORGETOWN and FLORENCE of the second col-
umn to a different state later specifically identified as Texas, and
the GEORGETOWN of column three to a third state, New
Mexico. Of course, in reading the states, the reader makes use
not only of metaphorical processes but also of synecdochal operations in situating the town in its whole. These second rhetorical operations move to the level of the signified and are referentially based (if one knows the geography of the southwestern
United States, one does not need to wait for Butor to mark explicitly the name of the state). Similarly, the reader can associate
the phrases *Bleu nuit, Les monts la nuit, Le réveil sonne* thanks to
their shared use of italics and location in column one. This association serves as a point of departure for reading a mininovel
within the text, the dreams and nightmares of an unidentified
white couple from the South. Once again, the recognition of the
content of the novel depends on additional rhetorical operations
on the level of the signified. For example, *nuit* and *le réveil* suggest that someone is sleeping and has to get up.

Larger Textual Units

In the above examples, the rhetorical processes were used to link
individual words. Even in those cases where the operation resulted in a trace involving numerous terms, the constitution of
the trace required a series of word-to-word associations. Readers work with larger textual fragments, however, and regardless
of the size of the elements in question, rhetorical operations continue to enter into play as readers notice combinations of signifiers. In each case, the metaphorical nature of the process depends on a mixture of similarity and difference.

Traditional analysis of poetry offers numerous examples of
metaphorical operations performed at the level of the signifier.
One recognizes *formal structures* by identifying at least one common element between stanzas. Such structures can range from
the simple, where two stanzas have the same number of lines, to
the more complex, for example, a ballad, which requires not
only repetition of a certain number of lines but also of a refrain,
to the very complex, for example, a *pantoum*, where, in addition
to the repetition of lines and rhymes, entire signifying chains are

repeated. *Metrical patterns* depend on the repetition of a certain number of phonemes while allowing for differences both in the number of graphemes and in the nature of the sounds involved. *Syntactic structures* similarly require that the reader recognize a repetition in the order in which certain categories of signifiers, such as nouns, verbs, and prepositions, appear in the text. In all these instances, the preliminary metaphorical operation which reveals these formal aspects of the poem serves as the foundation for other rhetorical operations which may well involve not only signifiers but signifieds. In the first stanza of du Bellay's sonnet

> Si notre vie est moins qu'une journée
> En l'éternel, si l'an qui fait le tour
> Chasse nos jours sans espoir de retour,
> Si périssable est toute chose née

> [If our life is less than a day in the eternal / If the year which goes around / Chases away our days with no hope of return / If everything born is perishable]

the regularity of the metrical pattern (4–6) and the repetition of the syntactic pattern (three subordinate clauses introduced by *si*) complement the central theme of the stanza, the brevity of human life. At the same time, the reader also becomes aware of certain differences—the absence of accord between metric patterns and syntax (*enjambement*), and changes in word order within each *si* clause. The combination of similarity and difference on the level of the signifier helps the reader discover a progression within the signifieds of brevity, fleeting time, and death.

Because such analyses based on the interplay of signifier and signified are commonplace in dealing with poetry, readers of prose have tended to adopt the terminology and methodology of poetry when they have analyzed prose style. In the following paragraph from Chateaubriand's *René*, one might associate metaphorically the rhythm of the sentences, linked metaphorically by the parallel syntax, to the repeated tolling of the bell:

> Les dimanches et les jours de fête, j'ai souvent entendu, dans le grand bois, à travers les arbres, les sons de la cloche lointaine qui appelait au temple l'homme des champs. Appuyé contre le tronc d'un ormeau, j'écoutais en silence le pieux murmure. Chaque frémissement de l'airain portait à mon âme naïve l'innocence des

moeurs champêtres, le calme de la solitude, le charme de la religion, et la délectable mélancolie des souvenirs de ma première en-
fance. Oh! quel coeur si mal fait n'a tressailli au bruit des cloches
de son lieu natal, de ces cloches qui frémirent de joie sur son berceau, qui annoncèrent son avènement à la vie, qui marquèrent le
premier battement de son coeur, qui publièrent dans tous les lieux
d'alentour la sainte allégresse de son père, les douleurs et les joies
encore plus ineffables de sa mère! Tout se trouve dans les rêveries
enchantées où nous plonge le bruit de la cloche natale: religion,
famille, patrie, et le berceau et la tombe, et le passé et l'avenir.

[Sundays and holidays I have often heard, in the forest, through
the trees, the sounds of the distant bell calling to church the man
of the fields. Leaning on the trunk of an elm I would listen silently
to the pious murmur. Each vibration of the bronze would bring
to my naive soul the innocence of country ways, the calm of solitude, the charm of religion and the delightful melancholy of my
early childhood memories. Oh! what heart so poorly formed has
not quivered at the sound of bells from its native region, of those
bells which trembled with joy over one's cradle, which announced
the advent of one's life, which marked the first beat of one's heart,
which published all around the godly happiness of one's father,
the even more ineffable pains and joys of one's mother! All is found
in the enchanted reveries into which the sound of the native bell
plunges us: religion, family, country, both the cradle and tomb,
both the past and the future]

Similarly, in the following passage from *Madame Bovary*

Ils commencèrent lentement, puis allèrent plus vite. Ils tournaient:
tout tournait autour d'eux, les lampes, les meubles, les lambris, et
le parquet, comme un disque sur un pivot.

[They began slowly, then went faster. They were turning: everything around them was turning, the lamps, the furniture, the
wainscoting, the floor, like a disk on a pivot.]

the reader can discover several metaphorical associations of signifiers—repetition of words (*tournaient, tournait*), repetition of
sounds (*tout tournait autour*), alliteration (*les lampes, les meubles,
les lambris*)—which can be related, again metaphorically, to the
meaning of the passage: the repetition and the insistence on a
liquid consonant ([l]) suggest the regular, flowing movement of
a waltz.

Ricardou's readings of new novelists demonstrate the possibility of performing metaphorical operations on other aspects
of the signifier. Two examples will illustrate Ricardou's play with
signifiers. In the famous "la cafetière est sur la table" passage
from Robbe-Grillet's *Trois Visions réfléchies* (from *Instantanés*),
Ricardou points out a metaphorical relationship based on the
same unchanging order in which certain signifiers appear and
reappear in the text:

> La *cafetière* est sur la *table*. C'est une table ronde à quatre pieds
> recouverte d'une *toile cirée*. . . . Au centre, un carreau de céra-
> mique tient lieu de *dessous de plat*; le dessin en est entièrement
> masqué, du moins rendu méconnaissable, par la *cafetière* qui est
> posée dessus. . . . Il n'y a rien d'autre sur la *table* que la *toile cirée*,
> le *dessous de plat* et la *cafetière*. (Pp. 9–10; our italics)

> [The *coffeepot* is on the *table*. It's a round, four-legged table covered
> with an *oilcloth*. . . . In the center, a ceramic tile takes the place of
> a *hot-plate*: its design is completely hidden, or at the least made
> unrecognizable, by the *coffeepot* which is sitting on it. . . . There
> is nothing on the *table* other than the *oilcloth*, the *hot-plate* and the
> *coffeepot*.]

The orderly repetition of the signifiers *cafetière, table, toile cirée,
dessous de plat, cafetière, table, toile cirée, dessous de plat* is then connected, also metaphorically, to reflections, one of the main motifs of the text, as well as to the *Trois visions réfléchies*. Thus,
Ricardou reads the literal doubling of the signifiers in the text as
"reflecting" the thematic doubling of mirrors and reflected visions. A second example, drawn from Robbe-Grillet's *Le Voyeur*, shows how metaphorical operations can work semiana-
grammatically within the groups of words:

> C'est dans cette dernière armoire, la plus imposante, toujours fer-
> mée à clef, que se trouvait, à l'étagère inférieure, dans le coin droit,
> la boîte à chaussure où il rangeait sa collection de ficelles et de
> cordelettes.
>   Le corps de la fillette fut retrouvé le lendemain matin, à la marée
> basse.[8]

> [It's in the last dresser, the most impressive one, (which is) always
> kept locked, that was found, on the lower shelf, in the right-hand

corner, the shoe box where he kept his collection of strings and small ropes.

    The little girl's body was found the next morning, at low tide.]

Surprised by the apparently unmotivated transition from one setting, a room rented by the protagonist, Mathieu, to another, the rocks where the murder victim's body was discovered, the reader can establish a nondiegetic link by the play of signifiers—*ficelles, cordelettes → corps de la fillette*—through redistribution of many of the same graphemes.[9]

    In the previous examples, the common elements consist of phonemes and graphemes. The intermediary for a metaphorical relationship between textual fragments can also involve primarily typographical elements. One of the means by which Butor gives mobility to *Mobile* is by the interpenetration of ideograms. The reader becomes aware of the movement of the text by metaphorically relating each ideogrammatic configuration to previous ideograms. For example, when one comes upon the following fragment:

Harles à poitrine rouge,

        oeils d'or de Barros,

la mer,

        tourbillons,

                bécasseau semi-palmes,

grottes,

        archipels,

caps,

        macreuses d'Amérique,

sternes de Forster,

        rades.

[Red breasted mergansers,

        Barrow's gold eyes,

the sea,

        waterspouts,

                semi-palmated sandpipers,

caves,

        archipelagoes,

capes,

        American puffins,

Forster's terns,

        jetties.]

one can find in it two typographical patterns already seen: one
consists of bird names and forms a V shape on the page; the
other, beginning with the words *la mer*, contains things associated with the sea presented in a list of alternating pairs:

La mer,

                                                    hors-bord,
ski nautique,

                                                    plongeoirs,
toboggans,

                                                    bouées,
Grèbes de Holboell,
    puffins d'Audobon,
        pluviers des terres,
        plongeons communs
sarcelles à ailes bleues.

[The sea,

                                                    outboards,
water-skiing,

                                                    diving boards,
toboggans,

                                                    buoys,
Holboell's grebes,
    Audobon's puffins,
        land plovers,
        common terns,
blue-winged teal.]

   The similarity with the earlier isolated appearance of these
configurations allows the reader to recognize the basic difference
(the interpenetration of the two series). The trace established by
successive performances of this operation then permits linking
by metaphorical symbolization the changes in the typography to
changes associated with movement and eventually to one of the
main metaphors of the text—the mobiles of Alexander Calder.

Inclusion (Synecdochal Operations)

We have characterized synecdoche as "a semantic or referential
relationship of inclusion made possible by the fact that one of
the signifieds is also a semantic feature of the other signified."

When dealing with signifiers, the definition is adjusted to read "the inclusion of one signifier entirely in the other." Whereas metaphorical relationships can range from total identity to partial similarity, synecdochal operations require that an entire signifier—a word, a phrase, or a paragraph—be included exactly and completely in a larger textual unit. One can establish a metaphorical link between *vert* ([vɛr]) and *cher* ([ʃɛr]) or *pair* ([pɛr]); a synecdochal relationship would require that *vert* (and/or [vɛr]) be entirely present in the second signifier, for example, in *couvert* or *verrou* ([vɛru]). Because of this limitation, synecdochal operations on the level of the signifier are found less frequently than the metaphorical.

Individual Words

On the level of the signifier, metaphorical and synecdochal relationships resemble each other because both involve the co-possession of certain phonetic, graphic, and typographic elements. The difference resides in the fact that the shared elements in synecdoche constitute a signifying whole and that one of the signifiers involved coincides perfectly with that whole. The distinction can be illustrated by the final six lines of Michaux's *Glu et gli*:

> Ah! que je te hais Boileau
> Boiteux, Boignetière, Boiloux, Boigermain,
> Boirops, Boitel, Boivery,
> Boicamille,
> Doit de travers
> Bois ça.

> [Ah! how I hate you, Boileau, / Boiteux (Gimpy), Boignetière, Boiloux, Boigermain, / Boirops, Boitel, Boivery, / Boicamille, / Drink crooked / Drink that.]

Initially, the reader establishes a metaphorical trace based on the copossession of phonemes ([bwa]). But it is only when he arrives at the last two lines that [bwa] appears as a complete signifier in its own right, thus transforming the entire trace into a synecdochal relationship with [bwa] figuring in all the proper names. These first rhetorical operations form the basis of a metonymical figuration linking the end of the poem (*bois, boit*) to the title (*glu*, *gli*), the latter representing onamatopoetically the sounds, or effects, produced by the act of drinking.

In the above illustration, the inclusion involved only phonemic features; the following example of synecdochal reading bases the inclusion on both phonemic and graphic features. Analyzing the following passage from *Le Ravissement de Lol V. Stein*, "Lol rit parce qu'elle cherche quelque chose qu'elle croyait trouver ici, qu'elle devrait donc trouver et qu'elle ne trouve pas" [Lol laughs because she is looking for something that she thought she would find here, that she should find therefore, but that she does not find], Verena Andermatt sees in the repetition of *trouver* [to find] an insistence on the word *trou* [hole], "the absence, the hollow engulfing everything for ever." This synecdochal operation supports a metaphorical interpretation of the protagonist's situation: "With Lol in the middle as zero, nothingness, a hole, an absence—but a hole through which objects are engulfed and from which they emerge."[10] The reading is overdetermined by the signified because Lol finds nothing.

As with metaphorical relationships, one can also discover the second signifier of a synecdochal link dispersed over several lines of text. Numerous examples of paragrammatic analysis illustrate this process, ranging from Saussure's famous discovery of the name Aphrodite in the opening lines of Lucretius' *De Rerum Natura* to Jonathan Culler's reading of *hystérie* ([isteri]) in Baudelaire's phrase "je sen*tis* ma gorge serrée par la main *terri*ble de l'*hystérie*" [I felt my throat gripped by the terrible hand of hysteria].[11] In a more modern text, his own *La Prise/Prose de Constantinople*, Ricardou points out the paragrammatization of the name Isis: "Mais Berthold Toth préc*ise* qu'*il* *s*'agit plutôt, *si* *sa* mémoire est correcte, d'un obél*isque* br*isé* de Karnak, tel que peut le découvrir une observation suff*isamment scrupuleuse, à proximité du huitième pylône comportant des statues des pa*ys* vaincus par Thoutono*sis* III" [But Berthold Toth specifies that it is rather a question, if his memory is true, of a broken obelisk from Karnak, such that it can be seen by a sufficiently careful observation, near the eighth tower comprising statues from the countries conquered by Thoutonosis III]. The included, though dismembered, signifier—*Isis*—fits into a trace which the reader can establish between the textual paragrammatization of the name, the novel's dedicatory phrases ("à Isis, donc. Donc, à Isis") and Ricardou's theoretical essay "Le dispositif osiriaque," where Isis plays the role of "actrice de la contradiction" [actress of contradiction] in a reading of the myth of Osiris as an allegory for the problematic of writing.[12]

Larger Textual Units

When one moves to larger textual units, where the relationship involves more than one word, it is even more unusual to find examples of inclusion involving signifiers. In general, the *reprise de mots* takes the form of an exact repetition—for example, a refrain or a chorus. As such, the relationship is metaphorical rather than synecdochal. But in a few contemporary texts, one does find true examples of inclusion on the level of the signifier, particularly when the reader makes an association between one group of signifiers, originally constituted as a whole, and a second group of which the first has become only a part. In the first few pages of Ricardou's *La Prise / Prose de Constantinople* one encounters the following passage:

> A chaque déplacement de l'oeil, des arêtes, des rentrants imprévus,
> à chaque déplacement de l'oeil, des arêtes, des rentrants imprévus, des perspectives paradoxales se déclarent,
> à chaque déplacement de l'oeil, des arêtes, des rentrants imprévus, des perspectives paradoxales se déclarent selon un ordre incomplet qui pénètre l'esprit,
> à chaque déplacement de l'oeil, des arêtes, des rentrants imprévus, des perspectives paradoxales se déclarent selon un ordre incomplet qui pénètre l'esprit et y accrédite l'idée qu'il existe un point de cet espace d'où il est possible de percevoir simultanément la convergence des rythmes de toute la configuration et d'en pénétrer les arcanes en tous sens
> à chaque déplacement de l'oeil. (P. 8; our spacing)

[With each movement of the eye, ridges, unexpected recesses / with each displacement of the eye, ridges, unexpected recesses, paradoxical vistas come into view / with each movement of the eye, ridges, unexpected recesses, paradoxical vistas come into view

in an incomplete order which pervades the mind / with each
movement of the eye, ridges, unexpected recesses, paradoxical vistas
come into view in an incomplete order which pervades the mind
and sanctions the idea that there exists a point on this space from
which it is possible to perceive simultaneously the convergences
of the rhythm of the entire configuration and to see through its
secrets in all directions / with each movement of the eye.]

The reader recognizes the cyclical or canonical structure of the
passage by performing a progressive series of synecdochal operations involving, at each stage, the identification of a part as a
previous whole. Once the pattern is established, the reader can
link it metaphorically to numerous other passages having a similar structure. A further metaphorical operation has led one critic
to suggest that these passages serve, on the level of the signifier,
as metaphors of the entire text, itself structured cyclically or ca-
nonically.[13]

A second example, a typographical one, can be found in
Maurice Roche's *Circus*. The words and signs in parentheses on
page 73 (Fig. 7) first appeared on page 22 (Fig. 8) as part of a
larger text. Faced with the task of understanding the partial repetition (inclusion), the reader establishes a link with the final words
on page 73—*on coupe*—the section in parentheses having been
"cut out" of the text on page 22. The latter words enter into a
generative trace which involves pages 72 and 73, both "produced" metonymically by the various signifieds of *coupe(r)*.

Examples of inclusion within individual texts occur relatively infrequently. But if one shifts attention from the individual text to the domain of intertextuality, synecdochal operations
on the level of the signifier play a much greater role, as in the
recognition of quotations and citations. In such cases, the operation moves from the syntagmatic to the paradigmatic, and the
included segment, reprinted exactly, "stands for" the absent in-
tertextual whole. These quotations may name the source or remain anonymous; they may be detached from the flow of the
text, at the beginning or even the end of the book or chapter, or
be embedded in it. The quotations tend to come from works of
authors other than the writer producing the text in question. In

some cases, however, the writer uses his own texts. For example, Robbe-Grillet's *La Belle Captive* interweaves passages from the final chapter of his *Topologie d'un cité fantôme* and the beginning of *Souvenirs du triangle d'or*; Butor's series *Illustrations* takes up and interweaves texts published separately in small art editions. In the cases above, the synecdochal recognition of the quotation prompts other rhetorical operations which create an interplay between the part quoted and the new whole.

OPPOSITION (IRONIC OPERATIONS)

Irony on the level of the signified is characterized by a semantic and referential relationship of opposition made possible by the possession of one or more identical semantic features as well as of one or more contrary semantic features. When distinguishing between simple opposition, paradox, or contradiction on the level of the signifier, it is also necessary to make a distinction between relationships involving only signifiers (simple opposition) and those which link signifiers and signifieds (irony). Consequently, to discuss simple opposition (signifier-signifier relationships), the original definition shifts to read "a relationship of opposition made possible by at least one identical and one contrary phonemic, graphic, or typographic feature." For example, phonemically, *vert* and *père* can be linked metaphorically ([vɛr]) / ([pɛr]); *vert* and *inversion*, synecdochally ([vɛr] / [ɛ̃vɛrsjɔ̃]); and *vert* and *rêve*, by opposition ([vɛr])[rɛv], where there are identical phonemes in a reverse order.

Simple Opposition: Individual Words

In searching for examples of opposition between signifiers, the reader can follow strict constraints, where the reversals are perfectly phonemic (*cil / lisse*: [sil] / [lis]) or graphic (*les / sel*) or even phonemic-graphic (*cor / roc*: [kɔr] / [rɔk]). More frequently the reader looking specifically for *jeu des signifiants* moves freely back and forth between sounds and letters. Ricardou, in analyzing the generative production of Simon's *La Bataille de Pharsale*, points out the link between *jaune* and *nuage* based on

| Coupe | façonnée (............)
sertie de notes, faite avec le crâne

*l'avoir dans la main : tenir à ce trophée, à ce vase
plein de boue, de sang et de nuit.* Le retourner, le
vider de son contenu[1] : en avoir ras-le-bol de la vase

d'un ennemi (un adversaire)... Porter
un toast au futur : *l'exploit exem-
plaire reporté* au lendemain *sur l'exem-
plaire* introuvable *du Grand-Livre*

plein de fautes — à corriger sans faute. Faire le signe
(l'équivalent) conventionnel ? Une bonne correction ! —
ne plus pouvoir s'en remettre à la justice ! : (en somme,
doit avoir payé ! — Vérifier la balance du registre)

**du Monde, le livre, la phrase, la lettre unique, seule,
pour tout dire. Toucher à ce terme emblématique — à
l'idéogramme, hiéroglyphe d'un (dernier) soupir, d'un
souffle (contenant tous les sens — y compris celui de
l'histoire, de toutes les histoires possibles et imagina.bles).**
ir

Majuscule-Capitale par excellence la figure)m(on signe) du

rapportant une quête qui rapporte,
passant de mode avec l'illusion :

1. " pour la forme " désormais réduite au signe : omeN
étendue présage
(se) rendre (des) compte(s) à rebours. Trop tard : Nemo

Figure 7. Maurice Roche's *Circus*, pp. 72–73.

Légende perdue d'un dessin **secret** *éventé.*
Saga contant obscurément un désastre : **dire**
la *fin* **d'une bonne aventure** (:)

> buffon, rieur, toutes dents
> ttres $\left(\mathbf{C}\,^{r}_{a}\ \mathrm{n\ E} \right)$ dont ı
>
> tâter du test faute de
> car « no $ and doll »
> Écrase :mollu! sur bout
> tte, du ⊙ métaphc

faðiʀ aft faigian sunu.

Croire, tirant les cartes pour le fils
(décédé -   son avenir?), tirer les fils
d'un petit pantin pour qui il suffisait
d'être

l'homme à abattre

son jeu.

Se substituer à lui en lui subtilisant cet
« atout » qui prend la valeur que son
possesseur lui attribue : (Jolly) Joker
- masque de personne (efface face)
de camarade, compère du prestidigita
teur, l'   mot   ayant la main et
du jeu dans l^{a}_{e} manche. Pitre fou[tu
comme l'   de pique, *faisant le mort /*
une drôle de tête / pour rire. Etant fauché
passer à l'as (on n'y coupe pas *ici bas :*) on coupe

Entre le pouce et l'index ce qui se passe aussi
entre dans la tête. Sur toute la circonvolution
pariétale ascendante en arrière de la scissure
de rolando se trouve le centre de la sensibilité tactile; cette zone est probablement en rap-
port avec la sensibilité à la douleur. Examiner
le moule externe | un esquipot pourri de dons de
cauchemars valant son pesant d'histoire | : effet
de masque bouffon, rieur, toutes dents dehors.

— Grossièrement fait ? De cinq lettres $\left(C\ \overset{r}{\underset{â}{}}\ n\ E \right)$ dont une canine, celle de

l'œil. $\dfrac{\text{Démontable}}{\text{Incassable}}$ **|** En somme tâter du ⬚test⬚ faute de mordre la carne
car « no $ and doll » — Here hung those
lips that I have kissed — Écrase : m•ɴʉ$! sur bouche cousue penta-
cle de secrets (pierre de rosette, du ♋ métaphore à la lèvre).

Figure 8. Maurice Roche's *Circus*, p. 22.

the opposition [ʒ]au[n] / [n]ua[ʒ].[14] As one might expect, given the "acrobatics" needed to establish the reversal, the frequency of such oppositions remains relatively low.

On the other hand, more traditional readings of poetry lay heavy emphasis on phonemic opposition in the analysis of sound patterns. For example, after having established the rhyme scheme of Baudelaire's *Harmonie du soir*—[iʒ] (*tige, vertige, afflige, fige, vestige*) and [war] (*encensoir, soir, reposoir, noir, ostensoir*)—the reader usually opposes the two sets of sounds: clear front vowel [i] and fricative consonant [ʒ] versus dark back vowel [a] and liquid consonant [r]. This opposition in turn can be related to a series of oppositions in the meaning: pain versus harmony, day versus night, beauty versus melancholy. Theoreticians such as Jakobson, Grammont, and Cohen who have proposed varying systems for organizing sounds base their differing theories on the common notion of oppositions.[15] Given the number of phonemes and combinations, it is possible for a vowel or consonant to be opposed to several other sounds. For example, [l], [m], [n], and [r] share a common feature as liquid consonants, but [l] and [r] are opposed to [m] and [n] if one considers the question of nasality. Yet [l] and [r] can also be opposed to one another on the basis of continuity of articulation [l] versus interception [r].

Typographical considerations can also come into play, especially the position the signs occupy in the signifying chain. The physical position at the beginning and end of the text will at times suggest to the reader additional oppositions on the level of the signified. In Proust's *A la recherche du temps perdu*, the trace established by confronting the first word, *Longtemps*, and the last, *le Temps*, of the novel gives rise to a synecdochal operation which serves to underline the central subject of the work. In the two-page sequence of Rochu's *Circus* reprinted earlier (see Fig. 7) the generative role of the word *coupe* is stressed by a double opposition. When the reader confronts the first word on page 72 (*coupe*) with the last word on page 73 (*coupe*), the physical opposition of first-last is overdetermined by a typographical reversal: the first *coupe* is printed in black letters on a white background; the second, white on black. Struck by the typographical play, the reader can then turn his attention to the various links which one can establish between the signifieds of *coupe* and the other signs making up the sequence. Thus the reader can see not only how *coupe*, as "something cut out," leads to the section of musical score, but also how, as "cup," it leads to trophy, vase, and glass. In addition, one discovers how, as a verb, it leads to the idea of cutting cards and playing trump. Each of these associations generates other trains of thought which overlap, such as the musical score "faite avec le crâne" [made with the skull], the drawing of the skull, and the ideogram of the skull, containing also the word *crâne* and representing a part "cut out" of an earlier page.

Simple Opposition: Larger Textual Units

The classic example of opposition involving more than one-word-to-one-word associations is a palindrome—a series of letters which, when read from left to right and then from right to left, keep the same meaning: for example, "Esope reste ici, et se repose." Palindromes, because of the great technical difficulty which they present, rarely consist of more than a few words; moreover, they have scarcely been classified as literature. As part of the Oulipo experiments with "potential literature," however, Georges Perec composed a palindrome containing more than 5,000 words. The beginning and the end go as follows:

9691
EDNA D'NILU
O, MU, ACERE, PSEG, ROEG

Tracé l'inégal palindrome. Neige. Bagatelle, dira Hercule. Le brut repentir, cet écrit né Perec. L'arc lu pèse trop, lis à vice-versa . . .

. . . trépas rêve: Ci va! S'il porte, sépulcral, ce repentir, cet écrit ne perturbe le lucre: Haridelle, ta gabegie ne mord ni la plage ni l'écart.   Georges Perec.
Au Moulin d'Andé, 1969.

Without the assistance of the marker *palindrome* placed near the beginning of the text, the reader might well arrive, thoroughly confused, at the final few words before noticing the opposition

1969/9691, which would then give the impetus to work systematically back through the text verifying the presence of similar
graphemes in the reverse order of presentation.

Examples of opposition between sets of signifiers need not,
however, be limited to the experimental games of groups such
as Oulipo. Traditional rhetoric included a *figure de style*, classified
by Fontanier as *réversion*, for which he gives as illustrations the
proverb "Il ne faut pas vivre pour manger, mais il faut manger
pour vivre" [One must not live to eat, but rather one must eat
to live]; a couplet by Corneille on the subject of Richelieu, "Il
m'a trop fait de bien pour en dire du mal; / Il m'a trop fait de
mal pour en dire du bien" [He did too much good for me to
speak evil of him, / He did too much evil to me to speak well
of him]; and these lines from Voltaire's *La Henriade*, "Des li-
gueurs obstinés confonds les vains projets: / Rends les sujets au
prince, et le prince aux sujets" [Confuse the vain plans of the
obstinate conspirators: / Bring the subjects back to the prince,
and the prince back to the subject]. This figure is also known as
a chiasma, from the Greek *khiasmas* [crossing]. Whereas for Fontanier the use of *réversion* on the level of the signifier serves to
embellish, to "paint," to make stand out the thoughts expressed
by the signified, Ricardou reads a chiasmatic construction in
Robbe-Grillet's *Trois versions réfléchies* as another example of how
the text is produced. "Le Mannequin" begins:

> La *cafetière* est sur la *table*.
> C'est une *table* ronde à quatre pieds, recouverte d'une toile cirée
> . . . du moins rendu méconnaissable par la *cafetière* qui est posée
> dessus.
>
> [The *coffeepot* is on the *table*
> It's a round, four-legged *table*, covered with an oilcloth . . . at
> the least made unrecognizable by the *coffeepot* which is sitting
> on it.]

On the following pages one reads:

> L'*anse* a, si l'on veut, la forme d'une oreille, ou plutôt de l'ourlet
> extérieur d'une *oreille*; mais ce serait une *oreille* mal faite, trop ar-
> rondie et sans lobe, qui aurait ainsi la forme d'une *anse* de pot.

[The *handle* has, if one will, the form of an ear or rather of the outer rim of an *ear;* but it would be a badly formed *ear,* too round and lobe-less, which would have the shape of a pot *handle.*]

and

. . . l'image de l'*armoire* à *glace.* Dans la *glace* de l'*armoire* on voit . . .

[. . . the image of the *wardrobe with a mirror.* In the *mirror* of the *wardrobe* can be seen . . .]

These inversions lead Ricardou to suggest a metaphorical relationship between the chiasmatic structures and the thematic subject of the text, the former constituting "a maximum literal reflection" (*un miroitement littéral maximal*) which complements the metaphorical doublings discussed above.[16]

Moreover, Ricardou does not limit his readings to new novels. He points out, for example, that the first and last sentences of Rimbaud's *Le Dormeur du val*—"C'est un trou de verdure où chante une riviere" and "Il a deux trous rouges au côté droit" [It's a hollow (filled with) greenery where a river sings] and [He has two red holes in his right side]—contain a chiasmatic opposition: the third and fourth syllables are reversed (*trou de / deux trous*). From there, he proposes, by a metonymic reading, that the "crossed connection *trou de / deux trous* allows one to understand why the young soldier 'has two red holes in his right side' and not one, or three, or five, or six or seven, or eight, nine, or ten, as would be possible from the perspective of the meter." In other words, he reads the first line as the generator of the last.[17]

Opposition and Irony

Oppositions between signifiers cannot be ironic; irony requires a link between the signifier and the signified. We have already examined metaphorical relationships, where the signifier "reinforces" or "illustrates" the signified, and metonymical operations, where the signifier produces or generates the signified. An ironic relationship occurs when the signifier is opposed to the signified, when the "voice" of the narration talks against itself by presenting signifiers which undermine the apparent signified. Although he does not use the term *irony*, Mallarmé is particularly interested in this problem in his meditations on language. In his essay "Crise de vers," he complains about the inadequacies of the words *jour* and *nuit*: "What a disappointment, in the face of the perversity conferring to *jour* as to *nuit*, contradictorily, dark tones to the first, light ones to the second. The wish for a term of brilliant splendor, or let it be extinguished, inversely."[18] Mallarmé's suggestion here of a contradiction between the signifieds (*clear, shining; dark, extinguished*) and the phonetic signifiers ([ʒur] / [nɥi]) gives rise to irony in the very structure of language itself.

Poets often make use of this form of irony. Some critics, for example, have pointed out the disparity in Verlaine's "Art poétique" between the oft-quoted thematic statement "De la musique avant toute chose" [Music before all else] and the lack of musicality of this poem, especially when compared to the complex plays on phonetic signifiers in so many of Verlaine's other compositions. In a more immediately recognizable fashion bordering on parody, Rimbaud's sonnet *Vénus Anadyomène* offers a striking contrast to the subject matter usually associated with that poetic form. On the level of the signified, one finds the picture of a fat, misshapen, blotchy, smelly woman: "Et tout ce corps remue et tend sa large croupe / Belle hideusement d'un ulcère à l'anus" [And her whole body shakes and sticks out its broad rump / Hideously beautiful with an ulcer on the anus]. On the level of the signifier, however, one encounters many of the traditional traits of the sonnet: alexandrine verses, rhyme scheme, alliteration, recurring sound patterns. The opposition between the two levels serves to heighten the irony suggested already by the opposition between the title and the subject of the poem: the goddess Venus emerging from the water versus the decaying prostitute climbing out of a bathtub.

This notion of irony also helps explain the difficulty many readers have in reading the texts of plays, particulary those where stage directions are minimal or totally absent. Accustomed to dealing metaphorically with the relationship between signifier and signified, readers often fail to recognize the irony potentially present in a speech or scene. It is precisely the function of the director (the "first reader" of the play) to bring out the irony in production. Of course, the concreteness of theatrical signifiers—voices and bodies of the actors, lighting, stage setting, etc.—greatly facilitates the underlining of ironic oppositions. Two examples will illustrate how the signifier can play against the signified. One of the most comic scenes in *Tartuffe* (act 4, sc. 5: the table scene) often leaves inexperienced readers wondering where the comedy is. It is the presence of the signifier (seen by the spectator or imagined by the knowledgeable reader)—Orgon hiding under the table, Elmire's gestures and looks, Tartuffe's failure to notice the other signifiers—which both reverses the meanings of the signifieds and changes a serious situation (an increasingly aggressive attempt at seduction and coercion) into a classic example of dramatic irony. Whereas in *Tartuffe* the irony serves a comic end, in Musset's *On ne badine pas avec l'amour*, the effect is the opposite. The conversation in Camille's room (act 3, sc. 6) involves, on the level of the signified, a typical *badinage* between two characters who, despite their love for each other, are prevented by pride from declaring honestly their feelings. But the presence of a third signifier—the actress playing the role of the naïve young serving girl who, also in love with Perdican, has been hidden (with the knowledge of the spectators) by Camille behind a curtain—transforms the scene. The reader-spectator does not just follow the psychological skirmish between Camille and Perdican but, thanks to the dramatic irony, realizes the cruelty of the two characters who, in their egotism, willingly play with the emotions of an innocent third party.

Causality (Metonymic Operations)

Like irony, metonymy on the level of the signifier requires the involvement of the signified. Metonymy, however, does not have a counterpart, as does irony in the form of simple opposition, which can function purely on the level of the signifier. This difference can be understood, perhaps, by looking at the schematic drawings which illustrate the four basic rhetorical operations (Figs. 1, 3, 4, and 5). In metaphor, synecdoche, and irony, there is an overlap, a common ground which varies in degree and nature, but which nevertheless translates into the copossession of letters, sounds, or typographical characteristics. Metonymy, on the other hand, is characterized by "a semantic and referential relationship of causality made possible by the presence of the category of semantic feature *cause.*" Since there is no equivalent for the category *cause* on the "material" level of the sign, metonymy never functions solely between signifiers, but rather between a signifier and a signified.

Many of the reader's most "natural" responses to a text are actually learned conventions based on metonymical relationships. When one finds on the page a signifying chain divided into lines of unequal lengths (irregular number of type-spaces), one reads that typographical disposition as the agent for an action: writing poetry. Similarly, a signifying chain consisting of groups of irregular lines each introduced by a name in capital letters leads metonymically to the idea that one is reading a play. In each case, the reader then acts upon the text in accordance with the conventions of that particular genre. In a more general sense, within any genre, when the reader encounters quotation marks, he reads them as indicating the product of a producer other than the narrator. In such cases the metonymical operation, the recognition of the new producer, may well change the type of rhetorical operations affected upon the product, the quotation. These general metonymical readings, quickly and easily assimilated by most readers, can, in certain cases, play a very specific role in interpreting a text. In Flaubert's *Un Cœur simple*, a metonymical reading of the ellipsis (the three dots in the signifying chain) leads to a psychological explanation for Félicité's actions (see Chap. 3). On the other hand, in Sollers' *H*, it is the absence of all punctuation from the signifying chain that may well encourage the reader to look, from the very start, for an interpretation involving a revolutionary, contestatory attitude toward law, tradition, and authority.

Another type of metonymical operation is found in the generation or production of texts. In moving from one part of the signifying chain to another, one reads the signifiers as the products, not of some signifieds, such as ideas or meanings, but of other signifiers. Such an operation takes place on a second level or at a second stage. The metonymical relationship proposes an explanation or an interpretation of links established analytically by means of procedures involving similarity, inclusion, and/or opposition. Ricardou's metonymical readings of the *vocables producteurs*, or generators, in *La Bataille de Pharsale*, where *jaune* is a source or "cause" for effects such as *nuage, auge, nage, nue, eau*; in *Projet pour une révolution à New York*, where *rouge* produces *orgue, rogue, joue, roué, jour, gourre*; and in his own *La Prise/ Prose de Constantinople*, where *Isabelle* generates the *belle Isa, abeilles,* Dr. *Basile, Silab Lee,* depend on initial connections made by means of metaphoric, synecdochal, and oppositional operations.

The above examples involve only the individual text. Literary studies often lead the professional reader to make use of extratextual material; here again metonymical operations moving from signifieds to signifiers also play a role. In some cases, the activities represent an unconscious application of metonymical operations to the text, when critics and readers perform activities without recognizing their metonymic nature. Graphologists analyze the material aspects of handwriting to arrive at conclusions about the person who produced the loops and slashes; in analogous fashion, medieval scholars examine *ducti* to deduce source and date of a manuscript, and critics working with printed texts often return to manuscript copies to discover how the text was composed. In other cases, researchers are opening up new areas of investigation, seeking out causal relationships, or building theories on causal assumptions. Literary critics interested in psychoanalytic interpretations might use Ivan Fonagy's notion of the *bases pulsionnelles de la phonation*. For Fonagy, sounds (vowels and consonants) are linked to stages in the libidinal development of the child. These links depend on the place of articulation: thus, sounds involving the lips ([m], [n], front vowels) invest oral drives, recalling the act of sucking at the breast; sounds requiring glottal stops ([g],[k], back vowels) invest anal drives, because of the physiological link between the glottal and anal sphincters; sounds involving the tongue (especially [r]) are phallic. By analyzing the sound pattern of the text, the reader can propose an interpretation based on the fundamental drives presiding at its composition or production. In a different domain, critics interested in the sociology of literature can use the physical book itself (size, format, paper) as the starting point for metonymical discussions going from effect to cause (the book as product of certain economic and social factors) and cause to effect (the book as "producer" of certain kinds of readers).

4

THE RHETORIC OF

DISPLACEMENT AND

CONDENSATION

Sa barbe était d'argent, comme un ruisseau d'avril,
Sa gerbe n'était point avare ni haineuse;
Quand il voyait passer quelque pauvre glaneuse:
'Laissez tomber exprès des épis,' disait-il.
Victor Hugo, *Booz endormi*

At the end of his article, "Two Aspects of Language and Two
Types of Aphasia" (1956), Roman Jakobson suggests that metaphor and metonymy are at work in all symbolic processes. He
illustrates this notion by referring to dream analysis: "Thus, in
an inquiry into the structure of dreams, the decisive question is
whether the symbols and the temporal sequences used are based
on contiguity (Freud's metonymic 'displacement' and synec-
dochic 'condensation') or on similarity (Freud's 'identification'
and 'symbolism')."[1] This alliance of rhetorical and psychoanalytical terminology inaugurated a series of attempts to link these
two fields. Although numerous thinkers have seen the value of
such an association, they often have disagreed as to how exactly
the two domains intersect.

Some of the issues in the debate have crystallized around

the interpretation of a line from Victor Hugo's poem *Booz endormi*: "Sa gerbe n'était point avare ni haineuse" [His sheaves were not miserly nor spiteful]. Jacques Lacan associates metaphor with condensation and metonymy with displacement. For Lacan, the Hugo verse is a clear example of metaphor. When one reads *sa gerbe*, one superimposes or substitutes the name *Booz*; this superimposition or substitution represents precisely a condensation: "The *Verdichtung*, or condensation, is the structure of the superimposition of signifiers which is the field of metaphor, and its very name, condensing in itself the word *Dichtung* [poetry], shows how the process is connatural with the mechanism of poetry to the point that it actually envelopes its properly traditional function."[2] J.-F. Lyotard in *Discours, Figure* (1971) takes issue with Lacan. Lyotard begins by disputing Lacan's interpretation of the Hugo example as a metaphor: "It seems to me that *His sheaves were not . . .* is a good example of metonymy, *his sheaves* being taken as an emblem of *Booz*."[3] Lyotard then questions the link established by Lacan between metaphor and condensation. He argues that Lacan, although claiming to follow Jakobson and Freud, is actually playing with words. According to Lyotard, Lacan's use of the terms *metaphor* and *metonymy* is itself metaphorical and quite different from Jakobson's structural linguistics. Moreover, Lyotard maintains that Freud's notion of condensation is basically nonlinguistic, whereas Lacan claims that the unconscious and its processes are structured like a language.

More recently (1977), Christian Metz in *Le Signifiant imaginaire* has attempted to settle the argument. First, in the matter of the Hugo verse, he sides with both Lyotard and Lacan. Metz points out that Lyotard concentrates on the phrase *His sheaves*, while Lacan deals with the entire verse. Metz concludes: "Thus *sheaves* is metonymic. But in the sentence a dotted movement inscribes itself which appears to me typically metaphorical: *His . . . miserly . . . hateful*: the possessive, which evokes the possessor, the two adjectives, which fit people more than things.'"[4] Metz then proceeds to take issue with Lyotard's implicit refusal to unite psychoanalysis and semiotics. For Metz, the operations of displacement and condensation characterize both the conscious and the unconscious. Consequently, like Lacan, he sees

no problem in using these terms in connection with metaphor
and metonymy. But Metz does take issue with Lacan's rigid association of condensation with metaphor and displacement with
metonymy. He argues that these terms intersect in multiple ways
and that it is possible to speak of "condensation metonymies"
and "displacement metaphors" as well as of the categories proposed by Lacan. This opening and reworking of the rhetorical
processes represents an important movement away from Lacan's
reductions and serves as a needed corrective to studies derivative
of Lacan which simplified the rhetorical and psychoanalytic processes in binary tables.[5]

   While Lacan, Lyotard, and Metz have contributed immea-
surably to rejuvenating the study of rhetoric, their work cannot
stand as a finished model for a rhetoric of reading. As a whole,
it perpetuates the misunderstanding inherent in Jakobson's original use of the word *contiguity* and the consequent subordination
of causality and inclusion and the paradigmatic and the syntagmatic under the general notion of metonymy. In addition, ap-
proaching rhetoric from a psychoanalytic perspective, Lacan and
Metz, among many others, have argued that there is a psychoanalytic basis to rhetoric, but until they also demonstrate that
Freud's original writings in psychoanalysis have a rhetorical
foundation, their work is only half completed. Few people would
argue that the study of literature has not been informed by psychoanalysis; it is time to show that rhetoric can also inform and
explain Freud's notions of condensation and displacement. The
greatest modification to the French model is in a shift in perspective away from a psychoanalytic view centered on the relationship of the author and the text, to a view focused on the
reader and the role of condensation and displacement in the
symbolizations and figurations of reading.

FREUD'S CONCEPTS OF DISPLACEMENT AND CONDENSATION
Although Freud never provided fixed definitions of *displacement*
and *condensation*, his own discussions and later standardizations
by others can act as an entry into the material. In their dictionary, Laplanche and Pontalis define *displacement* as the "fact that
an idea's emphasis, interest or intensity is able to be detached

from it and to pass on to other ideas, which were originally of little intensity but which are related to the first idea by a chain of associations." *Condensation* is described as "one of the essential modes of functioning of the unconscious process: a sole idea represents several associative chains at whose point of intersection it is located. . . . Condensation should not, however, be looked upon as a summary: although each manifest element is determined by several latent meanings, each one of these, inversely, may be identified in several elements; what is more, manifest elements do not stand in the same relationship to each of the meanings from which they derive, and so they do not subsume them after the fashion of a concept."[6]

In *Jokes and Their Relation to the Unconscious*, Freud has recourse to the general theory of displacement and condensation as applied to dreams and discusses these two processes in the following manner:

> In the course of the dream-work the material of the dream-thoughts is subjected to a quite extraordinary compression or *condensation*. A starting point for it is provided by any common elements that may be present in the dream-thoughts, whether by chance of from the nature of their content. Since these are not as a rule sufficient for any considerable condensation, new artificial and transient common elements are created in dream-work, and to this end there is actually a preference for the use of words the sound of which expresses different meanings. . . . The fact of condensation is the piece of the dream-work which can be most easily recognized; it is only necessary to compare the text of a dream as it is noted down with the record of the dream-thoughts arrived at by analysis in order to get a good impression of the extensiveness of dream condensation.
>
> It is less easy to convince oneself of the second great modification of the dream-thoughts that is brought about by the dream-work—the process that I have named 'dream-*displacement*'. This is exhibited in the fact that things that lie on the periphery of the dream-thoughts and are of minor importance occupy a central position and appear with great sensory intensity in the manifest dream, and *vice versa*. This gives the dreams the appearance of being displaced in relation to the dream-thoughts, and this displacement is precisely what brings it about that the dream confronts waking mental life as something alien and incomprehensible.[7]

While Freud relies on these general definitions of displacement and condensation in *Jokes*, he carefully notes the great difference between dream and wit, and implicitly between the workings of condensation and displacement in the two realms:

> All these methods of displacement appear too as techniques of joking. But when they appear, they usually respect the limits imposed on their employment in conscious thinking; and they may be altogether absent, although jokes too have invariably a task to accomplish of dealing with an inhibition. We can understand the subordinate place taken by displacements in the joke-work when we recall that jokes always have another technique at their command for keeping off inhibition and indeed that we have found nothing more characteristic of them than precisely this technique. For jokes do not, like dreams, create compromises; they do not evade the inhibition, but they insist on maintaining play with words or with nonsense unaltered. They restrict themselves, however, to a choice of occasion in which this play or this nonsense can at the same time appear allowable (in jests) or sensible (in jokes), thanks to the ambiguity of the words and the multiplicity of conceptual relations. Nothing distinguishes jokes more clearly from all other psychical structures than this double-sidedness and this duplicity in speech. From this point of view at least the authorities come closest to an understanding of the nature of jokes when they lay stress on 'sense in nonsense'. (172)

Because wit is a conscious activity, its mechanisms are more clearly delineated than in dreams, where it is necessary to locate the representation which has been censured through the work of displacement. But consciously or not, wit points to the inhibitions by its nonsense.

To put it in more linguistic terms, condensation represents minimally one signifier which stands for two or more signifieds or, according to Freud, "the use of words the sound of which expresses different meanings." In everyday language, condensation can be said to exist in the word *fly*, which can mean either "to fly," the animal fly, or the fly on a pair of trousers. By extension, condensation can define the relationship between one sign and several other signs condensed into the first sign, as in the proper name *George*, which can have condensed in it a multitude of different individuals called George (George Washington, George Sand, George Holmes, etc.). Because the sign stands for other signs and acts as a nodal point, the operation of condensation is paradigmatic, going from a sign present to others absent. Thus, it can be related to the action of tropes.

A simplified diagram of the work of condensation in one isolated sign would take on the following configuration:

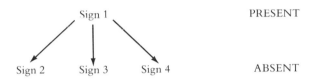

Displacement, as suggested by Freud's commentary, involves movements on both the syntagm and the paradigm. A movement from the "periphery" to the "central position" can be rendered in linguistic terms as a shift of attention from one sign (which appears more important or noticeable) to another sign in the text. Paradigmatically, the displacement is a shift from one meaning of the word to another, often unexpected or secondary. In both cases, the displacement can be sketched as

Freud tells the story of a medical friend who once said to the dramatist Arthur Schnitzler: "I'm not surprised that you've become a great writer. After all your father held a mirror up to his contemporaries" (37). For Freud, the play on words here is between the doctor's laryngoscope (literally a "larynx mirror") and Hamlet's declaration that the play, and by extension the dramatist, should "hold the mirror up to nature." Meaning is displaced from the doctor's mirror to Hamlet's metaphorical mirror. In discussing wit, Todorov defines two types of meaning at work: on one hand the given meaning ("le sens exposé") and on the other hand the imposed (or new) meaning.[8] The displacement thus shifts from the given, obvious meaning to the less obvious, new one of Hamlet's mirror.

In another of Freud's jokes, the shifts in meaning go beyond the single word: "Two Jews met in the neighborhood of the bath-house. 'Have you taken a bath?' asked one of them. 'What?' asked the other in return, 'is there one missing?'" (49). As Freud states, the joke works because of the displacement of meaning in the expression *to take a bath* and the resulting misunderstanding between the two interlocutors. One takes the words to mean "to bathe," while the other takes them to mean "to steal a bath." Todorov argues that the displacement in this example is purely syntagmatic, with emphasis shifting from the word *bath* ("to bathe") to the word *take* ("to steal"). There is surely movement along the syntagm, but the joke could not succeed without the second displacement from one meaning to the other.

In other examples given by Freud, the play extends to the signifier, which generates the play on meaning. The same signifier, on the phonetic level, is broken into different signifieds: "A young man, introduced into a Paris *salon*, was a relative of the great Jean-Jacques Rousseau and bore his name. Moreover he was red-headed, but he behaved so awkwardly that the hostess remarked critically to the gentleman who had introduced him: 'Vous m'avez fait connaître un jeune homme *roux* et *sot*, mais non pas un Rousseau [You have made me acquainted with a young man who is *roux* (red-haired) and *sot* (silly), but not a Rousseau]'" (30). As in the previous example, there is a double movement between the syntagm and the paradigm. On the syntagm the parts of sounds are displaced to the whole, and then paradigmatically the listener-reader displaces from the meaning *red-headed* and *fool* to the proper name *Rousseau*. The joke results from the clash between identical signifers on the phonetic plane and opposed signifieds.

In the above example, Freud insists that there is no condensation or "substitute formation." On the phonetic plane this may be true, but graphically the joke depends on the reader-listener condensing the three words, and from this condensation the reader-listener realizes the absurdity of the combination *Rousseau—roux/sot*. The play on words, if taken from the point of view of the reader-listener with the graphemes *rou sseau* as the starting point, illustrates nicely the work of condensation and the transformations involved:

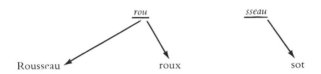

For the person familiar with the joke, future references to Rousseau might well bring to mind the two absent words, *roux* and *sot*, thus reminding us that condensation implies refocusing energy from one word in praesentia to two or more words absent from the text. The word or words present in the text act as nodal points for those absent.

For Freud, condensation often involves an ellipsis as well as a change in meaning. The remark "He has a great future behind him," according to Freud, is a condensation of the longer statement "That man has had a great future before him, but he has it no longer" (26). The change in meaning is the result of the substitution of opposites: "behind" replaces "before."

The process works quite often on the level of the signifier. In the famous lines from the Heine play, in which a character recounts meeting Solomon Rothschild ("I was next to S.R. and he treated me entirely as an equal, completely *famillionaire*"), meaning is displaced from *familiar* to the neologism *famillionaire* (19), where *familiar* and *millionaire* are condensed. As in the example of Rousseau, one signifier contains two (or more) signifieds. Other examples, such as the British *alcoholidays* (22) and *anecdotage* (*anecdote* and *dotage*—baby talk), work on the same principle.

Displacement and Condensation in the Reading Process

The Activity of the Reader

According to Freud, displacement and condensation are in the text. Condensation is formed and a displacement has been made from the author-speaker's mind to the text. For the reader a double strategy evolves from confrontation with these already existent phenomena. The reader can seek to understand them when displacement is followed back to the original signs, as when *famillionaire* is broken into two separate words. This act of understanding involved decondensing (breaking down the elements in the nodal word) and replacing (following the movement of displacement back to the original "place" or sign).[9]

The reader also has open the option of making further condensations and displacements from the text, of playing a game with the text and grouping traces into new nodal points and associations, of displacing from words in the text to words absent and in the reader's mind alone. In this game of associations further nodal points can be formed, mixing elements of the text and those of the reader's own fantasy world. These reading strategies can be schematized as follows:

WORDS ON PAGE   ACTION OF THE READER

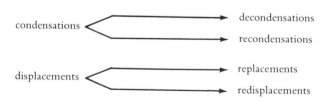

condensations   decondensations
                                           recondensations

displacements   replacements
                                           redisplacements

These strategies open to the reader are not fixed and are not always acted upon in a neat binary fashion. The reader may decondense (break down a metaphor, for example) and then form a new condensation. Or he may displace from the text to a single word. In Freud's example of *famillionaire* a reader might displace and decondense the neologism into fragments not suggested or thought of by Freud: the letters *fam* could become *femme* [woman], *famill* could generate *famille* [family], and the letters *lion* and *air* could be isolated into individual words. The displacements could continue along lines of the reader's personal associations (family-child-orphan-loneliness, etc.). They could also recondense around a fantasized or real family, or could return, be replaced, within the Freudian text, where the family would be associated with Freud's work on the Oedipal complex. Thus a new nodal point would be formed outside the original text. This multiple movement, not marked or explored in Freud's explanation, is possible because the reader might find the text and explanation (the extension of the joke-text) incomplete. The reader would activate and complete the elements present in the neologism.

Rhetorical Displacements

In our definitions of the four tropes, the notion of a transposition from one sign in praesentia to a sign in absentia implies the very idea of displacement from one sign to another. In metaphor, *robe* is displaced to *petals*, *drown* to *set*; in metonymy, *joy* to *son*, *vengeance* to *sword*; in synecdoche, *Paris* to *Parisians*, *steel* to *sword*; in irony, *heroic* is displaced to *coward*, *lovely* to *horrible*. In figurations, where the two signs are present in the text, the displacement can be said to be more direct, within the syntagm itself, as in "My love burns like a flame." The reader displaces semantic features from *flame* to *love* in order to arrive at the metaphorical sense of *love*.

In classical texts the displacement is often highly controlled, even at times rationalistic, and encoded by cultural and literary conventions. Balzac, for example, leaves little room for the reader to take initiative in displacements when he states in *Père Goriot* that Paris is like a mud hole, that "life is a theater," or that the maison Vauquer reflects the woman herself. But in all the declarations, the reader displaces from one sign to the other in order to attain meaning. And even within a highly encoded text, the reader has freedom in choosing the direction to take in many displacements. Displacement, as Freud suggests, means censorship, letting information through in transformed or distorted form (the very operation of going from one sign to another) and forgetting or repressing some information. A reader cannot retain all of a text and must displace (unconsciously) to certain signs and to certain parts of the text. The very establishment of traces[10] involves displacement from initial tropes and figures in the text to others not present before the reader's eyes. For a reader of Balzac's *La Duchesse de Langeais*, the metaphors of animality associated with the character Montriveau may become predominant traces throughout the text, without the reader's remembering *where*, at what point in the text, or *when* they became key traces. Thus the displacement is to the construct in the reader's mind of what came before. The actual moment of reading has been erased (displaced), with the trace remaining to show the flow of energy through the text. Conversely, other words are read and forgotten, traces discarded and relegated to the preconscious or the unconscious. Thus a reader can complete *La Duchesse de Langeais* with no memory of the play of colors or of the traces involving fire. Displacement also suggests a movement *away* from the text and from the relationships in it (a vertical movement initially). The reader often goes beyond the encoded text to displace an interpretation *onto* the text. In other instances, the movement away from the text creates a personal fantasy.[11] The traces of lions and the sado-masochism of *La Duchesse de Langeais* could lead a reader to a vivid fantasy of bestial sexuality, of Montriveau as a veritable lion assaulting the Duchess.

In many contemporary texts, where the encoded processes are broken down, the reader is allowed, even forced, to complete rhetorical operations where the displacement between signs is widened and the choice of absent signs to which the reader can move is enlarged. The following poem by Artaud retains elements of traditional poetry (rhyme scheme, division into stanzas of equal length) and on one level can be read without undue movement beyond the words in the text:

La Rue
La rue sexuelle s'anime
le long des faces mal venues,
les cafés pépiant de crimes
déracinent les avenues.

Des mains de sexe brûlent les poches
et les ventres bouent par–dessous;
toutes les pensées s'entrechoquent,
et les têtes moins que les trous.[12]

[The sexual street becomes animated / along the ill-begotten faces, / the cafés chirping crimes / uproot the avenues. / / Hands of sex burn the pockets / and the stomachs mud (a verb here) underneath; / all the ideas clash, / and the heads less than the holes.]

Although there is no direct reference in the poem to women, and in particular to prostitutes, a first reading, by metonymy and synecdoche, would construct a scene of prostitution in the street. The sexual street, the produce for sale in the street, the faces lining it, either of clients or women (by synecdoche), the noise of crime in the cafés, the clients' hands in pockets (a displacement from their sexual organs), and the final holes are all arrived at by simple displacement of either product-producer or part-whole. The displacements in the final stanza—parts of the body for other parts, the product (heat) for the producer (sexuality)—illustrate also the censoring of displacement, as the blatant sexuality is masked by figuration. This reading follows the configurations of that of many traditional texts.

In such a reading, the symbolizations and figurations are quickly perceived, because they are encoded into the culture with the commonplace image of Pigalle or the rue Saint-Denis found in popular songs, tour books, and literature. The displacements thus work systematically between terms present and absent, and the signs in the text easily form the whole of a street of prostitution. In these controlled movements, then, the reader assumes that there is an "original" term which has to be discovered by following the displacements to the original or primary sign(s). As such, the reader's movement toward understanding is replacement, a relocation of thought.

But on the metaphorical plane, the reader's displacements do not lead to such a neat understanding; instead they open the text to multiple readings, to multiple avenues of displacement (or redisplacements) not controlled by the rhetoric of the text. This metaphorical play begins with the title, which is a play on the two meanings of *rue*, either "street," the obvious meaning, or "citrus tree." A citrus tree provides a multitude of semantic features which lead through the poem: "vivacity" (in dry places), "heat" (the regions where the trees grow), the color, shape, and odor of the fruits (oranges, lemons, grapefruit). This reservoir of features and traces permits the reader to move (displace) in a variety of directions. The sexual street then is also a sexual tree which by metonymy and synecdoche has birds chirping in it: the chirping, a product, conducts us to the birds of the cafés, which are themselves part of the street. Displacing in another direction, the chirping can conduct us to trees, and by metaphor to cafés as trees containing the birds. These café-trees at the same time uproot (*déracinent*) the avenues. By yet another vertiginous displacement, the avenues, with roots, are plants, even trees themselves. Thus the poem opens up to hallucinatory movements between nature, sexuality, and people in the metropolis.

Rhetorical Condensations

Whereas displacement is central to the definition of all tropes and is contained in the notion of "transposition," the function of condensation is not readily perceived except in metaphor, where Metz, Lacan, and others have related it to "multiplicity of meaning."[13] Because condensation has not been symstematically located within metonymy, synecdoche, and irony, it is worthwhile to treat each of the four processes separately.

   Synecdoche. In synecdoche and the other three processes, it is necessary first to reconsider the notions of *replacement* and *substitution*, for neither one adequately describes the act of reading. In synecdoche, for example, when a person reads the work *sail*, he does not replace it on the page, but in the mind, by *boat*. Both *boat* and *sail* are present, one on the page, one in the mind. Because the substitution occurs across two different planes (that of the page and that of the mind), the two terms, in any tropes, are copresent. Thus the signifier *sail* sends the reader to two signifieds, *boat* and *sail*. The same process of copresence is evident in the movement from *steel* (on the page) to *sword*, or from *head* to *body*.

   This copresence or condensation of two signifieds on one signifier is not initially apparent, in part because many synec-

doches are highly encoded culturally, and the reader passes quickly
from the first signified to the second "without thinking," unconsciously. When the word *sail* is read, the conventional reflex is
to think of *boat*. But condensed in this movement are not only
the words *boat* and *sail*, culturally encoded, but other possible
traits which can come to the reader's mind: *mast, bow, rail, hull*.
Other parts of the boat are condensed and potentially available
to the reader in *sail*. In the Artaud poem just cited, the word
street has condensed, through cultural encoding, the prostitutes,
clients, cafés, and criminals. The reader quite possibly fills out
the parts of the synecdochal process with further additions to
the condensation by "seeing" specific people, shops, dress, or
trash in the street.

In examples beyond the trope, condensation operates in
synecdoche as in other symbolic and figural processes. The figuration whole-to-part of the word *room* brings to mind any
number of shapes, colors, and objects—parts of a room. Mention of the room in Balzac's *La Duchesse de Langeais* to someone
who has read the story brings to mind a series of more specific
signifieds composing the room: grey walls, a couch, the door,
the feet of a Sphinx, curtains, the colors red and green. Other
details—such as the two people in the room, a rug, a table covered with papers, two armchairs, a chest with an alarm clock on
it, the bed, a fireplace, and candlesticks—may be in the preconscious of the reader, or else relegated to the subconscious. But
there remain the various objects, the parts, which represent in
the reader's mind the ensemble of the room.[14]

Metonymy. As we have noted, Metz suggests that condensation works at times in metonymy, but he is reluctant to pursue
his presentiment very far. From the point of view of the reader,
condensation plays a key role as *potential* in metonymic operations. While there is no condensation in *discovered* metonymic
links, condensation resides in the *act of discovering* them. When
one reads "I saw him that night, this unfortunate Severus, / Vengeance in his hands, his eyes burning with anger," the phrase
vengeance in his hands has potentially condensed in it several instruments: gun, knife, poison, dagger, or even a document containing incriminating evidence. The "proper" instrument is often

encoded culturally and historically; thus for the reader of Corneille *vengeance* would lead to *sword*.

But such is not always the case, especially when we observe
metonymic processes along the syntagm. The detective story,
perhaps the metonymic form *par excellence*, is founded on the
potential of metonymic condensations and the act of discovering
the correct metonymic link. In the conventional model of the
detective story, a body is discovered (the effect of a crime) and a
number of suspects are identified (the agents of the crime). The
reader has condensed in his mind the possible metonymic links
springing from the body-effect. This example of the detective
story illustrates particularly well the fact that condensation is not
static; it consists of encounters, intersections, paths joining and
then separating around nodal points. As the reader progresses in
the detective story, he plays with the combinations, brings the
causal lines together (reestablishes nodal points), before decondensing and following (displacing) a path to a possible solution.
The pleasure of reading a detective story comes in large part
from this gathering of traces and elimination of paths, as suspects and instruments are eliminated in the story. The general
movement can be seen as from condensation to elimination (decondensation) to the reduction to just one suspect, where the
causal chain no longer permits any multiplicity.

Metaphor. Because multiplicity is almost synonymous with
metaphor, condensation is closely associated with the work of
the intermediary and the phenomenon of contamination. The
most highly encoded metaphors, where the reader passes from
one sign to the other without difficulty, function through condensation. In the banal expression "You are the flower of my
life," addressed to a woman, the relationship is not simply a one-
on-one contact between the word *flower* and *woman*, nor even a
simple displacement through a third word, an intermediary such
as *beauty*. Rather, condensed in the metaphorical relationship are
numerous intermediaries, or intersections of meanings, between
woman and *flower*: freshness, fragility, ephemeral beauty, odors,
colors, shapes, touch, and feel. These are the very condensations
which "contaminate" the word *woman*, giving rise to the image
of a flower-woman. Similarly, for the reader of Ronsard's "Dar-

ling, let us see if the rose . . . " these condensations also enter
into play. The text will eliminate some of the traits which are
condensed in the initial metaphor and which the reader condenses in the mind, whether consciously or unconsciously. In a poem
such as Ronsard's the reading process is in a sense both a decondensation (an isolation and elaboration of some of the features
suggested by rose-woman) and an elimination of some traits which
do not come into conscious play in the poem. Whereas Ronsard
shapes his poem around the ephemeral, beauty, and dress, he
leaves aside any elaboration of shapes, odors, and touch. Yet all
of these traits can continue to play in the reader's mind, particularly since Ronsard has written a love poem, a poem of seduction, where much of the sensuality condensed in the metaphor
rose-woman has been repressed. The reader need only bring these
repressed traits to the surface to reactivate interpretation of
the poem.

   Irony. In our discussions of irony, we have argued that when
a sign, or a group of signs, demands that the opposite sign be
read, the original sign does not disappear from the reader's mind,
but rests as a reminder to read ironically. The appellation *hero*
attached to the cowering Fabrice in Stendhal's *La Chartreuse de
Parme* triggers an opposite sign, but *hero* remains as the mark of
ironical opposition. In the process of reading ironically, we once
again have a clear example of movement before the final solidi-
fication of the irony. The various opposites of *hero* and their gradations—*coward, confused, aimless, weak*—converge in the reader's mind. Either the reader remains at this condensation, this
multiple selection, or else he goes down the path of selecting one
appropriate word to pinpoint the irony.

   Condensation and Displacement of the Four Processes
Condensation in its most extended form encompasses all four of
the rhetorical processes and is the intersection of the metaphorical, metonymic, synecdochal, and ironical paths of a text. In the
title of Baudelaire's *Les Bijoux* are condensed the paths of the
four rhetorical processes. The jewels metaphorically can refer to
the woman (they are as beautiful as the woman) or to the female
sexual organs (by a play on Diderot's *Les Bijoux indiscrets*).[15] Me-

tonymically, the jewels are a product, a sign of wealth, something purchased, while also the cause of the poet's excitement and ecstasy. As a synecdoche, the jewels are part of the woman and can be read either as the part which stands for the entire physical woman or as the part which erases the woman and becomes an entity of its own. Ironical chains form where the sexual metaphor clashes with the lexical features of hardness, rigidity, and impenetrability in the word *jewel*. The play of condensation in the title could continue endlessly as one recombines (makes new intersections with) the rhetorical processes and lets them form new chains.

But in the act of interpretation, as we have suggested, the play of condensation and displacement is stopped, and the chains are fixed. Often unconscious choices are made and some of the rhetorical paths are eliminated from the very beginning. The partiality of interpretation comes from the impossibility of sustaining the condensation, of immobilizing it, and of retaining all the elements flowing through it. The game is impossible particularly because there is not one static, global "condensation" called *les bijoux*; the nodal points in the title itself, as well as in the entire poem, continually shift, metamorphose, and form new intersections. Thus, the reader displaces, selects (consciously or unconsciously), and decondenses fragments of the poem. Because of condensation, multiple interpretations are possible; also because of condensation and displacement, each interpretation necessitates a repression or denial of some part of the text. Two paths cannot be followed at the same time all the way to the end. But a reader can "see" two at the same time.

THE RHETORIC OF FREUD

If displacement and condensation are integral parts of the rhetorical process, one might well ask to what extent the rhetorical processes function in Freud's original concepts of displacement and condensation. A return to the examples cited earlier shows clearly that the four processes function in displacement and condensation. Most of them are dominated by metaphor and synecdoche, as in the following:

1. In the story in which Schnitzler is compared to his father,

a doctor, rhetoric enters into play between the lexical and meta-phorical meanings of mirror. The father and the playwright are joined together by the laryngoscope and Hamlet's mirror. Two different types of mirror unite father and son by the *reflections*.

2. The examples in which the words *roux* and *sot* are con-densed into the proper name *Rousseau*, *millionaire* and *familiar* in *famillionaire*, *alcohol* and *holidays* in *alcoholidays*, and *anecdote* and *dotage* in *anecdotage* all work by synecdoche: the reader deciphers them by taking the parts (the two words) out of the whole word. The resulting words may form a metaphorical relationship, as in *familiar* and *millionaire*, which have some common and some dif-fering graphemes, but the process of deciphering is clearly sy-necdochal.

The metonymic process plays a key role in the double meaning of the question "Have you taken a bath?" The misun-derstanding in the reply can be deciphered as a confusion in causal chains. The word *bath* can be taken as an object, which can be stolen (an action) by one of the Jews (the agent). Or *bath* can be understood as part of an action (to take a bath, to bathe); the agent would remain the same (the other Jew), but the object would be the person himself (take a bath yourself, to bathe yourself).

The statement "He has a great future behind him" demands two rhetorical processes, synecdoche and irony. The synecdoche appears in the form of an ellipsis of the longer statement "That man had a great future before him, but it is not realized now." The irony comes in with the substitution of "behind" for "be-fore."

Irony needs special mention, because it is so closely related in Freud's thought to the very essence of wit: silliness and non-sense. Silliness and nonsense refer first to the initial encounter with a witticism, which is incomprehensible without a transfor-mation of meanings. In addition, Freud locates nonsense and sil-liness within a double discourse of wit:

> For jokes . . . insist on maintaining play with words or with non-sense unaltered. They restrict themselves, however, to a choice of occasions in which this play or this nonsense can at the same time appear allowable (jests) or sensible (jokes), thanks to the ambi-

guity of words and the multiplicity of conceptual relations. Nothing distinguishes jokes more clearly from all other physical structures than this double-sidedness and this duplicity in speech. From
this point of view at least the authorities come closest to an understanding of the nature of jokes when they lay stress on 'sense in
nonsense'. (*Jokes*, p. 172)

The nonsense in the double discourse leads to representations by
opposition and *contresens*—that is, to irony. Freud defines *irony*
as stating the opposite of what one wants to suggest, avoiding
contradiction by signals to the interlocutor, either by inflection,
a gesture, or stylistic markers ("small stylistic indications" [174]).
Any failure to perceive the marker risks incomprehension; in
Freud's terms, unresolved nonsense. For Freud, while irony may
not be the foundation of witticisms and jokes, it is nonetheless
at the very center of double meanings in wit, and it is the mechanism by which sense is produced from nonsense.

IMPLICATIONS FOR READING

Displacement and condensation are integral parts of the rhetorical processes, just as the rhetorical processes are part of displacement and condensation. It might be said that displacement and
condensation *are* the rhetorical processes, and vice versa. This
confluence of two disciplines has several paradoxical conse-
quences. On the one hand, it can be argued that it justifies a
psychoanalysis of literature. At the same time the confluence explains other types of interpretations, those which are not psychoanalytical. The aim of the psychoanalytical reading is to establish, to find, to locate the Other, the primary processes in the
text, or to go back to the absent origin, the Subject. Yet displacement and condensation as well as the rhetorical processes permit
the reader to go in another direction, to refuse to decondense the
text, to refuse to replace the displacements. One can displace
along the secondary or displace into one's own primary processes, as in fantasized readings.

The two activities, of reading a text critically (of
decondensing and replacing) and of allowing the free flow of
condensations and displacements from the text, are not as for-

eign to one another as one might think. Because of the psychoanalytical and rhetorical processes, in both strategies, the text before the reader's eyes becomes a pre-text, from which the reader creates a new mental text. For the "naïve" and free reader, the text before the eye is a pre-text for a series of displacements to personal fantasies. For the critic, whether psychoanalytical (looking for the primary in the secondary) or other (seeking to relocate the text in different areas of the secondary), the text before the eyes is a pre-text for a displacement to analogues (metaphors), sources (metonymies), the larger whole of which the text is but a part (synecdoche), or opposites (possibly ironic).

The real difference is between reading and interpreting. Gratuitous reading permits a full deployment of the rhetorical operations and a complete freedom to displace and form nodal points, whether they be from elements in the text or elements suggested (via rhetorical operations) by the text. Reading can permit the reader to be, not just the Duchess of Langeais in Balzac's novel, but a lion about to devour the hero Montriveau as it pursues him him through the desert. (A simple metaphorical operation and a change in sexual roles give us this fantasy.) Reading also permits us to expand the mud in Artaud's *La Rue* from the muddying stomachs ("les ventres bouent") to the entire poem and beyond into Balzac's mudhole of Paris. It is quite often only after this pleasurable free reading that the critic returns to confining, decondensing, and replacing the fantasy of traces in order to construct an ordered text on literature.

5

RHETORICAL READING:

TRUTHS AND PLEASURES

In her introductory essay to *The Reader in the Text*, a collection of essays on audience-oriented criticism, Susan Suleiman points out the quiet revolution that has occurred over the last decade in literary theory and criticism. "The words *reader* and *audience*, once relegated to the status of the unproblematic and obvious, have acceded to a starring role."[1] In attempting to organize the vast landscape of reader-centered criticism, Suleiman distinguishes six approaches: rhetorical, semiotic and structuralist, phenomenological, subjective and psychoanalytic, sociological and historical, and hermeneutic. Despite the overlap in name, the rhetorical theory we propose in *Rhetorical Poetics* has little to do with the rhetorical criticism identified by Suleiman, who uses as an exemplary representative Wayne Booth. His work, along with that of Stanley Fish and Mary Louise Pratt, is classified "rhetorical" according to the following criterion: "Any criticism that conceives of the text as a message to be decoded, and that seeks to study the means whereby authors attempt to communicate certain intended meanings or to produce certain intended effects, is both rhetorical and audience-oriented" (10). This kind of criticism places emphasis on the traditional notion of rhetoric

as the art of persuasion (manipulation) rather than on the rhetorical processes. Nor does *Rhetorical Poetics*, despite its obvious
semiotic and structuralist grounding, fit Suleiman's second category. Critics such as Gerald Prince, Gérard Genette, A. J. Greimas, and Michael Riffaterre are much more concerned with elements in the text which determine its readability than with the
reading processes.

The rhetorical reading proposed in this book is, in many
ways, most closely linked to the third of Suleiman's categories,
the phenomenological approach. Exemplified in the work of
Wolfgang Iser, "a phenomenological approach to literature concentrates . . . on the convergence between text and reader; more
exactly, it seeks to describe and account for the mental processes
that occur as a reader advances through a text and derives from
it—or imposes upon it—a pattern" (22). Yet, two basic differences distinguish our theory of rhetorical reading from Iser's
theory of aesthetic response. First, although Iser examines the
process of reading a text and explains *what* a reader does (reten-
tion and protension along the moving viewpoint, consistency-
building, acts of constitution stimulated by blanks and nega-
tions), he does not show *how* (on what basis) the reader makes
syntagmatic and paradigmatic connections. Second, Iser's major
concern is interpretation. He takes for granted the basic aspects
of reading a text (the understanding of the plot, the recognition
of motifs) and conducts his analysis at a higher level, where he
deals with the interplay of conflicting perspectives (for example,
those of author, characters, narrator, reader). A theory of reading based on figuration and symbolization, on the other hand,
addresses the question of *how* a reader can make a connection; it
examines the fundamental relationships that allow selection and
combination. It begins at the smallest level possible, the individual word, and yet is applicable to all levels of the text. It is above
all *materialistic* because it brackets higher categories of textual
structure (characters, the narrator, scenes, etc.) and explores the
word-by-word unfolding of the reading process. Consequently,
one might say that the theory of reading presented in *Rhetorical
Poetics* logically precedes the other forms of reader-oriented criticism, for it offers an analysis of the basic processes at work in

all forms of reading activity. In other words, other types of criticism, and not just audience-oriented criticism, use both the products and the processes of rhetoric to arrive at their interpretations.

While rhetorical reading underlies various kinds of criticism (reader-oriented, text-centered, author-directed), it also leads to interpretation in its own right, as we demonstrate in Part II of this book. The fundamental operations put into service at the simplest levels of the text continue to function, establishing traces, traces of traces, traces of traces of traces, and so forth. Interpretation is a metarhetorical process, whether it is placed under the direction of an "outside" theory (psychoanalytical, Marxist, structuralist, etc.) or allowed to trace out its rhetorically based paths. Whatever the route, one is faced with an age-old critical question: Is there a single interpretation of the text—a meta-meaning, a super trace, a rhetorical whole—which includes every part by means of similarity or opposition or causality? Or is interpretation a purely subjective, impressionistic act, which accepts as legitimate any and all interpretations? Both of these extremes require questioning. Iser, in the opening chapters of *The Act of Reading*, cogently attacks the first extreme, the idea that there is a single meaning buried in the text by the author and left for the reader to uncover. To this notion of a hidden truth, Iser opposes a theory of multiple meanings: "We can safely say that the relative indeterminacy of a text allows a spectrum of actualizations." [2] This spectrum, resulting from the tension that the reading process establishes between the determinacy of the discourse (the givenness of the signifiers of which it is composed) and the indeterminacy of the reader (the freedom and individuality which he brings to the text), guarantees the relative plurality of the text. At the other extreme, one finds the "absolute" plurality posited by Barthes in *S/Z*. His position espouses the idea of nonmeaning, of the refusal to interpret; he rejects the notion of structure in favor of an accumulation of isolated, fragmented "points." His absolutism is mitigated (and to an extent undermined) by the realities of his practical criticism, where implicit structures lead finally to explicit meanings. [3]

Although we are sympathetic to Iser's notion of avoiding

the two extremes of a "spectrum of actualization" (a variety of truths), we are unwilling to limit ourselves, as does Iser, to the domain of the signified. We take literally, perhaps even more so than she herself does, Lucette Finas's description of a Mallarmé poem, "indéfiniment ouvert, multiplement clos" [indefinitely open, multiplely closed].[4] Reading through figuration and symbolization involves opening the process of reading to the free play of signifiers and signifieds. Each meaning—partial and fragmentary as it may be—can signal the need to begin again. It is from this continuing process of play and meaning, of multiple traces and fragmented interpretations, that one discovers the truths of the text.

It is also through this continual process of play and meaning that one finds the pleasures of reading. Traditionally, reading pleasure has been tied to the reader's identification with (introjection of) the fantasy content of the text, a notion given theoretical form by Norman Holland.[5] Contemporary theorists such as Barthes and Julia Kristeva have argued, on the other hand, that the pleasure (*jouissance*) provided by reading comes from the reader's *bodily* contact with the text, his physical interaction with the sounds and rhythms of the work's language.[6] If the pleasure of reading is thus associated with nonintellectual, prelogical responses to literature, it would appear that, whichever of the above views one accepts, critical analysis and interpretation, those activities based on the rhetorical operations studied in this book, have no link with reading pleasure and, in fact, serve as obstacles to enjoying what one reads. Such a view receives constant reinforcement in the traditional student complaint: "Why must we ruin the book by analyzing it?" Nevertheless, rhetorical reading, in the form of metaphorical, metonymical, synecdochal, and ironic operations by the reader, carries with it the potential for pleasure, a pleasure which rivals the nonanalytic pleasures mentioned above.

Chapter 4 demonstrated how rhetorical operations are based on a combination of displacement and condensation. The latter, in turn, depend on Freudian theory on the economic thesis of a psychic apparatus capable of transmitting and transforming energy. With displacement, the energy invested in one representation can be detached and reattached to a different representation. In condensation, one representation is invested with the sum of energies of several other representations. In both cases, the energy liberated from one source is bound to another. Since the excitation produced by its liberation is reduced by attaching it to another object, one has a feeling of pleasure. Translated into the terms of our rhetorical model, the process would function as follows: an increase in excitement or tension—provoked either directly (incompatibility) or indirectly (incompleteness) by the text—is reduced because of a combination of displacement and condensation (a rhetorical operation) producing a new *liaison* (a trace). In this perspective, one can understand the pleasure felt by the reader–critic who suddenly figures out a difficult line or discovers a previously unseen opposition or connects several disparate elements to form an interpretation.

This pleasure can be produced by operations at work on any level of the text: a one-word trope or an extended passage, the signified or the signifier, a thematic trace or a typographical pattern. As such, it includes, *but is not limited to*, the violations, transgressions, and derogations which served as a source for Kristeva and theoreticians such as Lyotard.[7] Moreover, this pleasure is not reserved for the critic or professional reader. Although the examples we have used in this book tend to come from that corpus known as "Literature," the same processes are involved in ferreting out the clues in a mystery novel or in choosing which one of the characters in a historical romance will have your sympathy. In other words, these operations need not (although they well may) involve complex and esoteric associations.

Reading is not a mechanical application of a limited set of processes, nor does it involve the same degree of pleasure in every text. Freud's notion of binding (*liaison*) clarifies the relationship between pleasure and interpretation. According to Laplanche and Pontalis, Freud's writings seem to refer to two types of liaison: "One, known for a long time, which is coextensive with the notion of ego; the other, closer to the laws ruling unconscious desire and the ordering of fantasies, laws which are those of the primary process: unbound energy itself . . . is not a massive discharge of excitement, but rather circulation along representational chains implying associative 'links.'"[8] Coupled with the notion that primary processes involve a greater degree of pleasure (quantity of energy) is the idea that the more a reading is closed (i.e., characterized by an effort to combine traces into one coherent supertrace), the more it represents the first kind of binding and the lesser the degree of rhetorical pleasure involved. On the other hand, the more a reading is open (characterized by a multiplication and a diversification of traces), the more it approximates the "free circulation" of the second kind of binding and the greater the degree of rhetorical pleasure.

Such a notion must be tempered, however, by two additional remarks. First, one should not confuse open and closed reading with modern and traditional texts. Although certain works, at least initially, lend themselves to open readings and others to the quest for a single meaning, the reader need not feel constricted by these givens. As the criticism of the past twenty years has amply demonstrated, the most classic of texts holds the possibility for multiple rereadings. Consequently, one should not be surprised that Balzac or Zola can provide as much (if not more) opportunity for rhetorical pleasure as Sollers. Second, when children first learn to read stories, the simple operations of following the narrative and identifying basic similarities and oppositions in order to understand the moral, provide all the pleasure one might wish. Moreover, children's desire to read repeatedly the same texts indicates the high degree of pleasure which is present. Repetition as a psychological principle is paradoxical: source of pleasure (and therefore of life), it also leads to stasis (and therefore to death). Consequently, at some point, the reader feels the need for new readings and, in the case of some readers, new ways of reading. For the critic/professional reader, it may mean the search for new ways and places to perform the rhetorical operations; for other readers, it may take the form of an ever greater reliance on the other sorts of reading pleasures. In both cases, the pleasure processes continue, as is shown by the fact that, despite the frequent proclamations of the "death of literature," readers still read, and critics still analyze.

Part Two

Rhetorical Readings

6

BALZAC'S DUCHESS

It is understandable that critics have followed Jakobson's cue and treated the novel as predominantly metonymic. Early novels, usually recounting the lives and adventures of a central character, present a succession of causes and effects as the hero or heroine wanders about the world. Education novels offer a series of causes, formative events in the life of the main character, leading to one major effect, the development of a world view. Political and historical novels explore the effects brought on by various conflicting causes, the differing ideologies of the protagonists. No novel form exemplifies the metonymical base of the genre more clearly than does the mystery story. This type of fiction reverses the normal causal order, however; detective novels present first the effect (the crime) and then invite the reader to explore metonymic chains in search of agents ("who did it?"), instruments ("how did they do it?"), and causes ("why did they do it?") Although Balzac is not normally considered a mystery writer, he often makes use of the metonymic particularities of that form to engage the reader, to give false leads, and to string out causal chains until the final chapter of his novels. A good example of such metonymic manipulations is the short novel *La Duchesse de Langeais* (1834), in which Balzac offers a further variation of the mystery structure by beginning in the middle of the story but well before the "crime."

117

The first scene opens in a Carmelite convent, an impenetrable fortress built on the rocks of a Mediterranean island. A
French general has managed to gain access to the convent for an
interview with one of the nuns, Sister Thérèse. In the course of
the conversation, the reader realizes that the general and the nun
have once been in love. But although their passion is still alive,
Sister Thérèse refuses to go away with him. At this point, Balzac
introduces a long flashback, the major part of the novel, which
explains the two characters' pasts. Before becoming Sister Thérèse,
the heroine was one of the luminaries of the Faubourg St-Germain,
the Duchesse de Langeais. The general, the Marquis de Montriveau, had spent two years in captivity in the African desert. Upon
his reentry into Paris society, he immediately fell in love with
the duchess. He courted her according to the rules and conventions of their milieu. She encouraged the general, yet always
stopped short of giving herself to him. Exasperated by the way
she was torturing him, Montriveau had her kidnapped. He did
not harm her; rather, he symbolically asserted his superiority
over her. From then on, the tables were turned, and the duchess,
madly in love with the general, risked her reputation in vain
attempts to see him. A final desperate meeting, which might
have brought them together, did not take place because of a misunderstanding. The duchess left Paris for an unknown convent,
and Montriveau spent the following years traveling in search of
her. Finally, he locates her in the island convent. The last chapter,
after the closure of the flashback, finds Montriveau returning to
the island a second time in order to kidnap Sister Thérèse. The
general and his friends scale the rocks and gain entrance to the
convent only to discover that she has just died.

Balzac concludes the opening frame-scene of the novel by
having Montriveau say to himself that he must take Sister Thérèse
away ("l'enlever d'ici"). The narrator adds: "Voici maintenant
l'aventure qui avait déterminé la situation respective où se trou-
vaient alors les deux personnages de cette scène" [We will now
relate the adventure which had brought about the situation in
which these two persons found themselves involved].[1] As a result, the reader is confronted by a double symbolic metonymic
relationship. On the one hand, the narrator states that the island

scene is an effect and that he will now fill in the absent cause
(why Montriveau and the duchess were separated, why he went
to the island to find her). On the other hand, Montriveau suggests by his statement that because he has seen his beloved and
because she still loves him, he will take her, by force, from the
island convent. The reader thus anticipates that the remainder of
the novel will complete this second causal chain by describing
the absent effect (the kidnapping from the island and its conse-
quences) of the present cause (the encounter on the island). Figure 9 illustrates this double metonymic relationship. The reader
is thus given a double metonymic task: to look not only into the
story's past but also into its future.

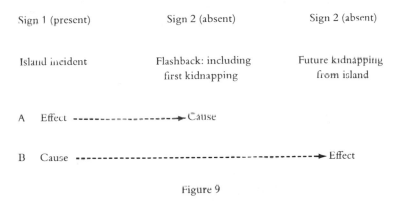

Figure 9

The search is complicated in two ways, however. First, in
order to discover the future effect the reader will have to await
the final chapter,[2] the greater part of the text (approximately 80
percent) being devoted to the flashback. Second, when one begins the main part of the text, expecting no doubt to read about
Montriveau and the duchess, one discovers a considerable amount
of text (almost twenty pages) devoted to a discussion of the Faubourg St-Germain. Thus, an ambiguity is introduced. When the
narrator states, "Voici maintenant l'aventure qui avait déterminé
la situation . . . ," the "adventure" in question is not just that of

the duchess and the general; it is also the adventure of the Faubourg St-Germain, the forty-year story of the Great Aristocratic Families. The mystery is not only a personal one, but a social and political tale as well. What appears at the beginning as only a love story between a Carmelite sister and a French general is at the same time the story of the aristocrats' failure to take command during the Restoration and to prevent the Revolution of 1830.

Although the love story of the duchess and Montriveau concentrates on a period roughly from 1818 to 1823, the sociopolitical adventure which interests Balzac goes back to the French Revolution, to the period when the Faubourg St-Germain became "what the Court used to be." In analyzing the role of the aristocracy during the first third of the nineteenth century, Balzac underlines the causes of the nobility's failure to play its appointed role. Among these causes, the most important is contained in the aphorism *Sint ut sunt, aut non sint* [May they be as they are, or may they not be]:

> Ces belles paroles pontificales peuvent servir de devise aux Grands de tous les pays. Ce fait, patent à chaque époque, et toujours accepté par le peuple, porte en lui des raisons d'état: il est à la fois un effet et une cause, un principe et une loi. (925)

> [These fine pontifical words may serve as a motto for the grandees of all countries. This fact, palpable in all periods and always accepted by the common people, carries reasons of state within itself: it is at once an effect and a cause, a principle and a law.]

For Balzac, the Great Families held their destiny in their own hands; they were either aristocrats or they were not. These self-created and self-perpetuating masters of society lost control when they failed to "be themselves." They should have, above all else, retained power, even if it were necessary to hide the fact. They failed to do so, however:

> Au lieu de jeter les insignes qui choquaient le peuple et garder secrètement la force, il [le Faubourg St-Germain] a laissé saisir la force à la bourgeoisie, s'est cramponné fatalement aux insignes et a constamment oublié les lois que lui imposait sa faiblesse numérique. . . . De nos jours, les moyens d'action doivent être des forces réelles, et non des souvenirs historiques. (928)

[Instead of jettisoning insignia obnoxious to the people while quietly holding onto the power, it allowed the middle class to lay hands on the power, and with fatal obstinacy clung to the insignia, and consistently forgot the laws imposed on it by its numerical weakness. . . . In our days, the means of action lie in real forces, and not in historic memories.]

In this passage Balzac extends the notion of metonymy far beyond narrative into social conduct when he suggests the Greats could have retained their position in society if only they had perpetrated a "metonymic lie" on the people. The aristocrats needed only to throw off the more noxious signs of their powers, the secondary effects, while retaining secretly the means of staying in power: power itself. They acted at being powerful when they had no power; they should have pretended to be weak when they were really strong. Just as "being what one is" contains its cause and effect, power is both the means and end, if handled correctly. By remembering too well the *ancien régime* and by trying to retain the meaningless attributes of their position, the aristocrats of the Faubourg St-Germain failed to adjust to the new age and thus lost their power.

But what has happened to the duchess, Montriveau, and their tragic love? Despite first appearances, they have not been lost. For Balzac, the sociopolitical background determines the fate of the lovers: "Ces idées [au sujet du Faubourg St-Germain] veulent des développements qui appartiennent essentiellement à cette aventure, dans laquelle ils entrent, *et comme définition des causes, et comme explication des faits*" (927, our italics) [These ideas call for a development which appertains essentially to the adventure here being recounted: *it relates to it both as a definition of causes and as an explanation of the facts*]. For the reader, the metonymical "reading" emphasized by Balzac can point the way to another possible reading: *La Duchesse de Langeais* as a double story of personal love and social tragedy in which the love story is a metaphor of the failed aristocrats' adventure. Such a reading throws into question Jakobson's identification of the realistic novel and metonymy. Certainly, metonymy plays a crucial role in the novel, but it offers only a partial reading. *La Duchesse de Langeais* contains a complicated and highly elaborate conceptual rhetoric in which metaphor, synecdoche, and irony as well as metonymy play a role. The text superimposes a second story on top of the conventional metonymic chains which make up the love story of the duchess and Montriveau. The second "adventure" or mystery demands that one find rhetorical links between Restoration society and the personal love story. In this search metaphor—in particular, the networks of interlocking metaphorical traces generated by the text—plays a principle part.

THE HARMONIES OF MUSIC

The reader can begin tracing one of the principle metaphors of the novel in the dedication which follows the title: "A Franz Liszt." The name, of course, suggests music, a suggestion reinforced in the very first paragraph:

> Mais nulle autre part que sur ce rocher à demi européen, africain à demi, ne pouvaient se rencontrer autant d'*harmonies* différentes qui toutes concoururent à si bien élever l'âme, à en égaliser les impressions les plus douloureuses, à en attiédir les plus vives, à faire aux peines de la vie un lit profond. (906; our italics)

> [But nowhere more surely than on this rock, half European, half African, could so many varying *harmonies* have been brought so perfectly into conjunction in order to elevate the soul, to cool its most burning fevers, bring relief to its sharpest anguish and guide its griefs into a deep channel (bed).]

The sentence seeks to harmonize several metaphorical associations that will be developed throughout the novel. The island itself is a metaphorical ground, bringing together the unlikely notes of Europe and Africa. Above all, it succeeds in harmonizing conflicting emotions, the liveliest and the saddest, and in so doing, metamorphoses a new metaphor in which suffering finds a "deep bed" (*lit profond*). It takes little imagination to conclude that the harmonious bed may well be a deathbed, especially since the narrator has just stated that the convent's austere rules attract women "qui soupirait après ce long suicide accompli dans le sein de Dieu" (906) [whose souls yearned for the lingering suicide to be accomplished here in the bosom of God]. Whereas the metonymies of the text point the reader to the material problem of power and to the necessity of dissimulation, the first paragraph contains a metaphor of spirituality, musicality, and death. At the same time, the fact that the island as metaphor can bring together very different things—sadness and liveliness, Africa and Europe—suggests that the metaphorical (here, the harmonies) can function to mediate such opposites as the materiality of power and the spirituality of the convent.

Several pages after the above passage, the general and the reader find themselves in the convent's chapel, where they are introduced to a superior form of communication emanating from the organ. The harmonies of the organ transcend their musicality to open up to a full play of synecdoche, metonymy, and metaphor. The organ is "un orchestre entier . . . il peut tout exprimer" [a whole orchestra . . . it can express all things]:

> N'est-ce pas, en quelque sorte, un piédestal sur lequel l'âme se pose pour s'élancer dans les espaces lorsque, dans son vol, elle essaie de tracer mille tableaux, de peindre la vie, de parcourir l'infini qui sépare le ciel de la terre? (912)

> [Is it not as it were a pedestal from which the human spirit leaps into space when, taking wing, it strives to sketch a thousand pictures, to paint man's life, and to explore the infinity which separates earth from heaven?]

Just as the island brings together Africa and Europe, the organ unites the heavens and the earth, while also painting life and acting as an instrument of flight for the soul.

The narrator then goes on to establish an affinity between music and the poet, restating in this comparison the metaphorically communicative power of the organ's harmonies:

> Plus un poète écoute les gigantesques harmonies, mieux il conçoit qu'entre les hommes agenouillés et le Dieu caché par les éblouissants rayons du sanctuaire les cent voix de ce choeur terrestre peuvent seules combler les distances, et sont le seul truchement assez fort pour transmettre au ciel les prières humaines dans l'omnipotence de leurs modes, dans la diversité de leurs mélancolies, avec les teintes de leurs méditatives extases, avec les jets impétueux de leurs repentirs et les mille fantaisies de toutes les croyances. (912)

> [The more a poet listens to its titanic harmonies, the more readily he conceives that, between man kneeling in adoration and the God hidden behind the dazzling rays of the sanctuary, only the hundred

voices of this terrestrial choir can fill in the distances, are the only
interpreter powerful enough to transmit human prayers to heaven
in the omnipotence of their modes and the diverse moods of their
melancholy, with the varied tints of their meditative ecstasies, the
impetuous spurts of their repentances and the thousand fantasies
of human creeds.]

Although the harmony of the island can bring together different
continents, the harmonic powers of the organ are the only ones
capable of bringing together mixed emotions and the "thousand
fantasies of all religions." Combined with the music of the choir,
the sounds of the organ reveal God's attributes: "Là, le jour af-
faibli, le silence profond, les chants qui alternent avec le tonnerre
des orgues, font à Dieu comme un voile à travers lequel rayon-
nent ses lumineux attributs" (912) [The dim light, the deep silence, the chants alternating with the thunder of the organ are
like a veil through which the luminous attributes of God Himself shine forth].

If music expresses the spiritual, it also speaks to the earthly
emotion of love. The latter serves in turn as an intermediary
linking music and poetry, an association overdetermined by the
fact that both are "texts":

> La musique, même celle du théâtre, n'est-elle pas pour les âmes
> tendres et poétiques, pour les coeurs souffrants et blessés, *un texte*
> qu'elles développent au gré de leurs souvenirs? S'il faut un coeur
> de poète pour faire un musicien, ne faut-il pas de la poésie et de
> l'amour pour écouter, pour comprendre les grandes oeuvres mu-
> sicales? (914; our italics)

> [Is not music, even the music of opera, for tender and poetic souls,
> for suffering and wounded hearts, *a text* which they develop at the
> bidding of things remembered? If a poet's heart is needed to make
> a musician, are not poetry and love needed for one to listen to and
> understand great works of music?]

Balzac uses this key metaphorical relationship to establish his
own rhetorical system within *La Duchesse de Langeais*. In this
system, three elements of existence—religion, love, and music—are united into one expression of our causal relationship to
the divine:

La Religion, l'Amour et la Musique ne sont-ils pas la triple expression d'un même fait, le besoin d'expansion dont est travaillée toute
âme noble? Ces trois *poésies* vont toutes à Dieu, qui dénoue toutes
les émotions terrestres. Aussi cette sainte Trinité humaine participe-
t-elle des grandeurs infinies de Dieu. . . . N'est-il pas le principe
et la fin de nos oeuvres? (915; our italics)

[Are not religion, love and music the threefold expression of one
fact: the craving for a fuller existence which works as a leaven in
all noble souls? These three *forms of poetry* all lead to God, who
unravels the tangles of all earthly emotions. Thus this holy trinity
in the human sphere has its part in the infinite greatness of God. . . .
Is He not the beginning and end of all our strivings?]

Although religion, love, and music are brought together as
three types of poetry, the reader is warned not to see them as
identical expressions of the soul. The relationship between the
three expressions is one of inclusion as well as similarity; they
are part of the same meta-expression, a "holy Trinity," and
therefore different from one another. The narrator underlines the
difference when he has the French general guess that "la reli-
gieuse s'était emparée de la musique pour y jeter le surplus de
passion qui la dévorait. Était-ce un hommage fait à Dieu de son
amour, était-ce le triomphe de l'amour sur Dieu?" (914) [the nun
had seized on music in order to throw into it the abounding
passion which was consuming her. Was she thus sacrificing her
love to God, or did this represent a triumph of love over God?].
By "reading" the musical text, the general (as well as the narrator and the reader) can answer these questions and construct the
sister's past. In other words, an initial "poetic" gesture permits
the narrator (and the others) to understand that music is indeed
a text to be read like a book. After making this "metaphorical
leap," one can then decipher the music and see it as an expression, a metonymy. The harmonies produced by the musician
(Sister Thérèse) reveal both her present spiritual state and its past
causes: "Le jeu de la musicienne lui dénonçait une femme aimée
avec ivresse, et qui s'était profondément ensevelie au coeur de la
religion et si soigneusement dérobée aux regards du monde" (910)
[The organist's style of execution was identifying her as a woman

madly loved, one who had buried herself so deep in the bosom
of religion and so carefully concealed herself from the eyes of
the world].

   Although music reveals the psychological and the divine
and functions as a language similar to verbal language, it does
have one crucial advantage over its metaphorical analogue; it can
communicate the incommunicable:

> Les sensations que lui causèrent les différents morceaux exécutés
> par la religieuse sont du petit nombre de choses dont l'exécution
> est interdite à la parole, et la rend impuissante, mais qui, sembla-
> bles à la mort, à Dieu, à l'Eternité, ne peuvent s'apprécier que dans
> le léger point de contact qu'elles ont avec les hommes. (909)

> [His feelings as he listened to the various pieces played by the nun
> are to be counted among the small number of things which human
> speech is powerless to express and which like certain concepts—
> death, eternity, God—can only be evaluated in relation to the slen-
> der point of contact they have with men.]

Music can thus put humanity into a metaphorical relationship
with these three unknown and ineffable absolutes: Death, God,
Eternity. One might say the music is the mediator (in rhetorical
terms, the intermediary) which brings together two opposing
realities: finite humanity and the infinite.

   Despite its metaphorical force within an individual's soul,
music is notably less successful in mediating between two people.
The duchess and Montriveau never manage to strike a purely
harmonious chord. Music fails as an intermediary in their love
story largely because the duchess *uses* music to keep love and
religion separate. Music expressed directly rarely appears in the
flashback section of the novel. All such occurrences belong to
the "*religious* phase" (Balzac's italics) of their courtship, where
the duchess has recourse to playing the piano in order both to
sublimate her feelings and to calm the ardor of her suitor:

> Si cette femme se sentait piquée par une fantaisie assez insistante
> pour la compromettre, elle savait alors sortir de son boudoir: elle
> quittait l'air chargé de désirs qu'elle y respirait, venait dans son
> salon, s'y mettait au piano, chantait les airs les plus délicieux de la
> musique moderne, et trompait ainsi l'amour des sens, qui parfois

ne lui faisait pas grâce, mais qu'elle avait la force de vaincre. En ces moments, elle était sublime aux yeux d'Armand: elle ne feignait pas, elle était vraie, et le pauvre amant se croyait aimé. Cette résistance égoïste la lui faisait prendre pour une sainte et vertueuse créature, et il se résignait, et il parlait d'amour platonique, le général d'artillerie! (967)

[If she then felt pricked with a fancy which might provoke her enough to compromise her, she knew the moment was ripe to leave her boudoir. She withdrew from its desire-laden atmosphere, went to her salon, sat down at her piano, sang the most delightful melodies of modern music, and in this way cheated the sensual love which sometimes gave her no quarter but which she was still strong enough to overcome. At such moments Armand thought her sublime: there was no pretence but only truth in her, and the fond lover believed he was loved in return. Her egoistical resistance made him take her for a saintly and virtuous creature. He grew resigned and talked of platonic love: he, a general of artillery!]

The harmony suggested here is false and impure: music serves to blind both Montriveau, consciously, and the duchess, unconsciously, to the real situation.

THE LADY AND THE LION: VEILS, GRILLS, AND PREDATORS
The failure of music to mediate between the duchess and Montriveau can also be attributed to the great differences between the two characters. On one side, there is the duchess—twenty-four years old, daughter of the Duc de Navarreins, married in name only to a young aristocrat, educated to play at being a "lady of fashion" (femme à la mode) in the salons of the Faubourg St Germain. On the other side, one finds Montriveau—older, son of a Republican general, brought up after the death of his father to serve in Napoleon's artillery, survivor of an ill-fated scientific expedition to the deserts of Africa. The differences suggested by these biographical details are complemented in the text by a series of metaphorical traces which act as a harmonic to the metonymic chains making up their adventure.

The first description of Montriveau, listening to the music

in the convent chapel, depicts him as "un homme ardent, un homme à coeur et face de lion, un de ces hommes à crinière, qui imposent et communiquent à ceux qui les envisagent une respectueuse terreur" (911) [a man of fiery spirit, a man with the heart and face of a lion, one of those imposing men with a mane who excite terror in the hearts of those who look upon them]. The lion metaphor reappears at other intervals in the text: "Il était petit, large de buste, musculeux comme un lion" (946) [He was small, broad in the chest, and muscular as a lion]; "souvent aussi le général secouait sa crinière, laissait la politique, grondait comme un lion, se battait les flancs, s'élançait sur sa proie" (967) [often the general shook his mane, thrust politics aside, growled like the lion he was, lashed his tail, pounced on his prey]. To the leonine trace can be added allusions to other powerful and voracious animals. He is alternately described as having "des yeux de lynx" (920) [lynx's eyes], "des yeux calmes comme ceux des panthères" (953) [eyes as calm as those of panthers], "yeux . . . comme ceux d'un tigre sûr de sa proie" (989) [eyes . . . like those of a tiger sure of its prey]. He has a "cou de taureau" (987) [bull's neck] and "griffes de tigre" (920) [tiger's claws]. He is also represented as being "cousin germain des aigles . . . il vous emportera dans son aire" (960) [first cousin to the eagles . . . he'll carry you off to his eyrie].

Opposed to this metaphorical image of power and predation is not, however, its logical counterpart: the lamb, the dove, the fawn. If one did find such an animal opposition, one might expect that music would succeed as a metaphorical intermediary, soothing the savage beast and causing the lion to lie down with the lamb. But only a single animal allusion is connected with the duchess: she has a "cou de cygne" (958) [swan's neck]. Instead, the metaphors associated with her organize themselves around the notions of protection and concealment. The first description of the duchess appears in the text at the moment when Montriveau manages an interview with Sister Thérèse:

Parvenus au fond de cette longue galerie, le prêtre fit entrer son compagnon dans une salle partagée en deux parties par une grille couverte d'un rideau brun . . . le rideau brun se tira; puis il [Mon-

triveau] vit dans la lumière une femme debout, mais dont la figure
lui était cachée par le prolongement du voile plié sur la tête: suivant la règle de la maison, elle était vêtue de cette robe dont la
couleur est devenue proverbiale. (917–18)

[When they had reached the end of this long gallery, the priest
introduced his companion into a hall divided into two parts by a
grille draped with a brown curtain . . . the brown curtain was
drawn aside. Then the light enabled him to discern a woman who
was standing, but whose features were hidden from him by the
veil draped about her head and falling over her face: in accordance
with the community rule, she was clothed in the brown habit whose
colour has become proverbial.]

A veil, a curtain, a robe: materials designed to cover, to hide, to
mask. Whereas one expects Sister Thérèse to wear a veil and a
habit, the duchess, when Montriveau visits her home for the
first time, is also, surprisingly, wearing a brown robe (brown is
the Carmelite color) and a veil:

Il trouva sa nébuleuse sylphide enveloppée d'un peignoir de cache-
mire brun habilement bouillonné, languissamment couchée sur le
divan d'un obscur boudoir. Madame de Langeais ne se leva même
pas, elle ne montra que sa tête, dont les cheveux étaient en dé-
sordre, quoique retenus dans un voile. (951 52)

[He found his nebulous sylph wrapped in a peignoir of brown
cashmere, skilfully flounced, and languidly reclining on a divan in
a dimly-lit boudoir. Madame de Langeais did not even rise to her
feet, and showed only her head, with her hair dishevelled though
caught up in a veil.]

Later in the text, the narrator picks up the metaphor again and
underlines its link to the story: Montriveau "put penser avec
quelque raison que tant de querelles capricieuses formaient des
voiles avec lesquels une âme céleste s'était vêtue, et qu'il fallait
lever un à un, comme ceux dont elle enveloppait son adorable
personne" (979) [had cause to believe that so many whimsical
quarrels were the veils in which an angel's soul was dressed, and
that they had to be lifted one by one, like the ones with which
her adorable person was wrapped].

If one returns to the original description of Sister Thérèse's first appearance, a second metaphorical trace becomes evident. The curtained grill separating the two parts of the convent *parlor* can be linked to the grill, behind which hangs a brown curtain, separating the choir from the rest of the church. This impassable barrier protects the nuns from the other churchgoers just as the impenetrable walls and unscalable rocks protect the convent from the rest of the world. Once again, one is not surprised to find a convent protected in this fashion. However, both the duchess and Sister Thérèse also erect barriers to protect themselves from siege. At first, it is part of the Parisian game of coquettry for the duchess, who

> voyait, dans la passion de cet homme vraiment grand, un amuse-ment pour elle, un intérêt à mettre dans sa vie sans intérêt. Elle se préparait à élever autour d'elle une certaine quantité de redoutes qu'elle lui donnerait à emporter avant de lui permettre l'entrée de son coeur. (954)

> [saw that the passion of a truly great man would be an amusement for her and bring some interest to her dull life. She was already therefore very skilfully preparing to throw up round herself a se-ries of barriers which he had to carry by assault before she allowed him to gain entry to her heart.

Then, as Montriveau's passion grows, the barriers are needed for defense: "Aussi Madame de Langeais s'entoura-t-elle bientôt d'une seconde ligne de fortification plus difficile à emporter que ne l'a-vait été la première. Elle évoqua les terreurs de la religion" (966) [And so Madame de Langeais soon girded herself with a second line of fortification, more difficult to take away than the first had been. She invoked the terrors of religion].

A further "metaphorical leap" allows one to join the veil and the grill, metaphors of the duchess's efforts to hide her feel-ings and protect her body. Just as the veils have to be lifted (*en-lever*), so must the grill be taken away (*enlever*). Here the meta-phors help to generate the story, for Montriveau has the duchess kidnapped (*enlever*). When she regains her senses, she finds her-self imprisoned in Montriveau's bedroom, which is separated from a mysterious second room by "une porte cachée par un rideau" (992) [a door hidden by a curtain]. Thus, the tables have been turned: she is surrounded by barriers erected by another and by curtains concealing someone else's intentions. The reversal does not, however, eliminate the metaphorical gap between the lady and the lion. When the latter refuses to drop *his* veils and remove *his* barriers, the lady responds by literally putting on a veil (that of the Carmelite order) and by surrounding herself with walls and grills (those of the convent). The second kidnapping overcomes these barriers (the rock is scaled, the grill is sawed through) and removes these veils (a false nun, Montriveau's friend in disguise, symbolically pulls down his veil as they enter Sister Thérèse's room), but what the kidnappers find is only a corpse.

The lady, veiled and hidden, and the lion, voracious and on the prowl, are not, however, just pure metaphorical constructs. As individuals they also stand for wholes. The synecdochal function of the duchess, as representation of the Faubourg St-Germain, is underlined by the narrator when the duchess is first presented to the reader:

Lorsque, dans un temps quelconque, il se trouve au milieu d'une nation un peuple à part ainsi constitué, l'historien y rencontre presque toujours une figure principale qui résume les vertus et les défauts de la masse à laquelle elle appartient. . . . Au commencement de la vie éphémère que mena le Faubourg St-Germain pendant la Restauration, et à laquelle, si les considérations précédentes sont vraies, il ne sut pas donner de consistance, une jeune femme fut passagèrement le type le plus complet de la nature à la fois supérieure et faible, grande et petite, de sa caste. (934)

[Whenever, at any time, there exists in the midst of a nation a people apart thus constituted, the historian almost always meets with a principal figure who sums up in himself or herself the virtues and defects of the group to which he or she belongs. . . . At the beginning of the ephemeral life of the Faubourg Saint-Germain during the Restoration, a life to which, if the preceding considerations are valid, it failed to give any consistency, one young woman was for the time being the most complete type of the nature, at once superior and feeble, great and petty, of her caste.]

The synecdoche has, however, a metaphorical base. The descriptions of the nobility are also descriptions of the duchess. Thus, speaking of that national instinct which "a dominé depuis trois siècles la noblesse" [has for three centuries dominated the nobility], the narrator describes the Frenchman thusly: "Quoiqu'il ait beaucoup de coeur, il préfère trop souvent écouter son esprit" (929) [although he may be a man of much heart, too often he prefers to listen to his mind]. The duchess is presented as a woman who "ne sentait rien et réfléchissait à tout" (976) [felt nothing and thought about everything]; as being "tout tête, elle ne sent que par sa tête, elle a un coeur dans la tête, une voix de tête, elle est friande par la tête" (982) [all head: she feels only with her head, she stores her heart in her head, her voice is in the head, and her tastes are in her head]. Moreover, both the aristocrats and the duchess misuse their heads: the Great Families waste their time on frivolous, superficial signs of power; the duchess plays at veiling her feelings and her body. As a result, neither manages to attain its goals. The duchess, like the society which produced her, is "pleine de sentiments élevés, mais manquant d'une pensée qui les coordonnât" (935) [full of lofty sentiments, but lacking ideas to coordinate them]. The personification of her world, it is no wonder that the duchess is a "reine de la mode" [queen of fashion].

Montriveau, on the other hand, does not come from the Faubourg St-Germain. He does, however, have a synecdochal function. As an individual he represents precisely that small group of individuals, exceptional people, who seem to stand above and apart. "C'était un de ces grands hommes inconnus, assez philosophes pour mépriser la gloire, qui vivent sans s'attacher à la vie, parce qu'ils ne trouvent pas à y développer leur force ou leurs sentiments dans toute leur étendue" (941) [He was one of those unknown great men, philosophical enough to be scornful of glory, who live without laying great store to life because it gives them no opportunity to develop their powers of mind or heart to their full extent]. Like the lion, he was feared, esteemed, but little loved. Like the eagle, he flew over the heads of common men, morally pure, intellectually superior. Each stage of his life had set him apart: orphan, member of Napoleon's artillery (a corps apart in the Emperor's army), leader of a scientific expedition to Upper Egypt and the unknown parts of Africa. A stranger to life, not having found a way to realize all his potential, he is also an outsider in the society of the Faubourg St-Germain. Moreover, it is precisely because of his "strangeness" that he gains access to the aristocratic *salons* and attracts the attention of the duchess.

THE NUMBER 3

The binary opposition (the duchess versus Montriveau) at the base of the story contrasts in turn with another metaphorical trace based on the number 3. The first appearance of 3 is found in the opening section of the novel, where it intersects the musical trace. The narrator talks of those "three forms of poetry"— Religion, Love, and Music—united in a harmony which reflects divine perfection. These metaphors—*harmony* and *three*—reappear in the long description of the Faubourg St-Germain. There, the narrator begins by proclaiming the need for "political harmony" (*harmonie politique*):

> Aux masses les moins intelligentes se révèlent encore les bienfaits de l'harmonie politique. L'harmonie est la poésie de l'ordre. . . . La concordance des choses entre elles, l'unité, pour tout dire en un mot, n'est-elle pas la plus simple expression de l'ordre? (925)

> [Even to the least intelligent masses the benefits accruing from political harmony can be made clear. Harmony is the poetry of order. . . . Now is not the cooperation of all things with one another, unity in a word, the simplest expression of order?]

He then associates the metaphor with social classes (*les peuples*), developing a series of interlocking triangular concepts which should constitute the harmonious society. This society is divided into three classes: the aristocracy, the bourgeoisie, and the workers (or people). The classes play respectively three different roles: the aristocrats are the "head," the bourgeoisie, the "heart" and the "hands," and the people, or workers, the "organism" and the "action" (925). Power is inscribed within a three-sided figure composed of art, science, and wealth (928). It is the role of the head to assume this power, to know how to utilize these forces in order to organize and control society, to create social harmony. The people, moreover, expect the aristocrats to play such a role: "Le peuple veut toujours leur voir aux mains, au coeur, et à la tête, la fortune, le pouvoir et l'action; la parole, l'intelligence et la gloire. Sans cette triple puissance, tout privilège s'évanouit" (926) [The people always want to see them holding in their hands, their heart and their head, fortune, authority and action: speech, intelligence and glory. Without this triple might, all privilege vanishes].

Such is the ideal society. But in the imperfect society of the Restoration, the aristocracy, according to Balzac, has not recognized its role. Hating art and religion, incapable of generating money and of thinking scientifically, the Great Families of the Faubourg St-Germain used their heads only to think of themselves. The aristocrats produced nothing outside themselves; as a result they had to stand by as the bourgeoisie, their former instruments, took their places, acquiring money, science, and art for themselves (927–32). The harmonious unity—where the spiritual would extend into the physical, where the power of the aristocracy would be reflected in all classes, where the head would produce art, science, wealth for the rest of the body—gave way to the disintegration of the triangles and to rivalry between the parts.

Metaphorically, this disintegration is repeated on the individual level with the duchess, the symbolic representative of the aristocracy. She appears in the novel in three guises: the Duchesse de Langeais, the *femme à la mode*; Sister Thérèse, the Carmelite nun; and Antoinette de Navarreins, the young woman. Just as the aristocracy failed to unite the social forces of the nation into a harmonious whole, so the duchess is unable to integrate the aspects of her personality. Both she and the nation are fragmented. As a woman of nobility, the duchess allows the artificiality characteristic of her class to repress the sexually vibrant woman. When she finally recognizes and accepts her true feelings (Balzac entitles the third section of the novel *La Femme vraie* [The Real Woman]), Montriveau ignores her, and she hides again, this time in the prison of Sister Thérèse. In this role, she sublimates her passion by playing the organ. But the holy trinity (Music, Love, Religion) also fragments: she is unable to resolve the conflict between love and religion except through death.

This division of the duchess into three separate characters metaphorically parallels the fragmentation of her relationship with Montriveau. Repressing the physical (body) and the emotional (heart), the duchess relies exclusively on her head to toy with Montriveau's affections. He, on the other hand, falls madly in love: "En ce moment, monsieur de Montriveau fut à la fois saisi par un violent *désir* . . . et par un mouvement de *coeur*" (950; our italics) [And so, at that juncture, Monsieur de Montriveau was at one and the same time seized with a violent *desire* . . . and with a surge of *passion*]. Thus, although the elements (head, heart, body) are all there, they are split: the harmony needed for the love affair to succeed is missing.

THE EXECUTIONER AND THE AXE

The failure of the duchess and Montriveau to realize a harmonic whole both in their individual lives and in their relationship mirrors metaphorically the failure of the aristocrats to unite the "head," the "heart," and the "hands" of the country. By refusing to take cognizance of the post-Napoleonic world, the aristocrats tried to live in the past. By trying to retain their meaningless attributes and by frittering away their time in social rituals, they became, in Balzac's view, vulnerable:

> Tissue dans le pays, elle [l'aristocratie] devenait indestructible; acculée dans son faubourg, adossée à son chateau, étendue dans le budget, il suffisait *d'un coup de hache* pour trancher le fil de sa vie agonisante, et la plate figure d'un petit avocat s'avança pour donner ce coup de hache. (932; our italics)

> [As part of the texture of the country, it would have been indestructible; but, cornered in its faubourg, leaning back against the royal palace, spreadeagled over the Budget, *one stroke of the axe was enough to cut the thread of its ebbing life*. The commonplace figure of a little barrister came forward to deal the blow.]

The historical reference is to the law passed in 1831 banning the inheritance of peerages. The metaphorical allusion to an axe blow signals a trace which functions as the central rhetorical figure of the text.

The original title of the novel was to be *Ne touchez pas la hache* [Touch Not the Axe]. The phrase appears, italicized by the author, in a scene just preceding the first kidnapping of the duchess. Montriveau is talking to a stranger, but he aims his words at the duchess:

> —Monsieur, lui disait-il, l'une des choses qui m'ont le plus frappé dans ce voyage . . .
> La duchesse était tout oreilles.
> . . . Est la phrase que prononce le gardien de Westminster en vous montrant la hache avec laquelle un homme masqué trancha, dit-on, la tête de Charles Ier en mémoire du roi qui les dit à un curieux.
> —Que dit-il? demanda madame de Serizy.
> —*Ne toucher pas à la hache*, répondit Montriveau d'un son de voix où il y avait de la menace.
> —En vérité, monsieur le marquis, dit la duchesse de Langeais, vous regardez mon cou d'un air si mélodramatique en répétant cette vieille histoire, connue de tous ceux qui vont à Londres, qu'il me semble vous voir une hache à la main. (989)

> ["Monsieur," Montriveau was saying to him, "one of the things which struck me most during my stay in England . . . "
> The duchess was all ears.
> ". . . was the words which the guide at Westminster, as he shows you the axe with which, so they say, the masked executioner cut off the head of Charles I, quotes in memory of that king, who spoke them to an inquisitive person."
> "What were they?" asked Madame de Sérisy.
> "*Touch not the axe*," Montriveau replied in a tone of voice which had a menacing note in it.
> "In truth, Monsieur le Marquis," said the Duchesse de Langeais, "you are looking at my neck with so melodramatic an air as you repeat that old story, known to all who visit London, that I seem to see you with an axe in your hand."]

The association of England's Charles I with the axe is due both to his brutal efforts to reestablish royal power and to his death by beheading. Earlier in the text, the narrator refers to the "époque à laquelle Louis XVIII, éclairé par la révolution des Cent-Jours, comprit sa situation et son siècle, malgré son entourage, qui, néanmoins, triompha plus tard de ce Louis XI moins la hache, lorqu'il fut abattu par la maladie" (936) [period when Louis XVIII, enlightened by the revolution of the Hundred Days, came to understand his situation and his century, in spite of his entourage which none of the less later got the better of this Louis XI minus the axe, once infirmity struck him down]. Later, the narrator describes the aristocracy as follows:

> Tels étaient les représentants de cette grande noblesse qui voulait mourir ou rester tout entière, qui méritait autant d'éloge que de blâme, et sera toujours imparfaitement jugée jusqu'à ce qu'un poète l'ait montrée heurcuse d'obéir au roi en expirant sous la hache de Richelieu, et méprisant la guillotine de 89 comme une sale vengeance. (1012)

> [Such were the representatives of this high nobility which was intent either on dying out or preserving its integrity, which was as worthy of praise as of blame and which will never be fairly judged until some poet has revealed it as it was: happy to obey the king by perishing under Richelieu's axe but despising the guillotine of 1789 as a base instrument of vengeance.]

The axe is associated, in apparently contradictory fashion, with both the successes and the defeats of the monarchy and the aristocrats. The contradiction can be resolved, however. The negative allusions involve either the absence of the axe (Louis XVIII, enlightened but powerless) or the use of the axe by the "wrong" class (the enemies of Charles I, the revolutionaries of 1789). The positive allusions show the axe being used, even against one's own class when necessary, to establish order (Charles I, Louis XI, Richelieu). The man with the axe in *La Duchesse de Langeais* is Montriveau, whose attitude towards its use proves to be ambivalent. Willing to threaten but unwilling to execute his threats, Montriveau settles for a symbolic assertion of his power over the duchess. As a result, he gains neither of his ends: his vengeance is unsatisfactory, and he fails to achieve harmony with the woman he loves.

The rhetorical trace organized around the axe can be extended synecdochally to include the material of which the axe is made: steel. Montriveau's friend, the marquis de Ronquerolles, describes the duchess as "ce système d'acier femelle" (983) [this female steel contraption], an image which the narrator picks up again: "Armand de Montriveau sentit alors la dureté de cette femme froide et tranchante autant que l'acier" (985) [Only then did Armand de Montriveau feel the hardness of this woman, as chilly and as cutting as steel]. This trace leads then to the passage where Montriveau makes the decision to act against the woman who has been toying with him. He says to himself: "Je te prendrai par le chignon du cou, madame la duchesse, et t'y ferai sentir un fer plus mordant que ne l'est le couteau de la Grève. Acier contre acier, nous verrons quel coeur sera plus tranchant" (987) [I will take you by the nape of the neck, Madame la Duchesse, and you shall feel a blade that is keener than that of the guillotine. Steel for steel: we will see which one of us will have the most cutting heart]. His vengeance consists of kidnapping her and threatening to brand her with "une croix de Lorraine adaptée au bout d'une tige d'acier" (998) [a cross of Lorraine fitted to the end of a steel shaft].

The axe trace can be further extended, this time metonymically, by linking the instrument (the axe) to its agent (the executioner). The first stages of the relationship between Montriveau and the duchess place him in the role of victim, her in the role of torturer or executioner. The narrator makes the image explicit with a simile:

> Jouet de ses caprices, Montriveau devait rester stationnaire tout en sautant de difficultés en difficultés comme un de ces insectes tourmenté par un enfant saute d'un doigt sur un autre en croyant avancer, tandis que son malicieux bourreau le laisse au même point. (954)

> [He was to be a plaything for her whims; he was to surmount one obstacle after another while making no advance, like an insect which, teased by a child, hops from one finger to another in the belief that it is getting away, while its malicious tormentor keeps it stationary.]

Ronquerolles, when apprised of the nature of Montriveau's affair with the duchess, advises him to rebel: "Sois inflexible comme la loi. N'aie pas plus de charité que n'en a le bourreau. Frappe. Quand tu auras frappé, frappe encore. . . . Les duchesses sont dures, mon cher Armand, et ces natures de femme ne s'amollissent que sous les coups" (982) [Be as inexorable as the law. Show no more charity than the executioner. Strike and when you have struck, strike again. . . . Duchesses are tough, my dear Armand, and women of her kind only soften up with blows]. Montriveau, taking in part the advice of his friend, acts. When the duchess is brought to him, he tells her: "Ici, vous serez ma victime" (992) [Here, you will be my victim]. He then makes an allusion to executions: "Madame, dit-il après une pause, lorsque, dans Paris, le bourreau devra mettre la main sur un pauvre assassin, et le couchera sur la planche où la loi veut qu'un assassin soit couché pour perdre la tête . . . " (994) [Madame, he said after a pause, when, in Paris, the executioner has to lay his hand on a wretched murderer and strap him to the plank on which the law stipulates that a murderer must be laid for his head to be cut off . . .]. Thus, the situation is reversed, and Montriveau, symbolic axe in hand, can dominate his victim. At this point, a complete switch takes place: Montriveau, the childlike lover, the victim of his heart, becomes the cold, unfeeling torturer; the duchess, the cerebral coquette, becomes the child,[3] victim in turn of her passion.

In her final letter to Montriveau, the duchess complains: "Dans cette terrible aventure qui m'a tant attachée à vous, Armand, vous alliez du désert à l'oasis, mené par un bon guide. Eh bien, moi, je me traîne de l'oasis au désert, et vous m'êtes un guide sans pitié" (1026) [In the terrible adventure which befell you and which tied me so closely to you, you moved, Armand, under competent guidance, from the desert to an oasis; but I am being dragged from an oasis to the desert under your pitiless guidance]. This sentence, underlining the reversal which has taken place, refers to a story Montriveau told the first night she met him. This anecdote, at first reading apparently gratuitous, can be seen, in retrospect, to complete the axe-steel-executioner trace. While on an expedition in the Upper Nile Valley, Montriveau had to cross a desert unexplored by nonnatives of the region. During the long and arduous crossing, his guide repeatedly promised a specified time of arrival, only to frustrate the hopes of Montriveau. Angered by the guide's calm reassessments of the time remaining, Montriveau accused the guide of deceiving him, to which the latter replied: "Nous avons encore cinq heures de marche, et nous ne pouvons plus retourner sur nos pas. Sonde ton coeur, si tu n'as pas assez de courage, voici mon poignard" (946) [We have another five hours in front of us, and it's too late to turn back. Probe your heart, if you don't have enough courage, here is my dagger]. Five hours later Montriveau could still see nothing when suddenly the guide hoisted him on his shoulders and carried him the last hundred yards to a lake surrounded with trees. During the telling of the anecdote the guide is specifically compared to an executioner: "Puis il se remit en route, suivant avec peine l'Africain impitoyable auquel il semblait lié par un fil, comme un condamné l'est invisiblement au bourreau" (945) [Then he set off again, painfully following the pitiless African to whom he felt as if he were tied by an invisible tether, as a condemned is to the executioner]. Thanks to the guide-executioner, "ce géant d'intelligence et de courage" (946) [this titan of intelligence and courage], Montriveau feels himself reborn. The executioner-guide is thus seen in positive terms as the source of power and thus order. In the light of this rhetorical chain, Montriveau's unwillingness to use his axe other than symbolically—his refusal to brand the duchess with his steel or to take her physically—marks his failure to play satisfactorily his role as guide-executioner for her.[4]

POETRY

The end of the desert anecdote also intersects the music trace. The final words of Montriveau's story suggest a mediation between two opposites: "Il voyait d'un côté l'enfer des sables, et de l'autre le paradis terrestre de la plus belle oasis qui fût en ces déserts" (946) [He saw on one side the hell of the sands, on the other earthly paradise: the most beautiful oasis there was in the deserts]. The link to the music trace is reinforced by the narrator's introduction to Montriveau's desert story:

> Monsieur de Montriveau ne comprenait rien à ces petites singeries parisiennes, et son âme ne pouvait répondre qu'aux sonores vibrations des beaux sentiments. Il eut promptement été laissé là, sans *la poésie* qui résultait de ses aventures et de sa vie. (944)

> [Monsieur de Montriveau understood nothing of these little Parisian affectations and his soul could only respond to the ringing vibrations of genuine feeling. He would have readily been dropped at that point had it not been for the *poetry* resulting from his adventures and his life.]

Poetry is one of the intermediaries creating the harmony of Religion, Love, and Music (*ces trois poésies*). Moreover, poetry is the link between harmony and political order: "L'harmonie est la poésie de l'ordre, et les peuples ont un vif besoin d'ordre" [Harmony is the poetry of order, and the people have a definite need of order]. And harmony, order, poetry, are precisely what the Restoration lacks: "Ce fut une époque froide, mesquine et sans poésie. Peut-être faut-il beaucoup de temps à une restauration pour devenir une monarchie" (939) [It was a cold, shabby, unpoetic period. Perhaps much time is needed for a restored monarchy to become a genuine one].

Poetry—tied metaphorically to harmony, political order, courage, adventure, and intelligence—reappears at the end of the novel. Having helped Montriveau carry off the dead body of the duchess, Ronquerolles suggests that they tie a cannonball to each of her feet and throw her overboard; Montriveau agrees: "Oui, dit Montriveau, car ce n'est plus qu'un poème" (1037) [Yes, indeed, said Montriveau, for only a poem remains]. Recalling the links, suggested at the beginning of the novel, between poetry and music, love, religion, one might be tempted to see this metaphor in positive terms: in death, the duchess finally achieves the harmony which she lacked in life. Other rhetorical traces refute such a reading, however. In the rhetorical structure of the text, harmony is associated with the number three. The conflict *within* the Duchess opposes two against one. Music can express both love and religion, but cannot join them into a realized whole. The head can unite with the heart in the convent, but the body must perish. In similar fashion, the conflict *between* the duchess and Montriveau finds three elements unable to unite into a whole. Initially, the head (the duchess) is opposed to the heart and the body (Montriveau). After the kidnapping, the opposition still exists: Montriveau has become the head, coldly refusing to respond to the duchess's entreaties, and she has become the heart, desperately trying to see the man she loves. Yet this opposition is not an exact mirror of the previous one. After the scene in Montriveau's room, there is no physical contact between the two except in the convent, where they are separated by a grill, a habit, and a veil. The two "virgins" remain intact. The body has disappeared from the triangle, or if it remains, it is only as a corpse. In this context, Montriveau's "ce n'est plus qu'un poème" can be read ironically. For Balzac, poetry is seen as energy, activity, performance.[5] Like the duchess's dead body, a poem is inert, passive, a result rather than an action. The absence of harmony, the failure of the love affair, can then be understood to have a double cause: during the first part of the adventure, the fault lies with the duchess, who, indoctrinated with the superficial values and concerns of her class, misuses her head; during the second part, the blame falls on Montriveau, who, unwilling to act "poetically," is content with a symbolic affirmation of his power.

LOVE AND POLITICS

As suggested at the beginning of the chapter, the adventure of the duchess and Montriveau is a metaphor for the adventure of the nobles during the Restoration. Synecdochally, the duchess represents her aristocratic class. Metaphorically, she is linked not only to the Faubourg St-Germain, but also to France as a whole. Balzac speaks of France as "le pays le plus femelle du monde" (930) [the most feminine nation in the world]. He asserts that "la France, femme capricieuse, veut être heureuse ou battue à son gré" (930) [France, a capricious woman (or wife) wants to be happy or to be beaten as fancy takes her]. Just as the duchess is presented as a woman needing a strong man to make her fall in love, to strip off her veils and become "the real woman," so France, and the aristocracy as its "head," needs a strong leader to push the nobles into playing their appointed role and to reestablish France as a harmonious political whole. Montriveau at first seems to be this man, this leader: leonine, eaglelike, he has the potential to combine aristocratic breeding and Napoleonic energy. He remains fragmented, however, unable to combine head and heart, unwilling to act until it is too late. Thus, of the duchess, the Faubourg St-Germain, and France there remains only "a poem."

7

BAUDELAIRE'S JEWELS

Mallarmé's declaration that the poet should "peindre non la chose mais l'effet qu'elle produit"[1] is most often taken as an example of the esthetics of suggestiveness, allusion, and ambiguity. Taken literally, Mallarmé says much more, as he defines poetry as cause and effect, product and producer, or, in rhetorical terms, as metonymical tropes. This reading of Mallarmé can be disturbing, since poetry generally has been considered metaphorical, and the ambiguity and suggestiveness of Symbolist poems are not readily associated with causality. There is little question that metaphor plays a major role in poetry, but it is also true that just as poetry is governed by conventions, the *reading* of poetry is governed by its own conventions. One of these conventions is that poetry should be read metaphorically. Mallarmé's statement suggests that there may be another way—the metonymic way—to explore poems.

This chapter will examine metaphorical and metonymic responses to one poem, Baudelaire's *Les Bijoux*. To begin, an analysis of two diametrically opposed readings of the poem, by Judd Hubert and Leo Bersani, will demonstrate the possibilities and limits of metaphorical readings.[2] Hubert interprets the poem as "an almost mystical vision of absolute beauty," an example of "tranquillity of the poet's soul" (217), and Bersani regards the poem as an example of "violent metaphoricity of sexual fantasy [which] has become a fantasy of sex as literal physical violence" (66).

METAPHORICAL READINGS

Judd Hubert appears to base his interpretation on lines 23 and 24:

> Et pour la [mon âme] déranger du rocher de cristal
> Où calme et solitaire, elle s'était assise.

[And to upset it (my soul) from its crystal rock / Where, calm and solitary, it had rested.]

Hubert reads the poem as a drama with three protagonists. The poet as tranquil soul is the center of the drama. The mistress, in her sinuous lewdness, represents seductiveness. The jewels provide a means for avoiding the woman's sensuality as they attract the poet (*attirail*) and "turn attention away from the woman and fix it on an inanimate object" (214). Whereas the woman's seductiveness is related to movement, the attractiveness of the jewels is found in immobility and Beauty. The poet, the woman, and the jewels compose the poem, but they cannot be unified into a whole: the observer-poet, according to Hubert, must decide between sensuality and Beauty.

In the lines central to his interpretation—lines 17 to 24—Hubert insists on metaphorical readings in order to detach the poet totally from the mistress and to release him from all contamination of sexuality. In these stanzas, where the woman is moving and trying different poses, she becomes the sea through words related either to the ocean or to liquids; *vague* (meaning, Hubert says, "wave," not "vague"), *lubricité* ("sliding" and "oily," not "lubricious"), and *onduleux* ("wavy"). On the other hand, the poet, as he looks at the plastic scene before him, resembles the rock upon which he (his soul) is seated. Hubert links this metaphor to a second one based on the same intermediaries (*detachment* and *immobility*): the poet's soul "strangely resembles the radiating jewels and the clairvoyant eyes" (216). In other words, the metaphorical chain poet-cliff-jewels suggests that the poet sees the woman through "such great artistic objectivity that all means of seduction are inoperative" (216). The metaphor of plasticity (the woman is like a painting) is reinforced by an allusion to a painting of Antiope by Correggio: the words are a simulation of a painting and justify an artistic interpretation of the poem as a whole.

To complete this reading, Hubert revises the conventional metaphor of fire and passion which can be found in the final stanza. Rather than read the sighing fire and the extinguished lamp as sexual, in either poet or woman, Hubert reads the fire as the remains of ardor and desire, detached from the poet, "while the poet continues his contemplation and the woman definitively takes on the aspect of a work of art" (217). Although Hubert does not explain the metaphor of woman-art, we can assume that the intermediaries are the final two words: *couleur* [color], recalling painting, and *ambre*, recalling the jewels or artifacts. In the end, the woman is united with the jewels, but as such she is no longer a woman: Beauty has triumphed over sensuality.

In order to read the poem as a "distraction" or a *détournement* from sensuality, away from the physical and toward Beauty, he represses or transforms all references to sexual desire and sexuality in the poet. At the same time, he selects parts of the poem which fit into a paradigm located outside the text. Part of a chapter on Baudelaire's erotic ambiguities, Hubert's reading deals with the poem as an example of immobilized sexuality. Within this paradigm, the mataphors of plasticity, the artistic, and the objective rest on an external metaphorization pointing to the absent signs of painting and art. Although the jewels, for example, are never given attributes in the Baudelaire text, they are attached, through Hubert's tropological reading, to the larger paradigm of art and stillness.

In contrast, Leo Bersani finds in the poem a violent drama based on desire and the fear of castration. Whereas Hubert works on a triangular model of man-woman-jewels, Bersani barely mentions the latter, subsuming them into the "pieces" (parts) of the woman's body which pass before the poet's eyes. The conflict would thus seem to take place between two selves: the poet-man, on a "rock of crystal," with a clear-sighted and serene gaze, "settled in peaceful solitude," and the other self, a fragmented, castrated, dispersed, moving woman. Bersani concentrates on the final two stanzas of the poem. The penultimate stanza is where desire goes too far, is "excessively available," when the Antiope's hips join a young boy's torso. Recoiling from this androgynous body (a fantasy of the poet himself), the poet resorts to "literal violence" in the final stanza, or rather the final line: "The light from the fireplace is 'poured' on the woman's skin; it is as if each instance of spreading light were a bloody ejaculation. The violent metaphoricity of sexual fantasy has become a fantasy of sex as literal physical violence" (66).

As does Hubert, Bersani chooses parts of the poem which fit into an absent paradigm—in this case, a complex Freudian model, which can be schematized as two series of mutually exclusive metaphorical chains:

fantasy of wholeness—arrest of desire—immobility—lack of meaning—the coherence of self—*the literal*

fantasy of castration (the detached phallus and other detachable objects)—desire—mobility—meaning—metamorphosis—*the metaphorical*

In discussing *Le Beau navire*, Bersani asserts that the woman's body—described variously as a ship, an armoire, and a snake—"*becomes* that which is different from it" (56), and the metaphorical operation is "a leap into an otherness equated with the same" (57). The woman remains woman while also being ship and armoire. This leap, Bersani emphasizes, "is a kind of violence—but it is of course the violence of energetic metaphorical activity" (64). He then adds: "Baudelaire will have only to interpret the violence of a desiring consciousness in order to close his work to the dynamics of desire. This is what *almost* happens in *Les Bijoux*" (65). In other words, Bersani reads *Les Bijoux* as a misunderstanding by Baudelaire of the violence of metaphorical activity. Metaphor taken too far, with too much displacement and too much fragmentation, results in an unanchored and scattered identity "which appears to raise the specter of a more literal violence" (65). Dispersed metaphor and desire, pushed too far, cause one to jump to the opposing series of metaphorical traces: arrest of desire—immobility—lack of meaning—the coherent self—*the literal*. Such a leap occurs at the end of *Les Bijoux*.

Thus, two paradigmatic metaphorical approaches lead to very different interpretations: for Hubert, the victory of art and tranquillity; for Bersani, the explosion of literal physical violence.

Metonymic Links

The very idea of treating a poem metonymically flies in the face of tradition, since poetry is "by definition" metaphorical. Yet Hubert and Bersani rely on certain metonymic operations to develop their interpretations. First, they both assume, despite the fact that there are no proper names and almost no nouns referring to the two protagonists, that the *je* is a man. They assign names and attributes to "him," thus releasing a paradigmatic metonymy of producer and product. The *je* is for them a product in the text, a creation of the "poet," and they endow him with the attributes of Baudelaire (the producer), be it his (Baudelaire's) aesthetic theory or his personal sexual problems. Second, both Hubert and Bersani reconstruct a narrative which is told by the poem. Hubert's story revolves around a dialectic of active-passive: in the beginning the man is active, willing the woman to perform a seductive dance for him; in the ensuing antithesis (lines 13–24), the woman intensifies her seduction and causes the man to retreat into passivity; in the synthesis of the final stanza, both are passive, as she is rendered pictoral and he tranquil. Bersani's story apparently works around a dialectic also: at first, the woman is active, her fragments moving before the man in an act of seduction; at the end of the poem, the man's desire for coherence translates itself into action as he commits violence upon her. However, Bersani reads this story as the product of the man's fantasy, for it is he who has projected his own fragmented desire upon the woman. Thus, the dialectic is proven false. Both narratives depend upon the play of metonymical relationships: cause-effect, agent-action, producer-product. Yet the metonymical reading remains, for both Hubert and Bersani, partial and implicit. Each "chooses" his story by repressing and/or transforming other possible metonymical links to suit the metaphorical relationships at the basis of his aesthetic or psychoanalytical interpretation.[3] In other words, the paradigmatic apparatus each brings to the poem tends to obscure or deform the syntagmatic sequences of the text. It therefore seems useful to attempt a more complete and explicit line-by-line exploration of the metonymical chains in *Les Bijoux*. This reading has a double focus: (1) to show the importance of metonymic operations in reading poetry and (2) to underline the necessity of reading syntagmatically as well as paradigmatically.

1   La très-chère était nue, et connaissant mon coeur,
2   Elle n'avait gardé que ses bijoux sonores,
3   Dont le riche attirail lui donnait l'air vainqueur
4   Qu'ont dans leurs jours heureux les esclaves des Mores.

[The cherished one was naked, and knowing my heart, / She kept only her sonorous jewels, / Whose rich finery gave her the victorious air / Of Moorish slaves on their happy days.]

The opening stanza reveals a complicated, almost circular chain of causal relationships. *Chère* [dear, expensive] can connote a prostitute, or at least an expensive woman, as has been suggested by Martin Turnell.[4] The subservient woman will act as the man's instrument and, like a slave, will obey her master. She wears only jewels to please the man, and the jewels then become her instruments. In turn, they initiate a new causal chain, as their attractiveness (*attirail*) creates the air of victory (*air vainqueur*), and this air redefines the woman as a cause herself. Completing the chain, we would have the man, a vanquished victim, as the effect, the jewels as the instrument, and the woman as the agent. From the beginning Baudelaire ties the reader in a metonymic knot, where the cause can become effect and the effect cause.

Only the word *air*, underlining the metaphorical and therefore hypothetical nature of the victor-woman, saves us from complete circularity.

5   Quant il jette en dansant son bruit vif et moqueur,
6   Ce monde rayonnant de métal et de pierre
7   Me ravit en extase, et j'aime à la fureur
8   Les choses où le son se mêle à la lumière.

[When it throws in dancing its clear and teasing sound, / This radiant world of metal and stone / Delights (ravishes) me into ecstasy, and I love furiously / Things where sound and light merge.]

The man, who had put the metonymic machine in operation, is now the recipient. The jewels, having become a "world," are the cause of his ecstasy and love. The woman, as agent, disappears.

9   Elle était donc couchée et se laissait aimer.
10   Et du haut du divan elle souriait d'aise
11   A mon amour profond et doux comme la mer,
12   Qui vers elle montait comme vers sa falaise.

[She was then recumbent and let herself be loved, / And from high on the couch she smiled with joy / At my love profound and gentle as the sea, / Which rose toward her as to its cliff.]

A reversal of causal patterns takes place as the woman reappears. But the man is now the agent of change: his love for her causes her to smile. At the same time, she lets herself be loved (by him).

13   Les yeux fixés sur moi, comme un tigre dompté,
14   D'un air vague et rêveur elle essayait des poses,
15   Et la candeur unie à la lubricité
16   Donnait un charme neuf à ses métamorphoses;

[Her eyes fixed on me, like a tamed tiger, / Vague and dreamy she tried poses, / And candour mixed with lewdness / Gave new charm to her metamorphoses.]

Whereas the first stanza was complicated by the syntagmatic metonymies, the complication now arises from blatantly paradigmatic metonymical relationships. The eyes (*les yeux fixés sur moi*) watch the poet's reaction to see what effect her poses have on him. His reaction, in turn, will be the cause of a new movement: she adjusts her movements to accommodate his re-actions. The verb *gave* (*donnait un charme neuf*. . .) brings the causal chain back to the man, as it affects him, and we assume, causes him to become excited.

But several ambiguities upset the visual dialogue of cause and effect. We have overlooked (suppressed) the simile *comme un tigre dompté*, which does not negate the above reading, since a tamed tiger will watch its master and follow his orders. But the tiger will also watch for the instant when it can attack. The eyes, then, symbolize the present submissiveness (instrument of the man's pleasure) and potential domination, as in line 2 (*d'un air vainqueur*).

The words *vague et rêveur* carry the idea of submissiveness one step further, by suggesting that the woman is detached from her movements. Her detachment produces the vague, dreamlike mood. A further metonymic step would suggest that she is a professional, detached from her work.

    17   Et son bras et sa jambe, et sa cuisse et ses reins,
    18   Polis comme de l'huile, onduleux comme un cygne,
    19   Passaient devant mes yeux clairvoyants et sereins;
    20   Et son ventre et ses seins, ces grappes de ma vigne,

[And her arm and her leg, and her thighs and her back, / Polished like oil, sinuous like a swan, / Passed before my clairvoyant and serene eyes; / And her belly and breasts, grapes of my vine,]

Hubert and Bersani see the man in this stanza as either de-tached or passive, present only through his eyes. While the ad-jective *serein* suggests that the man is little affected by the woman, *clairvoyant* connotes the opposite: a causal trace in which the eyes can predict the future, see into things, and as such control cause. The return of causality to the male is overdetermined in the last hemistich with the words *ces grappes de ma vigne*. Clearly, the man is the source of the dance of breasts and belly before his eyes. Thus, if his eyes are detached and unaffected, his "vine" is producing.

21 S'avançaient, plus câlins que les Anges du mal,
22 Pour troubler le repos où mon âme était mise,
23 Et pour la déranger du rocher de cristal
24 Où, calme et solitaire, elle s'était assise.

[Advanced, more caressing than Angels of evil, / To disturb the repose where my soul was seated, / And to upset it from its crystal rock / Where, calm and solitary, it had rested.]

For the first time in the poem, the end of the fifth stanza does not mark the end of a clause. The first verb in the sixth stanza, *s'avançaient*, has as its subject belly and breasts. The syntactical fusion of the two stanzas suggests a causal confusion, and, in fact, the breasts and belly are suddenly the cause, the agents. Compared to Angels of evil, the breasts and belly, paradigmatically, take on a diabolical force to create havoc and destruction. The causal powers of the fragmented woman are emphasized by the repetition of *pour*. Read in relation to the Angels of evil, they would mean "in order to," rather than "as a consequence of." But such logic is out of the question now. Both readings are possible. Since line 13 (*comme un tigre dompté* . . .), the causal links have been ambivalent; in the last lines, they have become absolutely entrapping. To reconstruct: the man's vine (his desire, his phallus, his physical powers, his creative powers?) produces the breast-belly fruits, which in turn take on diabolical powers to trouble and upset the man's soul, detached not only from the sensual scene, but from his body. As the woman is fragmented, so is the man, except that he is the cause of his own destruction (vine acting on soul through the female body).

25 Je croyais voir unis par un nouveau dessin
26 Les hanches de l'Antiope au buste d'un imberbe,
27 Tant sa taille faisait ressortir son bassin.
28 Sur ce teint fauve et brun le fard était superbe!

[I thought I saw united in a new design / Antiopes' hips and a youth's bust, / Her waist made her pelvis stand out so much. / On that fauve and brown complexion the paint (color) was superb!]

Whereas vision in preceding lines suggested control, the eyes lose their powers as the man "thought" he saw. Now he cannot even control his own vision. The final breakdown in the causal chain is marked by a totally foreign design, as the woman becomes *like* an Antiope and a pubescent boy. As the fragmented female body becomes completely metaphorical, a remnant of a causal chain is left, tied to the woman by the intermediary *tant* ("so much so")—her waist puts into relief the lower torso, which creates the androgyny and appears about to create yet another design.

> 29   —Et la lampe s'étant résignée à mourir,
> 30   Comme le foyer seul illuminait la chambre,
> 31   Chaque fois qu'il poussait un flamboyant soupir,
> 31   Il inondait de sang cette peau couleur d'ambre!

[—And the lamp having resigned itself to die, / As the hearth alone lit the room, / Each time it uttered a flaming sigh, / It flooded with blood that amber-colored skin.]

It is possible that the final stanza is the "new design," but it has almost no direct relationship to the causal links of the previous lines. Although the links were complex and self-destructive, they were centered first on the man as primary cause: at the beginning of the poem, in line 11 when the woman reacted to his love, and around line 20, the grapes of his vine. This chain was then broken in line 27, when the woman's waist generated an image. But now the two generating forces are absent except for *skin*, which is obviously being acted on, and *blood*, which inundates the skin. Except for this link and the personifications, people are replaced by objects, and the objects each act independently: the lamp goes out and the fire sighs and inundates. The two actions have an ambiguous causal relationship to each other. They can be read as simple sequences or as a causal chain. The lamp's extinction (it resigns *itself* to go out) is not a direct cause of personified events of the last two lines; but it might be said that because the lamp has gone out, the fire (effect) is now alone in lighting the room and is alone in covering it with its bloodlike colors.

THE LAST STANZA: THE REVERSAL OF TRACES

While Baudelaire marks the break between the last stanza and
the preceding lines of the poem with a dash ("—Et . . . "), it is
probable that few readers suspect the radicalness of the change:
a break in the metonymic chain, in the persons and objects, and
also in the décor.[5] Until now, the only mention of décor was in
line 10, the woman's divan, where she lay. It is as though we
have discovered another room, filled with objects not seen before and not similar to objects in the rest of the text.

One solution to this disparity between the last stanza and
the rest of the poem is to assign, as Bersani and Hubert do,
specific persons to the objects of the room—the lamp, the fireplace, the skin. Because *skin* is the most direct link to the past
stanzas (by synecdoche—part of the woman's body), it suggests
the continued presence of the woman. The gender of the other
words can help, by overdetermination, establish direct links with
the woman and the man: "*la* lampe," which resigns itself to dying,
can symbolize the woman, who has stopped the exhibitionistic
gyrations. "*Le* foyer," the fireplace, is equated with the man who
covers the woman's skin with his blood. If the word *blood* is
taken literally, he is dying, like the woman, in a sort of double
suicide, but one suspended in time, as he is continuously spilling
blood. Taken metaphorically, the man is sighing as he repeatedly
ejaculates and covers the woman's skin with his sperm. The
reading, which is compatible with Bersani's, also justifies the
self-destructive metonymic chains of the first part of the poem.
The man is once again the ultimate agent of destruction, whether
in suicide or in violent sexual activity.

If *le foyer* can be identified with the man and *la lampe* with
the woman, the very ambiguity of the pronouns and adjectives
also permits the reader to reverse the sexual attributes and to
read the lamp as the man and the fireplace as woman. This could
be justified in a number of ways and by a number of traces: the
flame of the lamp recalls the upright, crystal rock, the phallic
vine. The *foyer*, or fireplace, is a container, for flames, and a
recipient, like the female sexual organ. Traces then recall the waist,
the hips, the stomach, and cliff (which receives the sea). Other
traces run to the woman's liquidity (*onduleux, huile, lubricité*) and

to light (line 8). Such a metaphorical interpretation would lead
to seeing the death of the man—from exhaustion, satisfaction,
or lack of interest. The woman would be seen as killing herself,
inflicting wounds on her own skin, but there is almost nothing
in previous lines to substantiate a reading of her self-destruction.
She can also be seen masturbating, turning her seductive charms
onto her own flesh when rejected by the man and sighing as she
obtains satisfaction.

The lamp and fireplace can also be taken simply as personified elements of the décor. The man, as physical presence and
as source of desire, disappears, and only his eyes and the powers
of metaphorization (personification) remain. The woman too has
disappeared except for her skin, a fragment of the instruments
of her desire. Such a reading would relegate the stanza to the
role of an epilogue, and the penultimate stanza would stand as
the unification of the sexes, of the animallike woman and the
ornament ("sur ce teint fauve et brun le fard était superbe"). The
poem, excluding the epilogue, would be closed on the makeup
and its artificial qualities, thus suggesting other ornaments, particularly the jewels of the title.

Through metaphorical switching and through reestablish-
ment of previous traces, any of the above interpretations can be
"justified" in the text. By going outside the text, as Bersani and
Hubert do, the possibility of metaphorical interpretations becomes almost limitless.

But within the poem, the tracing of traces leads us to fragmentation and ambiguity, and, of greater consequence, to contradictions. The traces that we have sketched out are not "pure"
and do not carry one link through from the beginning of the
poem to the conclusion. For each of the traces, the opposite one
can be found. For example, the woman is a slave and a victor, a
tiger and a swan, an agent and an instrument, aggressive and
passive. The relationship of the last stanza to the rest of the poem
is contradictory also: it says the opposite of what we expect, or,
as Turnell says, "there is no connection." People disappear and
become objects, a new décor is introduced, sexual attributions
are further confused, ambiguity continues when we expect closure and finality. In more direct terms, the relationship of the

final stanza to the rest of the poem is paradoxical, and, in fact, the entire poem is a series of paradoxes, as different "truths" are posited for the same people and the same situations, without any resolution or revelation of the correct reading. No matter what traces the reader follows, what is eventually encountered is contradiction.

Two lines of the poem, 7 and 15, illustrate perfectly the unification of contrary elements, where Baudelaire designates clearly the paradoxical nature of the poem. Line 7 describes the man's emotional state:

> Me ravit en extase et j'aime à la fureur

An almost perfect equilibrium around the caesura permits Baudelaire to distribute his oppositions along the alexandrine:

me (passive)	*je* (active subject)
ravit (passive)	*aime* (active)
extase (detachment)	*fureur* (violence)
en (in)	*à la* (out)

Simultaneously the reader is confronted with a man both passive and active, submitting to the enchantment of the world of metal and stone and acting on it. The word *extase* suggests his detachment or transport out of his body, while *fureur* extends the activity of loving to the point of violence. Within the second hemistich itself, the reader can detect a collision between the verb *to love* and the violence, the anger, in the definition of the word *fureur*. Thus the man is at the same time violated (ravished) and violating.

In the fifteenth line, Baudelaire situates the woman in almost exactly the same manner, uniting within her two totally contradictory states:

> Et la candeur unie à la lubricité

Candeur, which originally meant "white," has all the connotations of purity and virginity: innocence, ingenuousness, naïveté. The attributes of *lubricité* suggest the experienced and even debauched woman such as a courtesan or prostitute: a strong penchant for *luxure* and lasciviousness. The word's original meanings, "oily" and "slippery," tend to overdetermine the lasciviousness of the woman in the face of her virginal whiteness.

Other traces of sexuality reinforce the split nature of the protagonists and extend the sexual paradoxes to the question of the very nature of sexuality. The reader can find pronouns and adjectives where sexual roles are reversed and where masculine becomes feminine, and feminine masculine. We have noted the play of genders in the words *la lampe* and *le foyer* in the last stanza. But from the beginning of the poem there is a mixture and reversal of masculine and feminine. *La très chère* of the first line is eclipsed by the masculine jewels, which in turn become a masculine world, with its aggressive sound (*bruit vif et moqueur*), before returning to the passive feminine in line 9 (*Elle était couchée et se laissait aimer*). In lines 9 to 12 the woman retains her femininity, as she is compared to a feminine *falaise*, while the man takes on feminine traits in the comparison to the sweet depths of the sea (*mon amour profond et doux comme la mer*). One might go so far as to make a play on the words *mer* and *mère* (mother), as the poet's love approaches that of a mother for her child.

In line 13 the woman is compared to a tiger, a word which has encoded into it all the male traits of strength, movement, cruelty, and violence. It might be argued that this reversal of sexual roles is but a preparation for lines 21 to 28, where the sexual reversals are most striking and complete. The woman's breasts and belly (masculine grammatically but not biologically) are compared to angels, masculine grammatically but neuter in religious mythology. A play on the words *mal* and *mâle* ("evil" and "male") would reinvest the woman with masculinity, as does her aggressiveness. The man is reduced to his soul, whose femininity is overdetermined: " . . . mon âme était mise, / Et pour la déranger . . . / elle s'était assise." The female soul sits astride a male rock. For an instant the insistence on the feminine shakes the reader's consciousness, and we can imagine man and woman exchanging roles and places. This interchange is finally realized in lines 26 and 27 as the haunches of the Antiope unite with the pubescent boy's bust.

Confronted with these reversals, with the contradictory definition of the protagonists, and with the broken metonymic chains in the poem, the reader has a choice: either to accept the poem as a *mise en jeu* of contradictions, thus leading to paradox, or to seek a resolution. Taking the seventh line by itself ("Me ravit en extase, et j'aime à la fureur"), we can say that Bersani and Hubert resolved the paradoxical situation by selecting one of the hemistiches: Hubert opted for the passive transport of the first six syllables, while Bersani sought the traces emanating from *fureur*. By selecting the first possibility, as we do, to read and interpret the poem as "an irony in suspension," as paradoxical, one allows the text to remain more complete in all of its division, contradiction, and ambivalence. With such a decision, a metonymical reading would lead, not to metaphorical unity, but to ironical dispersion.

The Surrealists taught us that metaphor permits writers and readers to bridge immense semantic gaps and to associate unlike words. Extended over a poem, metaphor invites the reader to establish a coherent reading. But metaphor can also obfuscate and conceal the disunity, fragmentation, and ambivalence which metonymy is able to convey. In an age of metaphorical thinking, according to Roman Jakobson (and of ironical modes, according to Hayden White),[6] and in a genre—poetry—where it is conventional to read metaphorically, a metonymic reading of *Les Bijoux* demonstrates that insistence on a limited and exclusive rhetorical strategy robs poetry of its fullness. At the same time, the ironical dispersion resulting from such a reading points out Baudelaire's position in the history of modern poetry, as a forerunner to Mallarmé in the effort to put into question the notion of literature as communication.[7]

8

MALLARMÉ'S CLOWN

In 1864 Mallarmé wrote a first version of a sonnet entitled *Le Pitre châtié*:

Pour ses yeux,—pour nager dans ces lacs, dont les quais
Sont plantés de beaux cils qu'un matin bleu pénètre,
J'ai, Muse,—moi, ton pitre,—enjambé la fenêtre
Et fui notre baraque où fument tes quinquets.

Et d'herbes enivré, j'ai plongé comme un traître
Dans ces lacs défendus, et, quand tu m'appelais,
Baigné mes membres nus dans l'onde aux blancs galets,
Oubliant mon habit de pitre au tronc d'un hêtre.

Le soleil du matin séchait mon corps nouveau
Et je sentais fraîchir loin de ta tyrannie
La neige des glaciers dans ma chair assainie,

Ne sachant pas, hélas! quand s'en allait sur l'eau
Le suif de mes cheveux et le fard de ma peau,
Muse, que cette crasse était tout le génie!

[For her (his) eyes, — to swim in these lakes, whose embankments / Are planted with lovely eyelashes that a blue morning penetrates, / I have, Muse, — me, your clown, — strode out the window / And fled our hut where your oil lamps are smoking. / / And, drunk with herbs, I have plunged like a traitor / Into these forbidden lakes, and, when you were calling me, / Bathed my na-

159

ked limbs in the white-pebbled wave, / Forgetting my clown's
costume on the trunk of a beech. / / The morning sun dried my
new body / And I felt refreshed far from your tyranny / The snow
of the glaciers in my purified flesh, / / Not knowing, alas! when
went off with the water / the grease of my hair and the makeup
of my skin, / Muse, that this dross was all of genius!]

Although particular words may be ambiguous, the sonnet
as a whole is comprehensible at a first reading. The poem describes the clown's betrayal of his Muse for a real woman. The
pronouns and the repetition of the word *Muse* leave no doubt
that the poem describes a triangle of the poet, the Muse, and an
"Other." The conventional trope of *eyes* for *woman* leads to a
reading of a rivalry between the spiritual muse and a real woman.
From the first word, *pour*, the metonymic chains of cause and
effect are stated explicitly. Because of the other woman's eyes,
the comedian flees his Muse, and for having swum in the eye-
lakes of the flesh-and-blood woman, he is punished by the loss
of his genius, the makeup of his craft. The explicit inscription of
the word *Muse*, a word more commonly associated with poetry
than theater, can easily lead readers to conclude that the "je" of
the poem is in fact the poet. A metaphorical reading of poet and
poetry for comedian and comedy opens the poem to a more
general reading of the conflict between the necessity of artifice
in poetic creation and the deceptive purity and naturalness of real
life. Read synecdochically, the woman's eyes stand as a part of
her entire attractiveness, and just as the comedian is read metaphorically as poet, the lakes can be read metaphorically as sexuality which brings rebirth in its forbidden waters.

Although the signifiers in the text mark it as a "poem," they
in no way distract the reader from quickly finding a meaning.
As in most poems before Mallarmé, syntax, sounds, verbs, and
graphemes reinforce meaning and contribute to the general es-
thetic pleasure of reading.

It is tempting to regard the second version of *Le Pitre châtié*,
published in 1887, as essentially the same poem, one in which
poetic devices make interpretation more difficult but still possible. The first version of the poem could then act literally as a
"version" or a translation of its more obscure successor:

Yeux, lacs avec ma simple ivresse de renaître
Autre que l'histrion qui du geste évoquais
Comme plume la suie ignoble des quinquets,
J'ai troué dans le mur de toile une fenêtre.

De ma jambe et des bras limpide nageur traître,
A bonds multipliés, reniant le mauvais
Hamlet! c'est comme si dans l'onde j'innovais
Mille sépulcres pour y vierge disparaître.

Hilare or de cymbale à des poings irrité,
Tout à coup le soleil frappe la nudité
Qui pure s'exhala de ma fraîcheur de nacre,

Rance nuit de la peau quand sur moi vous passiez,
Ne sachant pas, ingrat! que c'était tout mon sacre,
Ce fard noyé dans l'eau perfide des glaciers.

[Eyes, lakes with my simple drunkenness to be reborn / Other
than the (bad) actor who with gesture was evoking / As a quill
(feather) the ignoble soot of the oil lamps, / I have pierced in the
wall of cloth a window. / / With my leg and arms limpid traitorous swimmer, / In multiple bounds, renouncing the bad / Hamlet! it is as if in the wave I was innovating (creating) / A thousand
sepulchers to disappear into them virgin. / / Hilarious gold of
cymbal with fists irritated, / Suddenly the sun strikes the nudity /
Which pure was exhaled from my freshness of mother of pearl, //
Rancid night of the skin when over me you passed, / Not knowing, ingrate! that it was my entire consecration, / That makeup
drowned in the perfidious water of the glaciers.]

Numerous critics have assumed the second version is interpre-
table, and their interpretations show the strong influence of
the first poem. Robert Greer Cohen, for example, describes the
final sonnet in these terms: "A clown (representing, in a self-
deprecatory way, the artist) has abandoned his Muse in favor of
a real woman and plunged into the lakes, her eyes. He feels refreshed when the trumpery clown paint is washed off him in the
metaphorical water, which experience is a sort of baptism in love
(-death)—a rebirth. Alas, he discovers that the dirty paint was
essential to his art, was even 'all of (my) genius.'"[1] He takes into
account the reference to Hamlet by stating that Hamlet is the

"symbol of the poet with large aspirations who is impotent to realize his dreams" (40). The difficult wordplays coincide with the general interpretation of the poem. For example, *rance nuit* translates as the "love act seen in retrospect [which] is sour," and the *nuit de la peau* is the paint which darkens the skin (41). The word *glacier* refers to purity, while also containing the word *acier* [steel], a note of hardness and coldness (42). In a similar interpretation, Guy Michaud reads the final version as a metaphor of comedian for poet, in which the "pitre offers the first images of the Poet, that is really typical of Mallarmé as we have come to know him. . . . A naked poet is no longer a poet, and . . . pure poetry is perhaps a mirage and an illusion."[2]

If one applies freely Mallarmé's injunction that poetry should describe the "effet" and not the "chose," it could be said that by dealing with the two texts as treating the same subject matter, critics regard the final version as the "effet," or product, and the first version as the "chose," or the decoded message obscured by the later sonnet. But to treat the two versions in such a manner negates Mallarmé's work and diminishes the value of the second poem. The classically refined expression of the first *Pitre* did indeed engender a second text, but one in which differences outweigh similarities with the first text. The two texts can be understood only by looking at how they demand totally different reading strategies. The first *Pitre* is more similar to Baudelaire's *Bijoux* and even Balzac's *Duchesse* than to the later poem bearing the same title. The difference between them marks the gulf between classical nineteenth-century French literature and the modern poetic language of which Mallarmé is considered the founder.

Mallarmé's second *Pitre* is composed according to new concepts of rhetorical poetics, and it creates new conventions for the reader which exclude attributing one meaning or interpretation to the text. Barbara Johnson has stated that "Mallarmé's famous obscurity lies not in his devious befogging of the obvious but in his radical transformation of intelligibility itself through the ceaseless production of seemingly mutually exclusive readings of the same piece of language."[3] Johnson suggests that Mallarmé places the work of poetry between the two vast poles of intelligibility and nonsense. When reading Mallarmé's poetry it is fruitless to search for one meaning or message, and it is equally misguided to dismiss the work of the signified in his poetry as mere nonsense and focus one's attention on the signifier. A shift from seeking intelligibility to studying the production "of seemingly mutually exclusive meanings" suggests that we should indeed read Mallarmé on the level of the signifier as a starting point, to see best how he displaces and condenses meanings in the very form of his poems. Such a reading implies that the signifier does not reinforce meaning, but rather that the signifier fragments and undermines potentially coherent messages in the signified. If, in fact, Mallarmé questioned and revolutionized poetic language, this revolution should be most obvious in the figurations and symbolizations on all levels of the text. Mallarmé's unconventional poetics lead us to examine and read unconventionally his use of sound, graphemes, typography, syntax, and verbs even before looking for meanings.

THE PHONETIC SIGNIFIER

In her article on *Le Pitre châtié* Lucette Finas begins by playing with sounds paradigmatically. She reads the title out loud "et aussitôt tremble du pitre la vitre, bruit d'ondes, averse; Le pitre châtié / châtré; L'épitre châtié / châtré; Le titre châtié / châtré; La mitre châtiée / châtrée; La vitre châtiée / châtrée; Le prêtre châtié / châtré."[4] Finas's exploitation of the title is exclusively metaphorical (search for homonyms). But there is no need to go outside the text, as Finas does, to imagine an almost infinite number of sound associations; reading the poem slowly aloud and displacing the stresses and pauses brings out new words contained within the text:

YEUX	LACS	AVEC	MA	SIMPLE	IVRESSE	DE	RENAITRE
y	las	a	masse	sein	y	deux	maitre
ouy	laque			saint		est-ce	être
	là			sain	]		hêtre
		sa			pli		n'être
	a	s	a				

```
AUTRE     QUE      L'HISTRION  QUI    DU      GESTE    EVOQUAIS
O         queue    lisse              dû      thé      et
au                 tri                                 vos
                   on                                  quais
          lit                                          est
          lis


COMME     PLUME    LA          SUIE   IGNOBLE DES      QUINQUETS
me        plus me              suis   y       dès      quais
          plu me                      noble            est
          là                          I
          la


J'AI   TROUE   DANS     LE    MUR    DE    TOILE   UNE    FENETRE
jet    trou    dent           mûr          toi     lune   feu
geai   est                                 le             naître
jais                                                       n'être
                                                           être


DE    MA    JAMBE    ET    DES   BRAS   LIMPIDE       NAGEUR   TRAITRE
deux              jambée   dès          l'impie de              être
      mât                                             n'a


A         BONDS    MULTIPLIES      RENIANT      LE         MAUVAIS
ah        bon      mule            renie en                mot V
                   plié            nie                     mot vais
                                   ni                      mauve est


HAMLET    C'EST    COMME    SI      DANS    L'ONDE     J'INNOVAIS
          C                 six     dents   l'aune     "j" novais
                                            de         j'y novais
                                                       vais
                                                       est


MILLE     SEPULCRES       POUR      Y    VIERGE      DISPARAITRE
          ses pu          pourrie        vie         dix      hêtre
          ces pue                        erre-je     par
          c'est                                               être
```

HILARE	OR	DE	CYMBALE	A	DES	POINGS	IRRITE
y	hors		sein	balle	dès	point	y
l'art			saint	bas	dé		rit
I			sain	là			thé
lard				l'a			T

TOUT	A	COUP	LE	SOLEIL	FRAPPE	LA	NUDITE
	a	cou		sot		là	nue thé
	A	coule		sol est			T
				et			

QUI	PURE	S'EXHALA	DE	MA	FRAICHEUR	DE	NACRE
		sexe	deux		frais		acre
		à la					

RANCE	NUIT	DE	LA	PEAU	QUAND	SUR	MOI	VOUS	PASSIEZ
rends ce			là	pot	qu'en	sûr	mois		pas scier
	nuie								scié
									passe y et

NE	SACHANT	PAS	INGRAT	QUE	C'ETAIT	TOUT	MON	SACRE
	sache en		gras				mont	
								acre

CE	FARD	NOYE	DANS	L'EAU	PERFIDE	DES	GLACIERS
	phare	noyer	dent	l'O	père Fi de		glas
		noix			perd	dès	glace y est
		y et					scier

Several obvious patterns emerge from this initial play. Mallarmé
situates the sound [sɛ̃n]—*simple, cymbale*— in the middle of the
first and eighth lines, thus emphasizing the play of *sein-saint-sain*.
He also underlines a play on the *être* in the rhyming words of the
first eight lines before the sound disappears in the sestet. But
there is no coherent "second text" formed by these words, and
there is no unified pattern. Although some of the sound plays
can enter into a play of the signifieds, these secondary word sounds
serve above all to displace the reader's attention away from
grasping a unified sign in which a specific signifier denotes a

corresponding signified. Instead, meaning and sound float and suggest new combinations.

<h2>THE GRAPHIC SIGNIFIER</h2>

If the reader separates the graphic aspect of the signifier from the phonemic, anagrammatic variations of the text's signifiers appear. For example, if we exchange the last syllable of each noun in the title (pi*tre*, châ*tié*) and add an accent, we come up with *pitié, châtré* or *pitié (pour le) châtré*. Working with other elements of the poem, we discover a range of anagrams going from the exact (same letters, different order) to the approximate (similar letters, different order):

> nacre→crâne, carne, écran, rance
> ingrat→gratin
> sépulcres→crépuscule
> soleil→oseille
> passiez→sapiez
> sacre→crasse, écrase, écar(t)s

With anagrams, the focus remains on the grapheme as element in a word and on a paradigmatic operation.[5] It is possible, however, to focus on the grapheme as an isolated element and on syntagmatic relationships between graphemes. For example, the title contains, by opposition, the chiasma *IT/TI*—Le P*it*re châ*ti*é. The central element (*T*) can be linked to the first letter of the poem (*Y*) by similarity: the bar of the *T* can be transformed into the two branches of the *Y*. The *Y* in turn includes two other graphemes—the *I* of the original chiasma and *V*, which recalls the *T* (two straight lines). This triple association (*I, V, Y*) is in fact overdetermined by the text: *pour Y VIerge disparaître*.

The following patterns grow out of the entire poem:

a. *Y* appears only four times; however, these appearances frame the poem, since *Y* occurs in the first, eighth, ninth, and fourteenth verses (the beginning and end of the quatrains, the beginning and end of the tercets);

b. *I* appears frequently and consistently the length of the poem
    (stanza I, 11 times; II, 14; III, 7; IV, 7);
c. *V* appears primarily in the quatrains (I, 3; II, 3); there is a
    single occurrence (*vous*) in the tercets;
d. *T* appears frequently in the quatrains (I, 8; II, 6) and slightly
    less often in the tercets (III, 4; IV, 6); however, whereas
    twelve of the fourteen *T*'s in the quatrains are voiced, in
    the final tercet, four of six are silent, and the *T* is totally
    absent from the final line of the poem.

The discussion of the *T* suggests the impossibility of completely
dissociating graphemes and phonemes. A similar interplay can
be seen if one returns to the title.

From a graphic point of view, the center of the title is the
E—*le pitrE châtié*; phonetically, the [ə] must share this spot with
the [r]—[lə pitrə ʃatje]. The [r] is thus the sixth of twelve phonemes in the title just as, in the last line of the poem, another
phoneme—[o] (hidden in the form of *eau*)—occupies the sixth
position. The link between [o] and [r] finds graphic expression
in *O* and *R*: *j'ai tROué* and *hilare OR de cymbale*. Followed
throughout the poem, these graphemes reveal the following:

a. *R* appears with high frequency and is divided almost equally
    between stanzas (I, 8; II, 9; III, 9; IV, 7);
b. *O* also appears frequently with equal representation: five
    occurrences in each stanza;
c. the grapheme *R* is doubled by the phoneme [r] in thirty-
    one of its thirty-three occurrences (exceptions: *irrité* and
    glaciers);
d. the grapheme *O* does not correspond to the phoneme [o];
    the latter appears four times associated with different gra-
    phemes: *autre, mauvais, peau, eau*.

THE TYPOGRAPHICAL SIGNIFIER: POSITIONS IN THE POEM

Just as it is impossible to separate graphemes totally from phonemes, the linking of the *R* and *O* (as well as the analysis of the
role of *Y* in framing the poem) also suggests that one cannot

completely dissociate graphemes and phonemes from typographical considerations.

Like all poets, Mallarmé exploits the unique typographical arrangement of poems on the page. He uses the spaces around the beginning and ending of poems and the spaces between stanzas to make words stand out and relate to one another. If we consider *Le Pitre* as a whole, the first and last words (*Yeux, glaciers*) would seem at first glance unrelated. Phonetically and graphically, however, *glaciers* resembles *yeux, lacs*: note the [la] and [j] in [glasje] and [jø], [lak]. Moreover, *glaciers* contains phonetically *glace* [mirror], which can be linked metaphorically to *yeux* [eyes: light].

The first and last words of the first stanza, *yeux* and *fenêtre*, also share the semantic feature "light." *De ma jambe* [with my leg] and *disparaître* [to disappear] do not seem to offer any connection other than the initial grapheme *d*, unless one wishes to read *disparaître* as a signal of the missing leg (*une* jambe). The first and last words of the tercets reveal, however, some degree of similarity on the level of graphemes (hil*are*/n*acre*/r*ance*/gl*acier*).

From stanza to stanza (last word of the preceding to the first word of the following), the passage from I to II (*fenêtre* to *de ma jambe*) offers no immediate rhetorical connection. *Disparaître* (II) and *hilare* (III) share the graphemes *i, a, r,* and *e,* while *nacre* [mother of pearl] (III) and *rance* [rancid] (IV) are linked both anagrammatically and semantically (*acre,* a part of *nacre,* is a synonym of *rance*).

TYPOGRAPHY AND SYNTAX

Poetic convention requires that the syntax of a poem fit the metrical constraints of the formal structure chosen by the poet. Since the number and organization of verses and the length of line is translated on the page typographically, one can say that the syntactical grouping of words must conform to the typography of the poem. Usually this accord is marked by the coincidence of syntactical groups and lines of type. Ideally, each verse should

contain a complete thought or at least a complete grammatical
unit; moreover, in cases where the end of a verse does not mark
the end of a sentence, there should be a clear indication of the
syntactical link between the two lines. At the level of the stanza,
Le Pitre châtié poses no problem: there are three grammatical
sentences, one in each quatrain and the third covering the two
tercets. Moreover, there are only two instances of enjambement:
qui du geste évoquais / Comme plume la suie and *reniant le mauvais /
Hamlet.* But a problem arises for the reader when he tries to link
syntactical groups within the sentences.

The problem of syntactical linking is basically a rhetorical
question because the syntax of coordination and subordination
involves the four basic relationships: similarity, causality, inclusion, and opposition. Syntax performs rhetorical operations for
the readers by means of a combination of semantic and typographical markers. For example, in the typed or printed sentence
"The boy in the red shirt hit the little girl over the head with a
shovel because she called him stupid," the preposition *in* links
shirt synecdochally to *boy* (the shirt is a part of the boy's whole
configuration); the preposition *with* links *shovel* metonymically
to *hit* (the shovel is the instrument of the action); and the con-
junction *because* links *she called him stupid* metonymically to *he hit
her over the head* (the cause of the effect). In addition, in two of
the three cases typographical considerations (the position of word
not just on the page but in relation to other words in the signifying chain) plays an essential role. If *in the red shirt* and *with a
shovel* were moved from their places next to *boy* and *hit over the
head,* respectively, the meaning of the sentence would change:
i.e., "the girl in the red shirt" or "the girl with the shovel." Thus,
very often semantics and typography combine to perform for
the reader the necessary rhetorical operation. Although the examples from the model sentence involved synecdoche and metonymy (as would be expected in a conventional narrative statement), all four operations can be performed syntactically. In fact,
four of the connecting words in the first stanza of *Le Pitre châtié*
are based on the four rhetorical processes: *avec* expresses causality (agent); *autre que,* opposition; *qui,* inclusion (attribute), and

comme, similarity. Despite the presence of these syntactic-rhetorical guides, the reader still has great difficulty, because the typographical disposition in this poem works against the semantic markers, the latter frequently being separated from the words to which they refer.

NOUNS

The word *Yeux* remains detached from the rest of the poem because it is typographically isolated by its position at the head of the poem, because it lacks even a minimal semantic marker (an article, for example), and because the comma separates it from the rest of the sentence. Normal reading would anticipate that the eyes either belong to someone, to a woman perhaps, or to an audience watching the clown. It is conventional to assume that the first word of a poem has some relationship to the title, but Mallarmé forces us to provide the link. Either the eyes are looking at the clown, or the clown is looking into the eyes. In the juxtaposition *yeux, lacs* the "rhetorical comma" (the only suggestion of a syntactical relationship) provides material for a possible similarity (the eyes resemble the lakes) or a possible opposition (the eyes see, the lakes are seen). In addition, the "rhetorical comma" also raises a third possibility: a metonymical link between the eyes as producers of lakes, in the form of tears. It is at this point, however, that typography undermines syntax: *avec*, although juxtaposed to *lacs*, does not connect up with it. As a result, the phrase *yeux, lacs* is isolated (once again) from the rest of the sentence (and even from the rest of the poem). Although the reader will have problems reintegrating the phrase, the ambiguity marked by the comma serves both to allow and to force the reader to explore various interpretations not only of the phrase but ultimately of the entire poem.

At crucial moments throughout the poem, Mallarmé will take words out of their normal syntactical order and create for the reader similar theoretical choices, where the reader must decide not only which words can be joined, but also what relationships are possible between the words.

VERBS

Closely related to the multiplicity of meanings generated by
sound, graphics, and syntax is Mallarmé's use of verbs, where
the tense of the verbs is at least as important as their meanings.
The first stanza seems clear; *j'ai troué* denotes a precise act in the
recent past. However, a second verb, *évoquais*, lacks a clear subject. The reader must supply a pronoun, either *je* or *tu*. In addition, it is not at all clear if the imperfect *évoquais* expresses an
habitual action in the past or if it expresses a continuous action
which was interrupted by piercing the hole. Although there are
two separate actions, the causal and temporal links between them
are not spelled out.

In the second stanza, there is one main verb, the copulate
c'est, which links the first two and the last two lines in a metaphorical relationship, now in the present. Mallarmé confuses the
tenses when he does not provide an active verb for the first clause
("De ma jambe et des bras limpide nageur traître, / A bonds
multipliés, reniant le mauvais") and when he casts the subordinate clause in the imperfect, which suggests a continuous past,
even while the main verb (*c'est*) is in the present.

At the beginning of the first tercet, the ambiguity between
past and present seems resolved when the "soleil *frappe* la nudité" in the present. But this main clause is followed by three
subordinate clauses in past tenses. The last verb is the easiest, as
it establishes a clear equivalence between *ce fard* and *mon sacre* in
the past ("c'était tout mon sacre, ce fard"). The verbal form *vous
passiez* presents a problem of reference. The *vous* may refer to
the sun which *hits*, either once or continuously, after having passed.
But it could also refer to the *eyes* of the beginning of the poem.
The use of the imperfect can suggest either that the sun passed a
number of times (it "used to pass") or that it passed by only
once, in a slow, continuous motion. The other verb in the sestet,
s'exhala, fits into the past frame of reference, but by using a *passé
simple* for the first and only time in the entire poem, Mallarmé
throws the *je*'s actions into an historic past. By convention this
tense connotes an action which no longer has an effect on the
subject, and it creates a causal gulf between past and present.

This manipulation of the verbs is not entirely incoherent, because it does establish temporal references within the present and a broad past, composed of the immediate past and a distant historic one. In addition, the reader can discern a rough sequence of actions: in the first quatrain the *je* pierces a hole; in the second we are in a vague metaphorical frame which could be either past or present. The first tercet is placed squarely in the present when the sun hits, before the poem returns to the past. But within this temporal frame, the reader must select not only the causal chains, but also the various levels of past and present in which the verbs might be included. One is called on to ask if the poem refers to a single continuous block of time or to detached fragments. Thus the poem floats within vast temporal boundaries extending from the historical past to a metaphorical present.

TRACES: READING THE POEM

The words of the title establish several of the key metaphorical relationships for reading the body of the poem:

Le Pitre châtié

—*Pitre* can be linked metaphorically on the level of the signifier to *poète* (five graphemes, repetition of *p/t/e*) and on the level of the signified to other types of entertainers—*clown, farceur* [joker], *saltimbanque* [mountebank] (intermediary = performer, comic, costumed).

—*Châtié* gives rise directly to two signifieds—*punished, made pure or correct*—and indirectly to a third—a metaphorical link on the level of the signifier between *châtié* [ʃatje] and *châtré* [ʃatre], suggesting *castrated*. The title can then be anagrammatized to *pitié (pour le) châtré*.

—The previous metaphorical operations which transform "one" (*pitre or châtié*) into "two" (clown and poet / punish and make pure / punish and castrate) provoke a possible metaphorical play with numerical signifiers: 1 + 2 = 3 (the number of words in the title); 1 and 2 = 12 (the number of phonemes in the title); 1 and 3 = 13 (the number of graphemes in the title).[6]

Yeux, lacs avec ma simple ivresse de renaître
Autre que l'histrion

[Eyes, lakes with my simple drunkenness to be reborn / Other than the (bad) actor]

—With the exception of O the major graphemes of the poem are disseminated in the first line: "Yeux, lacs aVec ma sImple IVResse de RenaITRe."

—*Yeux*, syntactically isolated, can be linked to the title metaphorically by the intermediary "two" (the usual number of eyes). The phonemes and graphemes overdetermine, moreover, this association: *yeux* [jø], *deux* [dø]. The two of eyes contrasts with the singular (one) of *simple*, thus continuing the trace of 1 and 2. There still remains, however, a synecdochal ambiguity: to whom do the eyes belong?

—The rhetorical comma of *Yeux, lacs* (discussed above) poses a similar problem. The ambiguity continues as the rhetorical comma is followed by a rhetorical gap. At first, one sees no link between the signifieds of *lacs* and *avec ma simple ivresse de renaître*, despite the metaphorical relationship of signifiers (*lacs*, *avec*). *Avec* could signal a synecdochal association, but *lacs* can play neither the role of whole nor that of part for *ivresse*. It is only as the result of an extended metonymic operation—from effect (*ivresse* [drunkenness]) to cause (*s'envirer* [to get drunk]) to agent (*boisson* [beverage])—that the reader can establish a possible metaphorical link between *lacs* and *boisson* (I = liquid). This does not, however, resolve the syntactical role of *avec*.

—Because of the synecdochal linking of *ma simple ivresse* to *je* (attribute to possessor), a relationship marked semantically in the text by *ma, autre que* establishes a syntactic link of opposition between *je* and *l'histrion*: the *je* wishes to be reborn different from the *histrion*. The latter can be linked metaphorically to *pitre* both on the level of the signified (*bad actor, buffoon*) and the signifier (*histrion/pitre*). The previously established trace then allows one to associate *histrion* and *pitre*.

> *qui du geste évoquais*
> *Comme plume la suie ignoble des quinquets,*

[who with gesture was evoking / As a quill (feather) the ignoble soot of the oil lamps,]

—The opposition *je* versus *histrion* announced by *autre que* is immediately put into question by the form of the verb *évoquais*, which suggests that *je* is the *histrion*. The apparent contradiction is resolved by inscribing it in the trace of 1 and 2: the *je* is read as double, as a buffoon wishing to be other than a buffoon, and as a *pitre* willing to be "punished" (*châtié*) in order to be "made pure" (*châtié*).

—The typographical isolation of the phrase *Comme plume* as well as its polysemia (*plume* = "feather" or "quill" or even "pen") offers several possibilities: (1) a metaphorical reading: the soot resembles a feather; (2) a metonymic-metaphorical reading: *plume* (instrument) to *writing* (action); writing is similar to the act of evoking; (3) a synecdochal-metaphorical reading: *plume* (whole) to *encre* [ink] (part); the ink resembles the soot; (4) a second metonymical-metaphorical reading: *plume* (instrument) to *poet-writer* (agent); the *histrion* evoked the *suie* as would a writer.

—The phonetic signifier of *suie* [sɥi] inaugurates a trace which moves metaphorically to suis [sɥi] (I am) and then synecdochally to *être* (part to whole verb) and *renaître* [rənɛtr]. This trace, elaborated primarily on the level of the signifier, reinforces the opposition on the level of the signified: the desire of the *histrion* "to be" other than he is. On the other hand, the signified of *suie* is related metonymically to the *histrion* who, as the subject of *évoquais*, plays the role of producer. By the agency of his *geste* the *histrion*-producer conjures up the *suie ignoble des quinquets*. But what gesture? Writing? Another kind of gesture? The product of this evocation, the soot, can be attached to a second metonymical trace: *suie* (product) / *quinquets* (producers). The reader thus has the possibility of linking metaphorically the *histrion* and the *quinquets* (*I* = producer of *suie*). In the contamination associated with the metaphorical process, the *histrion-poète* becomes a producer (writer) who leaves behind a dark and ignoble waste material (his writings). But *quinquets* is also a popular expression for eyes, and this meaning of the word creates a new line of traces which works against the notion of the poet-producer. The *suie ignoble des quinquets* which the poet evokes may be the soot-filled eyes of spectators under the tent, now seen as part of his past. The eyes may also fit into the trace of 1–2 by their opposition to the eyes at the beginning of the poem. We now have two sets of eyes—dirty ones and the lake-eyes.

> *J'ai troué dans le mur de toile une fenêtre.*

[I have pierced in the wall of cloth a window.]

—The sounds of the words which enclose the fourth line—*j'ai troué* and *fenêtre* ([e] [tr] [ə]—relate metaphorically to the rhymes and to the title.

—The signified *trouer* gives the *histrion-je* the active role of creating the window himself. On the level of the signifier, *troué* carries with it, synecdochally, the product of the action—the *trou*. The latter can be related metaphorically to *renaître*: the hole (womb) from which one is born and, presumably, reborn. In addition, the syntactical position of *avec ma simple ivresse de renaître* finally becomes clear. The *je*'s *ivresse* (effect of his desire) will become the instrument with which he will make a hole in order to realize his desire.

—*Le mur de toile* evokes synecdochally the circus tent where the *pitre-histrion* performs.

—The play on the signifier of *fenêtre*—[fənɛtr]→[nɛtr] (*naître*) →[ɛtr] (*être*)—allows the reader to restate, on the level of the signified, the desire of the *histrion-je*: to find an opening in the wall that imprisons him, to be reborn, to be other. At the same time, the reader can see a first possible tie between *yeux* and the rest of the stanza. Metaphorically, *fenêtre* and *yeux* share the intermediary "opening which allows light to pass."

> *De ma jambe et des bras limpide nageur traître,*

[With my leg and arms limpid traitorous swimmer]

—The curious combination of singular (*ma jambe*) and plural (*les bras*) allows the reader to link this phrase metaphorically to the trace of 1 and 2. At the same time, the single leg and two arms

recall, again metaphorically, the grapheme *Y*, tipped on its
side to illustrate the position of the *nageur*.

—The combination *limpide nageur traître* also relates to the single-
double trace. Typographically, the reader finds *one* noun surrounded by *two* adjectives. *Traître*, linked metaphorically to
ignoble, can be opposed to *limpide*. This opposition in turn recalls the title: the "traitor" who is punished; the "other" who
is made pure (*limpide*). In addition, the opposition between
limpide and *traître* is reinforced by the relationship each has to
the metonymical role of the *histrion-je*: the *nageur-traître* is active, a producer of treason; the *limpide nageur* is passive, a non-
producer rendered pure by the clearness of the water.

> *A bonds multipliés, reniant le mauvais*
> *Hamlet!*

[In multiple bounds, renouncing the bad / Hamlet!]

—The metaphorical play on the signifier—*bonds* [bɔ̃] / *bon* [bɔ̃]—
permits an opposition between *bon* and *mauvais*. This opposition in turn can suggest a second metaphorical play: from the
phoneme [a] (*A*) to the grapheme *A*; from the phonetic combination [ve] (*mauvais*, [move]) to the grapheme *V*. The association of "good *A* (*A bon*) and "bad *V* (*mauvais V*),[7] can be
explained by having this trace intersect the single-double trace,
where we have already situated the grapheme *Y*. If we read
the *Y* as posing a conflict between one and two, the bar of the
A can be read, symbolically, to unite the two into one, while
the absence of a bar in *V* leaves the two separated (a situation
overdetermined by the reversal of Λ to *V*).

—By metaphorical association, *reniant le mauvais Hamlet* recalls
renaître autre que l'histrion (intermediary: refusal). This link allows the reader to establish a complex metaphorical trace: the
je-nageur disavows the bad Hamlet and, by extension, the *traître*,
just as the *je-histrion* refuses the *histrion* in himself. By opposition, one could then read that the *je-histrion* wishes to be
reborn other than the *histrion*; i.e., *limpide* (pure and clear) like
the other part of the swimmer. Does parallelism then allow
one to extend the metaphorical chain to include the *je-nageur*'s

acceptance of the "good" Hamlet? Who are the "good" and
"bad" Hamlets?

—The trace of signifiers pointed out previously—*être/renaître*—
reinforces the link between Hamlet and the question of rebirth. The problem remains, however: which Hamlet—"to
be" or "not to be"?

> *c'est comme si dans l'onde j'innovais*
> *Mille sépulcres pour y vierge disparaître.*

[it is as if in the wave I was innovating (creating) / A thousand
sepulchers to disappear into them virgin.]

—*C'est comme si* marks a metaphorical figuration linking *innover*
to *nager (nageur)*, thus consolidating the metonymical role of
the *je-histrion* as producer—*j'innovais / j'ai troué / (j')évoquais.*[8]

—A complex synecdochal and metonymic chain allows us to
piece together the missing parts of the narrative. The *onde* serves
as a container for the *nageur*, agent of the action of swimming.
The latter can be posited as the result of the *histrion* having
jumped through the window that he made in the canvas wall.
Onde also relates synecdochally to *lacs*, suggesting the possibility that the *histrion*, at this point in the poem, is swimming
in the lakes of the first stanza.

—*J'innovais mille sépulcres* presents an opposition—creation (*innover*) versus death (*sépulcres*)—which the reader can then associate metaphorically with the opposition, graphically and
typographically overdetermined by the rhyme, between *renaître* and *disparaître*: desire to be born anew versus prepara-
tions for disappearing.

—The juxtaposition of *YVI* (*y vierge*) can be added to the 1 and
2 (single-double) trace: *Y = V + I*. Moreover, these letters
can be linked to the *A* (*A = V*, reversed, *+ I*, as crossbar).
But whereas the bar of the *A* firmly unites the opposing sides
of the *V*, the *I* of the *Y* simply provides a point of contact or
conflict.

—*Vierge* can be inserted in the trace opposing *limpide* and *renaître*
autre to *mauvais / traître / ignoble / suie.* The absence of a semantic or syntactical marker for *vierge* raises a triple option

for the link between *vierge* and *disparaître*: metaphorical (disappear like a virgin disappears), synecdochal (disappear in a virginal state), or metonymical (disappear so as to become a virgin through the act of disappearing). The latter possibility can be tied metaphorically to the trace single-double, the single act of "being reborn" dividing into the double act of "disappearing" in order to "reappear."

—The sexual connotations of *vierge* suggest another possible trace, which finds support primarily (for the moment, at least) on the level of the signifier. Graphically, the initial letters of *vierge* suggest metaphorically the female (*V*) and male (*I*) sexual parts. One can then trace back through the poem a series of metaphorical associations: the single leg (*I*) of the *pitre*, the *I* rejoining the *V* in *Y*, which recalls the gestures of the swimmer and the *histrion* (making holes); the psychological and phonemic link between *la mort* [lamɔr] and *l'amour* [lamur]; the drama of Hamlet, who must avenge the death of his father by killing his uncle, who made love to his mother.⁹

> *Hilare or de cymbale à des poings irrité*

[Hilarious gold of cymbal with fists irritated]

—The *H* of *Hilare*, joined with those of *Hamlet* and *histrion*, suggests a third metaphorical solution to the opposition of single and double. Superior to the *Y* (which can offer only a single common point), but inferior to the *A* (which provides a double link), the *H* has a bar which joins yet maintains separate the double lines.

—*Or* contains the graphemes *O* and *R*. The *R*, and its phoneme [r], join the phallic trace mentioned above; the *O*, when read phonetically [o], suggests *eau* [water], which can be linked synecdochally to *onde* and *lacs*.

—The phonetic signifier of *cymbale* [sɛ̄bal] contains synecdochally the breast [sɛ̄], *sein*, which can be linked to *renaître* by a metonymical chain: *naître→nouveau-né* [newborn infant]→*lait* [milk]→*sein*.

—*Poings* recalls synecdochally *bras*. But the problem remains: whose fists? those of the swimmer? of the histrion? of some-

one else? The syntactical construction leaves the metonymical
relationship ambiguous: an action and an instrument without
an agent.

—Read on the level of the signifier, *irrité* suggests *I - ri - T*: the
pitre—by metonymy: he who makes people laugh [ri] (*ris, rire*),
between the *I* (single) and the *T* (double).

—The entire verse functions syntactically in opposition to *le soleil* of the following verse. The rhetorical comma serves to
make a metaphor: the sun resembles the *or de cymbale*. The
color of the gold and the shape of the cymbal form the intermediary for the metaphor which carries with it the "sudden
explosion" and "force" of the laughter as well as the "excitement" and even "pain" of the irritation.[10]

> *Tout à coup le soleil frappe la nudité*
>
> [Suddenly the sun strikes the nudity]

—The poem contains two verbs of action in main clauses: *frapper* and *trouer*. One can link the two verbs both on the level of
the signified (physical violence) and the signifier ([fr] [e] / [tr]
[e]). The parallel serves also, however, to establish an opposition: the *je-histrion* moves now from the active role of metonymic producer (*j'innovais / j'ai troué / (j')évoquais*) to a
passive role of direct object.

—*Frapper la nudité* also suggests, by paradigmatic metaphor, *fes-
ser* [to spank] Since the father traditionally spanks, this metonymical association leads to a metaphorical link between the
sun-father and the *je-histrion*-son. The first part of the relation
ship can be overdetermined by the traces already established
between sun and power, force, domination. Moreover, the
father-son link can interact, by opposition, with the allusion
to Hamlet: there, the son is supposed to strike the father. This
new trace can be linked to the double title: *pitre châtié* (punished) and *pitre châtré* (castrated), the father serving in each
case as the agent of the action.

—*Nudité*, by synecdoche, leads to the body of the *je-histrion*. This
first mention (albeit indirect) of the whole body contrasts with
the previous fragmentation: *poings / bras / yeux*.

Qui pure s'exhala de ma fraîcheur de nacre.

[Which pure was exhaled from my freshness of mother of pearl.]

—The syntactic subordination marked by the juxtaposition of *qui* to *nudité* encourages the reader to establish a metonymic trace from *nudité* to *fraîcheur* to *nacre*. *Fraîcheur* functions as the cause of *nudité*; *nacre* serves as the cause for *fraîcheur*; moreover, extratextually, *nacre* itself might suggest another cause: its parent mollusk. Once again, the *je-histrion* finds himself relegated to a passive role overdetermined also by the passive construction of *s'exhala* separated from the producer (*nacre*) by a synecdoche (*nudité* for *corps* [body]) and a metaphor (*nudité* similar to *nacre*).

—*Pure*—and with it *fraîcheur*, *nacre*, and *nudité*—can be added to the metaphorical chain of *vierge* / *limpide* / *renaître* / *autre*. We have already opposed this trace to the chain *mauvais* / *traître* / *ignoble* / *suie*.

—The numerous parallels between *ma fraîcheur de nacre* and *ma simple ivresse de renaître*—typographic (both at the end of a verse); syntactic (possessive + noun + *de*); phonetic ([ma] [fr] [nkr] / [ma] [vr] [ntr]—serve to overdetermine a metonymical link on the level of the signifieds: the *histrion* wants the rebirth to produce for him a new identity or self which is pure, fresh, virginal, like *nacre*.

Rance nuit de la peau quand sur moi vous passiez,

[Rancid night of the skin when over me you passed,]

—The graphic signifier *rance* is the anagram of the graphic signifier *nacre*; moreover, the latter contains synecdochally the signifier *acre* which, on the level of the signified, is a synonym of *rance*. *Rance* and *acre* can be added to the chain *mauvais* / *traître* / *ignoble* / *suie* and thus enter into opposition with the chain *nacre* / *fraîcheur* / *pure*.

—*Nuit de la peau* appears to bring a double contradiction: to the brilliant light of the sun it opposes the absence of light; to the pure whiteness of the nudity it opposes the darkness of the skin. At the same time, the whole body, discovered synecdo-

chally in the previous tercet, fragments again through a reverse synecdoche: *corps* (whole) to *peau* (part).

—If one reads *sur moi vous passiez* as referring to the sun (*vous*)
and and the je-histrion (*moi*), one can then explain metonymically the opposition *rance nuit de la peau* versus *fraîcheur de
nacre*: the sun causes the skin to lose its purity.

> *Ne sachant pas, ingrat! que c'était tout mon sacre,*
> *Ce fard noyé dans l'eau perfide des glaciers.*

[Not knowing, ingrate! that it was my entire consecration / That
makeup drowned in the perfidious water of the glaciers.]

—The syntactical ambiguity of *ne sachant pas*—does it refer to
vous or *je*?—introduces the possibility of two readings: the first
is a direct reproach to the *vous*, i.e., the sun; the second is an
ironic reproach to the *je*, victim of his own innocence or desire
for purity.
—On the level of signifieds, *ingrat!* seems to confirm the first
reading: the sun is ungrateful. But on the level of the signifiers, *ingrat!* can be linked metaphorically with *Hamlet!*—six
graphemes, repetition of *a* and *t*, nasal consonant, exclamation
mark. The link between Hamlet and the *histrion* underlines (as
does the ironic reading of *ne sachant pas*) the still-existent double
nature of the *je*: wanting to be "other" (pure, reborn) but still
the impure *histrion*.
—*Sacre* opens up multiple possibilities of association for the reader:
(1) It can be linked metaphorically to the chain *pure / nacre*
(graphic and phonetic overdetermination) / *limpide / renaître*.
The *sacre* would thus be read as the ceremony consecrating the
product of the rebirth—the new and other *je*. (2) *Sacre* can also
be related metaphorically to *sépulcre* because of the religious
resonances of the two words and because of the four graphemes (*s/c/r/e*) that they share. Such a relationship unleashes a
trace involving various synecdochal, metaphorical, and metonymical operations: the tomb contains the body of Jesus Christ
(the p*i*TRE as marT*y*RE) who dies on the cross (*T*). The signifier *sacre* is found synecdochally in *sacrements*; the first sacrament of the Church is baptism, now parodied by the *pitre's*

plunge into the lakes to be purified. (3) The signifier *sacre* [sakr] can also be found synecdochally in *sacrifice*, which permits a double metaphorical play: on the level of the signified, the *histrion-poète* sacrifices his art for his purity; on the level of the signifier, *sacrifice* [sakrifis] produces synecdochally the *sacre* of the *fils* [fis] (son).

—The play on signifiers *eau* [o] = O gives rise to a trace involving the feminine symbol for womb, maternity, mother: the O also relates metaphorically to *lacs* and even *yeux* (round shape). These traces suggest a metonymical reading in which the instrument of the rebirth are the eyes and/or the lakes and/or the mother's womb. The phoneme [o] also provides an intermediary for the trace *eau* [o] / *peau* [po] / *mauvais* [move] / *autre* [otr]. Reorganized into couples, these elements can be read as a metonymic (cause-effect) and synecdochal (part-whole) resumé of the poem: *autre peau*, but *mauvais(e) eau*.

—*Perfide*, on the level of the signified, can be inscribed into the series involving *traître*, thus creating an opposition between what the *histrion* finds (*perfide / ignoble / traître*) and what he was seeking (the desired *eau: pure / limpide / fraîche*). *Perfide*, on the level of the signifier, juxtaposes the O of the mother and the presence of the father: [pɛrfid]→[pɛr] (*père*).[11]

—On the level of the signified, *glaciers* contains the semantic feature "cold," which the reader can ironically oppose to the sought-for warmth of the womb. In addition, if one reads the *des* of *l'eau des glaciers* synecdochally (water as part of the glacier) rather than metonymically (water produced by the glacier), the water is not water, but ice (*glace*, graphically and phonetically overdetermined). On the level of the signifier, *glaciers* [glasje] contains synecdochally *glas* [gla], the sound of the bell announcing a death (*sépulcres*), a failure. This failure is "explained" by a second synecdoche on the level of the signifier, *scier* [sje] [to cut with a saw]. The reader can associate this action metaphorically to the father-son relationship: the status of the signifier, at the same time present (the grapheme *r*) and absent (the phoneme [r]), suggests the symbolic castration of the *pitre châtré*.

From Traces to Readings

Having established a multitude of traces and identified certain possible lines of interpretation, readers normally proceed to combine the various elements into readings or interpretations of the poem. Every reading, every interpretation represents a form of closure: the reader selects certain elements and disregards or downplays others; the reader favors certain operations and relationships at the expense of others. In this sense, every reading, every interpretation is partial, and, by being partial, implies the possibility of another reading. To demonstrate the partiality and diversity of interpretation, we propose to explore four possible readings of *Le Pitre châtié*. Each interpretation takes its departure from one of the major traces identified above: the drama of the poet, the drama of the unconscious, the paradoxical sacrament, the double and the search for unity.

The Drama of the Poet

Because of the influence of the original version of the poem, the reading we call the drama of the poet, although based on a minimal amount of textual evidence, has gained the greatest acceptance among critics. In it, the *pitre* represents the poet who wishes to be other. He desires to renounce his condition as an "ordinary" poet. He is not satisfied with the miserable poems he produces (*la suie ignoble des quinquets*) nor with the role he must play: actor-clown, forced to expose himself before a public which recognizes only the superficial (the *fard* made from *suie*, the poems that so far represent all he has been able to evoke). He desires to be reborn, to become a new poet, capable of attaining the perfection, the purity, the Ideal that he feels to be part of him. The *pitre châtié*—the *poète difficile*, the poet who wants to be made pure and perfect—becomes, however, the *pitre châtié*—the poet-buffoon punished for his desire. He makes the leap toward the Ideal, but after he has bared himself in his attempt to attain the Ideal, the Ideal (that part of himself which was buried under the *fard*) cannot support the glare of the Real. The *pitre* ironically admits that the Ideal is impossible, that all he has is the *fard*, the *suie*, his imperfect and ignoble poems.

But this interpretation is based on almost no direct references to the poet in the text itself and demands extensive metaphorical play by the reader to tease it out of the text. *Pitre* becomes *poète*; multiple meanings in *plume* are repressed to leave
only *pen*; the notion of the grimy, made-up performer is metaphorically transformed into the hard-working poet; and the *fard*
of the clown becomes the artifice of poetry.[12]

The Drama of the Unconscious

A second interpretation will depend, much more so than the
first, on a *va-et-vient* between our syntagmatic first-level traces
and a paradigmatic system, the Oedipal theories of Freud. In this
reading, the single-double trace (and particularly its graphic
configuration, the *Y* which "frames" the poem) represents the
son in relation to the mother and the father; in particular, it shows
the son divided between conflicting responses to the two par-
ents. The *pitre's* desire to be reborn expresses his desire to love
the mother and yet to remain pure; the plunge into the water
can be seen as an asexual (in ordinary terms) response to the
sexual drive toward the mother—a return to the warmth and
safety of the womb. However, the father (the superego, society,
the Law) proclaims a taboo against incest, transforming this pure
and virginal act (*la nudité / Qui pure s'exhala de ma fraîcheur de
nacre*) into *la rance nuit de la peau*. Consequently, the ironic conclusion of the poem shows the *pitre* expecting to find the warmth
of the womb, but discovering the *eau perfide des glaciers*; antici-
pating a victory, but ending up in passive defeat, punished and
castrated.[13]

This interpretation could be extended into a more blatantly
sexual one of interdiction, fulfillment of desire, and punishment.
The eyes of the first stanza would stand for the desired woman,
whom the poet penetrates. The metaphors of lakes, swimming,
and liquidity are conventional allusions to sexuality, which then
turns sour.

The Paradoxical Sacrament

A third reading takes as its point of departure a minimal number
of traces based on the connotations of the word *sacre* in line 12.
In such a case, one must do a rhetorical rereading of the text in

search of new first-level traces. Thus, the religious traces developed in line 12 can lead to a new metaphorical link between *pitre*
and *pretre* (PiTRE / PrêTRE). This relationship is metaphorically overdetermined by the notion of the priest as "actor" in the
"drama" of the Mass. Moreover, the graphic and phonemic link
sacre / sacrement leads to the metaphorical association of the plunge
into water and the sacrament of baptism. At first, one might be
tempted then to see the *pitre* as the "bad" priest who seeks to be
(re)baptized in order to cleanse himself of his sins, to wash off
the *suie*, the *fard*, of his earthly weaknesses. In so doing, he could
be reborn with the purity of Christ—evoked graphically and
synecdochally by the *T* of the cross, the *T* being the only consonant to appear twice in the title, where it is linked chiasmati-
cally (khiasma: crossing) with the *I* (IESUS); he would thus re-
gain his virginal status (the celibacy of the priesthood). The sestet
of the poem suggests, however, a different, more ironical reading, for the priest is punished by God (the sun, the Father) pre
cisely because he attempts this rebirth, because he denies his humanity, and seeks a spiritual perfection not possible on earth.
Thus, the ice-cold water of the baptism is qualified as *perfide*.
Read metonymically, this suggests that the water has received as
effect the attribute of the cause (he who has betrayed his faith,
the *pitre* who has denied the *fard* of the world). The *pitre-prêtre* is
thus punished for not having understood the meaning of his faith.[14]

The Double and the Search for Unity

The phonemic presence of être [ɛtr] buried in the rhyme scheme
as well as the allusion to Hamlet ("to be or not to be") suggest a
reading in which the *pitre* represents man. Presented as double
in the poem (*je-histrion*), he desires, in his search to be reborn,
to attain a new *être* [being]. The purity of this new state sym-
bolizes a unity, a wholeness, which the *pitre—limpide nageur
traître*—lacks. The very nature of his role as actor implies a di
vided self. In order to attain the desired unity, he must disappear:
rebirth implies death (*j'innovais mille sépulcres*). The *pitre* plunges,
disappears, and is reborn: nude, fresh, virginal. This new being
cannot survive as such in the world, however: unity represents
an impossible quest for man; there always exists an opposition

between the internal *être* and the external fard. The failure is underlined by a second death, buried like the *être* [ɛtr] of the rhymes: the *glas* [gla] of *glaciers*, tolling ironically the defeat (the punishment) of the *pitre*.

A similar drama unfolds on the level of the signifier. Phonemic unification—a rhyme scheme reduced to a bare minimum ([ɛtr], [akr], [e]); a continual reappearance of the sounds of the title throughout the poem ([tr], [i], [e], [a])—is opposed to syntactic dispersion (lack of unification between semantic and typographic markers) and rhetorical fragmentation (parts instead of wholes, actions without agents). Similarly, the graphemes play with various combinations designed to unite two separate elements: *A*, *H*, *Y*. In the end, however, there is a defeat on this level also: the *A*, *Y*, *H* give way to *O*, *R*, *I*; the [ɛtr] disappears totally from the tercets, and with it the new unified being (*être*) of the *pitre*.

These four interpretations are part of major interpretive trends of Western literature: the poetic, religious, philosophical, and psychoanalytic. It has been—or can be—argued that each of these major humanistic interpretations constitutes Mallarmé's poem. Through manipulating the traces in the text, the reader can in fact generate any of them, as well as others. Faced with these possible interpretations, what is the reader supposed to do? He can either fight for one interpretation or else democratically accept all the interpretations as valid, thus implying that Mallarmé's text could mean all things to all readers. But both these extreme approaches miss the point and overlook the true importance of Mallarmé's work. His work cannot "mean all things to all readers," because he obviously sets limits to what can and cannot be said about his texts. One would be hard pressed to show convincingly that the poem is about an imaginary voyage to the tropics, a meditation on the passage of time and the loss of love, or a description of the poetic anguish of creation. Unless one decides that reading Mallarmé is a mere excuse for paradigmatic fantasizing, the reader is constrained to accept negative limits by determining what the poem is *not* about. Conversely, Mallarmé's poem contains fragments of messages which the reader can develop into series of traces and possible interpretations. But his texts hide as much as they reveal and they fragment more than they unify. It is ironic that Mallarmé's Symbolist poems do not in any way direct the reader to precise and coherent Symbols. Rather, his poetic work is one which questions the long tradition of encoded, coherent, and unified figurations and symbolizations. By displacing the act of reading from the message and a unified sign to the production of meaning, Mallarmé calls on the reader to reexamine traditional rhetoric and traditional poetics. In poems where parts do not lead to wholes, where metaphors are incomplete, where the production of meaning overshadows the effect, and where letters on the page are reversed to produce new letters, the reader is in a continual and vertiginous flux of condensations and displacements. But in the end condensations do not decondense and the displacements do not find a stable resting place. Cut off from the past, they float on the page, defying the reader to stop their movement and give them meaning. The great secret of Mallarmé's poetry is that there is no secret except writing itself.

9

SIMON'S LESSON

In Chapter 6 ("Balzac's Duchess") we questioned the common association, based on a partial reading of Jakobson, between metonymy and the novel. The discussion underlined the central role played by metaphorical and ironic processes in the reading of *La Duchesse de Langeais*. It would be unfair, however, to discount completely Jakobson's suggestion, particularly if one remembers that for Jakobson metonymy also embraces synecdoche. An unspoken convention of the reading of any "traditional" narrative is the notion of continuity—that is, a plot or story to which all the elements of the text can be attached rhetorically. The usual means by which the reader integrates each scene (action, event, description) to other scenes and to a coherent whole are inclusion (synecdoche) and causality (metonymy). Thus, as the reader of *La Duchesse de Langeais* moves from paragraph to paragraph, two fundamental assumptions are at work. First, the paragraphs, whether describing a character or recounting an incident or dramatizing a scene, are included in the same story. Second, the paragraphs recount events or present scenes in a chronological order so that what is presented first can be read as the cause for the effect(s) that follow. Whenever one of these conventions appears to be broken for a moment, the reader expects to be able eventually to reestablish the synecdochal and/or metonymical links. Thus, if a scene or description seems unrelated to the story, the reader anticipates that the narration will at some point reintegrate the "digression."[1] Similarly, if the chronology is broken, the reader expects that the narrator (or the reader) will be able to reconnect the events as a flashback, that is, as a reversal in which effect precedes cause.[2]

Accustomed to such narratives, where the continuity of the story succeeds in masking the basic discontinuity of the signifying chain (punctuation within the sentence; division into sentences, paragraphs, sections; separation into chapters and parts), the reader who is unfamiliar with the New Novel will no doubt have difficulty reading a work such as *Leçon de choses* by Claude Simon.[3] Here, the signifying chain is much more continuous than in traditional novels: the book is divided into seven sections, each consisting of one long paragraph ranging from three to forty-three pages in length. However, the continuity of the signifying chain does not succeed in masking the discontinuity of the story, as becomes evident when one attempts to use synecdochal and metonymical processes to reconstruct the narrative.[4]

The first part of the novel, called "Générique," is a three-page description of a room (or of a painting of a room). The room is falling apart: wallpaper peeling, plaster chipped and fallen, objects (bricks, broken windowpanes, empty bag, bottle) strewn about the floor, a bare lightbulb hanging from the ceiling. The description presents itself as being both unfinished (it could continue indefinitely) and partial (no explanations are offered as to why the room is in this condition, no details given about sounds and smells). The second part, approximately forty pages in length, has as a title "Expansion." In it a description of a painting (a seascape, "l'image de l'immobile tempête" [the picture of the motionless storm]) leads to a description of a country scene viewed through a window: the painting is pinned on the wall next to the window. The beginning of the section seems therefore to deal with a single basic scene. It is wartime: a machine gunner, lying on a table in a farmhouse, alternately looks out the window (a quiet, uneventful rural scene) or at the wall next to the window (on which hang the seascape and also a postal calendar). During the first few pages, another soldier enters carrying two chickens to be plucked, and an officer stops by to verify the position of the machine gun.

To read *Leçon de choses* as a traditional text, it is necessary to establish a synecdochal and/or a metonymic link between the two parts. In fact, both are, at first glance, possible. The room in Part I can be seen as a *part* of the scene in Part II; the reader assumes that they are the same room. The room in Part I can represent the *effect* of the war described in Part II. As a consequence, Part II is identified as a flashback, thus accounting for the temporal inconsistency (the destruction of the room in Part I, its relatively normal state in Part II). But a major difficulty presents itself with such a reading. Three apparently unrelated passages interrupt at various points the narration of the war plot: (1) three women and a girl walking through a field of flowers; (2) two masons pounding on a wall; (3) a description of rocks and algae under the water. The rocks and algae could be part of the seascape hanging on the farmhouse wall; however, the painting represents a storm, while the rock bottom in the description undulates gently under the water (*ondule docement*). While the workmen could conceivably be pounding on the wall of another room in the house where the machine gunner waits, this would seem incongruous in wartime. As for the group of walkers, they could be what the soldier sees through the window, although their presence in a war zone would also be incongruous. Or they could be in a picture on the wall. In fact, the second mention of the women and the child places them on a calendar near the window. Yet the first mention has suggested movement ("L'une d'elles agite. . . . La bande avançant . . . " [16] [One of them waves. . . . The group advancing. . . .]), an idea which is reinforced by the very passage where they are linked to the calendar: "Le groupe insouciant des promeneuses continue à dévaler le coteau . . . les ombrelles oscillent aux rhythmes différents de leurs pas" (16) [the carefree group of the walkers continue to go down the hill . . . the parasols swing to the varied rhythms of their steps]. In short, as the reading proceeds, one comes to realize that there are three separate narratives—we will label them *war*, *walk*, and *work*—which cannot be tied synecdochally and metonymically into a coherent diegetic whole. Moreover, one gradually discovers how Simon, in manipulating these three narrative sequences, manages both to subvert and to displace the usual rhetorical work of the reader.

RHETORICAL SUBVERSION

The rhetorical subversion accomplished by Simon's text undermines precisely those operations which guarantee the diegetic continuity of the traditional novel, synecdoche and metonymy. Synecdochal continuity depends on the possibility of relating all parts, however numerous and diverse they may be, to a common whole. Thus, within a single paragraph of *La Duchesse de Langeais*, each new element (sentence or phrase) can be connected to the previous elements:

> ¹La duchesse pensait sans doute qu'en voyant le général la suivre au bal en bottes et en cravate noire, personne n'hésiterait à le croire passionément amoureux d'elle. ²Heureux de voir la reine du monde élégant vouloir se compromettre pour lui, le général eut de l'esprit en ayant de l'espérance. ³Sûr de plaire, il déploya ses idées et ses sentiments, sans ressentir la contrainte qui, la veille, lui avait gêné le cœur. ⁴Cette conversation substantielle, animée, remplie par ces premières confidences aussi douces à dire qu'à entendre, séduisit-elle madame de Langeais, ou avait-elle imaginé cette ravissante coquetterie; mais elle regarda malicieusement la pendule quand minuit sonna.

> [¹No doubt the duchess thought that no one who saw the general following her to the ball in boots and black cravat would hesitate to believe that he was passionately enamored of her. ²The general, happy to see the queen of elegant society willing to compromise herself for him, found his wit rising as his hopes increased. ³Confident of his powers to please, he gave full rein to his ideas and feelings, freed now from the constraint which had made him reticent the evening before. ⁴Had this more substantial and animated conversation, full of first avowals as sweet to utter as to hear, really charmed Madame de Langeais, or had she contrived this ravishing exchange of coquetries? In any case, when midnight struck, she threw a mischievous glance at the clock.]

The "queen of elegant society" and "the general" of sentence 2

are the duchess and general of sentence 1; the compromise re-
ferred to in sentence 2 is the idea, alluded to in sentence 1, that
the duchess might allow the general to accompany her to the
ball in dress other than formal. The "he" of sentence 3 is the
general of sentences 1 and 2; the "constraint" of the "evening
before" refers to an earlier scene. The "more substantial and animated conversation" of sentence 4 involves the "ideas and feelings" of sentence 3. "Madame de Langeais" is the duchess, the
queen of elegant society. And midnight is the hour when it is
too late to go to the ball mentioned in sentence 1. Thus, each
phrase contributes to the synecdochal unity of the paragraph,
which in turn fits into the scene, which in turn is part of the
flashback sequence, and so forth.

To subvert this kind of continuity requires only that the text
intermingle parts belonging to separate and unconnected wholes.
In a typical passage from *Leçon de choses* one reads:

> ¹A mesure que vont et viennent les machoires du vieil ouvrier, les
> saillies qui gonflent alternativement ses joues mal rasées diminuent
> de volume jusqu'à ce que sa pomme d'Adam s'élève et s'abaisse.
> ²Il saisit alors de sa main gauche la bouteille posée à côté de lui et
> boit au goulot en renversant la tête en arrière. ³De nouveau la
> pomme d'Adam s'élève et s'abaisse. ⁴Il repose la bouteille, s'essuie
> la bouche d'un revers de main et dit quelques mots à l'autre ou-
> vrier assis contre le pied du mur. ⁵Sa voix enrouée résonne en se
> répercutant sur les parois du local vide. ⁶Le maréchal-des-logis
> marche vers le lit et secoue le dormeur qu'il a saisi par les épaules.
> ⁷Le ronflement s'interrompt et fait place à des grognements inar-
> ticulés. . . . ⁸Le maréchal-des-logis fait brusquement demi-tour et
> sort de la pièce en marmonnant des paroles furieuses et inintelli-
> gibles. ⁹La petite fille se met à courir avec surexcitation et s'arrête
> brusquement, rappelée par la voix alarmée de la jeune femme. ¹⁰Sa
> silhouette tout entière se découpe sur le ciel. (42–44)

> [¹As the old workman's jaws go back and forth, the bulges which
> puff out first one then the other of his poorly shaven cheeks di-
> minish in size until his Adam's apple goes up and down. ²He then
> grabs the bottle sitting next to him and takes a swig by throwing
> his head back. ³Again the Adam's apple goes up and down. ⁴He
> sets the bottle down again, wipes his mouth with the back of his

hand and says a few words to the other workman who is seated against the base of the wall. [5]His hoarse throat reverberates against the walls of the empty building. [6]The cavalry sergeant goes toward the bed and shakes the sleeper whom he has grabbed by the shoulders. [7]The snoring is interrupted and gives way to some inarticulate groans. . . . [8]The sergeant suddenly turns around and goes out of the room muttering some furious, unintelligible words. [9]The little girl begins to run, overexcitedly, and stops suddenly, called back by the alarmed voice of the young woman. [10]Her whole figure stands out against the sky.]

The first five sentences can be linked synecdochally: the "he" is the old workman whose Adam's apple bobs up and down, who drinks from a bottle and talks to the other workman in the empty room whose wall they are in the process of knocking down. But the sixth sentence deals with two entirely different characters in a different situation: a cavalry sergeant and a sleeping soldier in a room with a bed. The seventh and eighth sentences continue this story: the snoring and grunting come from the sleeping soldier; it is the sergeant who angrily leaves the room. But sentences 9 and 10, again without transition, switch to two other characters in another location: the little girl and the young woman, who are outdoors. Thus, the reader encounters three parts belonging to three separate and discontinuous wholes; yet the sequences flow together without a single indication of a break.

Metonymical continuity depends on the possibility of establishing causal links between various elements of the text and of completing all the causal chains suggested by the story. Thus, in *La Duchesse de Langeais*, the long description of the Faubourg St-Germain explains *why* the duchess feels the need to play a role and mask her feelings; the anecdote concerning Montriveau and the guide in the desert suggests *why* the general makes such a strong initial impression on the duchess. The flashback sections offer the causes of the duchess's flight to the convent; the final return to the island is necessary to complete the chain begun by the general's promise to take the duchess away again. Consequently, the synecdochal subversion in *Leçon de choses* would not be total if one could somehow, as one can with the different sections of *La Duchesse de Langeais*, link the three "wholes" causally to each other. It is not possible, however. The three stories—the soldiers under attack, the workmen knocking down the wall, the walkers out for a stroll—do not intersect. The characters remain distinct, and the events of one story have no impact on the others. In other words, the metonymical subversion reinforces the synecdochal.

One might well object that to speak of three *stories* (albeit separate ones) is necessarily to imply the presence of synecdochal and metonymical relationships. To a certain degree this is true. Even though one cannot interrelate the three stories by synecdoche and metonymy, the reader is able to connect the various fragments of the separate narratives in a way which gives the impression of coherent units. The first five sentences of the passage analyzed above are continued two pages later: "Dans la bouteille qu'a reposée l'ouvrier . . . " [In the bottle that the old man has put down again . . .]. The next three sentences of that passage can be linked directly to three preceding passages (other stages or parts of the scene with the sergeant): "Le chargeur dit on les a vus passer là-bas sur la route ils sont en train de nous tourner pourquoi qu'on. Le maréchal-des-logis dit ou plutôt crie . . . " (41) [The gun-loader says we saw them go by over there on the road and they're going around us now why are we. The sergeant says or rather shouts . . .]; "Le maréchal-des-logis crie je me fous de tes explications" (38) [The sergeant says I don't give a damn about your explanations]; "Les ronflements du cavalier ivre continuent à s'élever avec régularité. . . . Au bout d'un moment le tireur se détend un peu, dit merde alors le salaud et est interrompu par l'irruption dans la pièce d'un personnage casqué lui aussi" (37) [The drunken soldier's snoring continues to be heard regularly. . . . After a moment the gunner relaxes a little, says shit that bastard and is interrupted by a person, also wearing a helmet, who bursts into the room]. Finally, the ninth and tenth sentences continue the story of the walkers from a previous passage: "Le chapeau de paille de la petite fille qui marche en tête se détache sur le ciel. La paille prend une couleur citronnée et un vent aux senteurs d'iode fait claquer les extrémités bifides du ruban qui entoure le canotier" (42) [The straw hat of the little girl who is leading the way can be seen against the sky. The straw takes on a lemony color and an iodine-smelling wind causes the split ends of the ribbon around the hat to flap]. This sequence

picks up again four pages after the analyzed passage: "Le vent
plaque la jupe de la fillette contre ses cuisses et la fait claquer
derrière elle comme un drapeau. Sur le bleu vaporeux du ciel sa
robe paraît presque blanche" (48) [The wind blows the little girl's
skirt against her thighs and causes it to flap behind her like a flag.
Against the hazy blue sky her dress seems almost white].

The "success" of these synecdochal and metonymical operations, which allow the reader to identify and to follow the
three narrative sequences, is not, however, total. Each of the
stories is in turn subverted rhetorically. The subversion is the
least apparent in the work sequence. It usually takes the form of
holes in the story—parts which are omitted and unaccounted
for.[5] Thus, as the workmen proceed through the day (they work,
have lunch, work again, wash and change clothes, leave the house;
the wall is at first a quarter, then a half, then three-quarters de-
molished), certain gaps appear. For example, on page 46 "les
deux ouvriers continuent à mastiquer dans le silence" [the two
workmen continue chewing in silence]. Yet previous sequences
(39, 44) have shown only the older workman breaking for lunch.
A more striking subversion, metonymical in this case, occurs on
pages 135–37, where a long description details the younger
workman peeling a hard-boiled egg. But the passage on page 73
(separated from the description of the peeling by several work
scenes) describes "le plus jeune des deux maçons [qui] tient per-
pendiculairement entre les doigts de sa main gauche réunis en
couronne *l'oeuf dur qu'il vient de peler*" (our italics) [the younger
of the two masons (who) is holding perpendicularly between the
cupped fingers of his left hand *the hard-boiled egg that he has just
peeled*].

The war sequence presents even greater anomalies. In addition to the three soldiers on duty in the farmhouse (the machine gunner, the supplyman, and the gun loader), at various
times two other characters populate the room: a wounded man
(24, 27, 28, 29, 76, 105) and a drunken soldier (37, 38, 41, 43,
145), both lying on a bed. On page 49, the sergeant supervises
the hanging of a mattress in the window:

> Le tireur est interrompu dans sa lecture par les deux autres cava-
> liers qui sous la direction du maréchal-des-logis ligotent un mate-
> las sur le vantail de gauche de la fenêtre. L'enveloppe du matelas

est faite d'une toile à petits carreaux bleu pâle, bleu foncé et blancs.
Une large tache d'un rouge foncé, visqueuse et brillante, s'étale à
peu près au milieu du matelas.

[The gunner's reading is interrupted by the two other soldiers who
are tying, under the direction of the sergeant, a mattress on the
left-hand shutter of the window. The mattress cover is made of a
cloth with pale blue, dark blue, and white checks. A wide dark-
red spot, viscous and shiny, spreads out about in the middle of the
mattress].

The sticky red spot (along with the fetid odor already mentioned) suggests metonymically that the wounded soldier has
died and that the mattress is being aired. But some fifty pages
and ten war sequences later, the same scene apparently takes place
again:

Le tireur perçoit dans son dos le bruit des semelles cloutées de
deux hommes portant sans doute un lourd fardeau. . . . Peu après
le chargeur et le pourvoyeur fixent sous les ordres du maréchal-
de-logis le matelas à carreaux bleus et blancs sur le vantail gauche
de la fenêtre. Le tireur regarde la large tache d'un rouge foncé,
gluante et brillante. (105)

[The gunner hears behind him the clumping of the hob-nailed heels
of two men carrying a heavy load. . . . Shortly afterwards the gun
loader and the supplyman attach, on the sergeant's orders, the blue
and white mattress to the left-hand shutter of the window. The
gunman looks at the wide dark-red spot, sticky and shiny.]

As for the drunken soldier, he makes his first appearance,
indirectly by metonymy, on page 18: "A l'intérieur de la pièce
s'élève la respiration embarrassée, comme un gargouillis, d'un
dormeur" [Inside the room can be heard the troubled breathing,
like a gurgling, of a sleeper]. Following a passage describing the
explosion of an artillery shell the drunk is replaced by the wounded
man: "Le gargouillis qui s'élève régulièrement dans le fond de la
pièce du lit où on a étendu le blessé" (28) [The gurgling that is
heard regularly coming from the bed, in the rear of the room,
where the wounded man has been laid]. The drunk reappears,
without warning, in the passage analyzed above, the scene in
which the sergeant has entered the room in order to complain

about a shot having been fired. Yet this effect (the sergeant's entrance) must wait almost a hundred pages to find its cause (the
shot, described on pp. 134, 135). The drunk is still there, as
indicated by the rest of the shot sequence: "A la fin il semble
prendre conscience des ronflements qui s'élèvent du lit dans le
fond de la pièce" (145) [Finally he seems to become aware of the
snoring coming from the bed in the rear of the room]. The "he"
is not the sergeant, however, but a young lieutenant. And rather
than furiously kick the empty bottle against the wall and fight
with the drunken soldier (as does the *maréchal-des-logis*), the lieutenant gingerly picks up the bottle, rolls it under the man's bed,
and leaves. Two separate incidents? Two versions of the same
scene? The reader's efforts at synecdochal and metonymical integration are stymied.

The major rhetorical subversion within sequences involves
the walk narrative. The sequence begins with three women and
a young girl walking down the hill of the orchard. At the point
where the young girl reaches the bottom of the hill, however,
the women (*promeneuses*) are transformed into a mixed group of
walkers (*promeneurs*): "Cependant que l'enfant atteint le bas du
coteau, les deux promeneurs qui marchaient en queue (un homme
et une jeune femme) se sont attardés (se sont laissés distancer)"
(26) [While the child is getting to the bottom of the hill, the two
walkers who were bringing up the rear (a man and a young
woman) have lingered (or have allowed themselves to fall behind)]. This walk continues the length of the text: they stop for
a snack (30, 34, 36); the girl runs ahead (44, 48); the group walks
along the top of a cliff by the sea (52); the man tries to make the
young woman speak to him (77); he gets her to agree to meet
him that night in the woods near the fence (80); the group sits
down to watch the sea and the shore (88, 91, 98 143, 149, 151,
154, 163, 171). On page 31, however, an apparently new sequence begins: "Elle s'agenouille sur le tapis et entoure de ses
bras le petit lit. Elle se penche sur l'enfant endormie" [She kneels
on the rug and puts her arms around the little bed. She leans
over the sleeping child]. The woman leaves the bedroom, ner-
vously breaks a glass in the kitchen (40), goes out of the house
into the woods (46, 50), and meets the man near the fence (51,

52). Thus, the effect, the meeting in the woods, has preceded the cause, the agreement to meet there, by almost thirty pages. The two segments of the walk sequence continue to alternate until the end of the text, the man seducing the woman and obliging her to participate in various forms of sexual activity. Two of the passages describing their lovemaking, separated from each other by twenty pages and four other moments of the same subsequence, offer synecdochal anomalies to accompany the metonymic reversal. The love scenes take place with the woman pinned against the fence or leaning over it; the lovers are observed by a cow and serenaded by frogs and crickets. However, on page 137 (and again on 160) the scene is different: they are in a room strangely reminiscent of the one where the masons are working. "Elle s'appuie en se cramponnant d'une main à l'une des *planches* rugueuses parsemées de menus éclats de *plâtre*. . . . Elle halète, elle dit oui moi aussi je vous je mais pas ici c'est plein de saletés de *gravats* . . . Elle glisse et se rattrappe au montant droit du *tréteau*" (137; our italics) [She leans over, clinging to one of the rough *boards* dotted with tiny bits of *plaster*. . . . she gasps, she says yes me too I you I but not here it's full of dirty pieces of *rubbish* . . . She stops and catches herself on the right post of the *trestle*].

These anomalies and reversals take place within the context of an even more radical subversion. The entire walk sequence begins under a cloud of ambiguity: the walkers seem to emerge from an image on a postal calendar ("Entouré sur le calendrier par les colonnes de noms de saints ou de martyrs, le groupe insouciant des promeneuses . . ." [18] [Surrounded on the calendar by columns of the names of saints and martyrs, the carefree group of walkers . . .]). Given life by the narration (i.e., promoted from a part of the war narrative to a sequence of its own), the walk or at least the subsequence involving all the walkers, thanks to a synecdochal reversal, is "captured"[6] in the middle of the text: "Le *peintre* aurait étalé [la pâte] sur toute la surface de la *toile* avec de faibles modulations, se contenant d'indiquer par quelques *taches* sommaires le canotier de la fillette. . . . La seule *note* soutenue est constituée par la veste d'alpaga noir du promeneur assis au bord du précipice. . . . Le chargeur lit lentement le titre de la *reproduction* punaisée sur le mur parmi les coquelicots géants: SUR LA FALAISE" (93; our italics) [The *painter* probably spread (the paint) over the surface of the *canvas* with slight modulations, being content to indicate by a few summary *strokes* the little girl's straw hat . . . The only sustained *note* is constituted by the black Alpaca coat of the man seated on the edge of the precipice . . . the gun loader slowly reads the title of the *reproduction* pinned on the wall amidst the giant poppies: ON THE CLIFF]. Thus, the walkers are seen as part of an image which is part of a calendar which is part of a room which is part of the war sequence. Shortly thereafter, the reversal is reversed: the walk comes alive again, only to be recaptured in the final short section of the text. There, the painting is not part of the postal calendar but of another poster on the wall (179). And again the capture is not permanent: the walkers are seen returning from their walk and going into a house under reconstruction.

RHETORICAL DISPLACEMENT

Confronted with these frequent subversions of traditional reading operations, the reader is obliged to recognize the synecdochal and metonymical discontinuity of the text. Yet if inclusion and causality fail to provide coherence, there remains the possibility of using similarity and opposition. In *Leçon de choses* metaphorical and ironic (oppositional) relationships do play a major role. They do not function, as they do in *La Duchesse de Langeais*, to determine meaning(s); rather, they operate at a more basic level, allowing the reader to establish a continuity from passage to passage in the text. In short, the "revolution" provoked by a text such as *Leçon de choses* involves the displacement from synecdoche and metonymy to metaphor and opposition as the rhetorical relationships functioning in the primary (first-level) decoding of a text.

The precise operation of this kind of reading can best be seen by examining a passage which extends over four pages. We will break the passage into six segments to analyze closely Simon's subversion of the text. At the point where our selection

begins (p. 22, in the midst of a fragment of the war sequence),
an officer has just left, leaving the machine gunner alone at the
window:

> Après le départ du gradé, le tireur inoccupé attire à lui un des livres
> restés éparpillés sur la table. La couverture cartonnée est d'un blanc
> verdâtre, ou plutôt amande, le dos est renforcé par une toile olive.
> Le livre a pour titre LEÇONS DE CHOSES. Sous le titre est
> porté la mention NOUVEAUX PROGRAMMES et, en bas, le
> nom de l'éditeur LIBRAIRIE GENERALE DE L'ENSEIGNE-
> MENT 1, rue Dante, 1. Le tout est encadré d'un filet noir qui
> dessine aux quatre angles des boucles serpentines, comme des ru-
> bans, des reflets ondulant dans l'eau, s'entrelaçant, et d'où se dé-
> tache, dans chacun des coins supérieurs, une tige, serpentine elle
> aussi, porteuse d'une fleur aux pétales refermés (ou peut-être quel-
> que baie), un peu comme les côtes bombées d'un minuscule melon
> ou d'un minuscule citrouille. (22–23)

[After the officer's departure, the machine gunner, having nothing
to do, pulls over one of the books scattered on the table. The
heavy paper cover is greenish white or rather almond-colored, the
back is reinforced with olive-colored cloth. The book has as a title
LESSONS ABOUT THINGS. Under the title is printed NEW
CURRICULA and, at the bottom, the name of the publisher LI-
BRAIRIE GENERALE DE L'ENSEIGNEMENT 1, rue Dante,
1. All of these are framed by a thin black line which outlines at the
four corners serpentine curls, like ribbons, [like] undulating reflections in water intertwining and from which stick out, in each of
the upper corners, a stem, also serpentine, bearing a flower with
closed petals (or perhaps some kind of berry), a little like the rounded
sides of a tiny melon or of a tiny pumpkin.]

This segment is clearly a *part* of the war sequence (in fact, there
is a synecdochal chain: the cover is part of the book, which is
part of the setting for the sequence) and can be related metonymically to what has just preceded: the departure of the officer is
the *cause* of an implied *effect*, boredom and inactivity, which in
turn functions as a *cause* for a new action, reaching for the book.
At the same time, it is possible to link this segment *metaphorically*
to earlier passages in the text. The books on the table in the
room (*livres restés éparpillés*) recall the scene outside the window

("parsemés d'objets, de débris éparpillés" [16] [strewn with objects, with scattered debris]), which recalls in turn the room in
Part I ("sont aussi éparpillés parmi les débris de plâtre divers
objets ou fragments d'objets" [9] [are also scattered among the
plaster debris various objects or fragments of objects]). This relationship is overdetermined by the graphic similarity between
débris and *livres* (both are six-letter words; they share four graphemes—*e, i, r, s*). The cover of the book can be tied, again metaphorically, to the two descriptions of seascapes at the beginning
of Part II. The colors *verdâtre* and *olive* can be associated by repetition and by anagrammatization to "Les flots verdâtres, les
rochers violets" [the greenish waves, the purple rocks]—*violet*
and *olive* share five identical graphemes. The cover design, serpentine curls compared to undulating reflections in the water,
can be linked to the description on page 21. "Sous l'eau couleur
d'huître, le fond de roches ondule lentement" [Beneath the
transparent, oyster-colored water, the rock bottom undulates
gently]. Here the relationship is by opposition: opaque water/
undulating reflections versus transparent water/undulating re-
fractions. The "berry" of the cover design can lead by polysemia
(same signifier, different signifieds) to all three narrative sequences. The signifier *baie* can have as a signified *berry* or *bay* or
opening in the wall for a door or window. These signifieds can be
found in the walk narrative (berries in the field), the war story
(the bay painted in the seascape on the wall), and the work sequence (the demolition of the wall). Finally, the title of the book
which the machine gunner is reading, *Leçons de choses*, suggests
the title of the book the reader is reading, *Leçon de choses*.

Les rubans qui entourent les chapeaux de paille des femmes sont
ornés de fleurs ou de fruits artificiels (des violettes, des pensées,
une grappe de cerises) qui se balancent au rythme de leurs pas. Le
bouquet que tient la petite fille est composé de scabieuses, de pis-
senlits et de marguerites des champs. Sainte Marguerite, Sainte
Gwaldys, Sainte Irène, Saint Pacôme, Saint Fulbert, Saint Stanislas . . . (23)

[The ribbons surrounding the women's straw hats are decorated
with artificial flowers or fruits (violets, pansies, a bunch of cher-

ries) which bounce up and down in time to their steps. The bouquet that the little girl is holding is made up of scabiouses, dan-
delions, and field daisies. Saint Margaret, Saint Gwaldys, Saint
Irene, Saint Pacome, Saint Fulbert, Saint Stanislas . . .]

This appears at first to belong to the walk sequence: the flowers
or fruits bouncing up and down suggest a "live" scene. But then
comes the list of saints and martyrs, continuing a list begun on
page 18 and therefore suggesting a link to the calendar (surrounded by saints' names), which is part of the war sequence.
This juxtaposition of "live" scene and "image" serves to underline the synecdochal subversion at work. At the same time,
metaphorical relationships within and without the segment work
at counterbalancing the apparent discontinuity. Thus, the fact
that the list begins with *Sainte Marguerite* relates it to the walk
sequence; there are daisies (*marguerites des champs*) in the little
girl's bouquet. Similarly, the ribbons (*rubans*) and the artificial
flowers and fruits (*fleurs ou fruits artificiels*) on her hat serve as
common features to link the walk narrative to the war sequence
(the design on the cover of the machine gunner's book).

> Tout en jetant de fréquents coups d'oeil en direction de la corne
> du bois, le tireur ouvre le livre orné d'illustrations. Il contemple
> l'une d'elles qui porte comme légende: Fig. 20. Roches à découvert
> sur le bord de la mer. Un phare se dresse au sommet d'une haute
> falaise aux parois noires, battue par des vagues grisâtres. A gauche
> de la falaise et presque sur la ligne d'horizon, on aperçoit un voilier
> à la mâture fortement inclinée. (23–24)

> [While glancing frequently towards the edge of the woods, the
> gunner opens the book, which is adorned with illustrations. He
> considers one of them which has for a caption: Fig. 20. Exposed
> rocks at the seashore. A lighthouse stands at the top of a high,
> dark-faced cliff lashed by greyish waves. To the left of the cliff and
> almost even with the horizon, one sees a sailboat with its mast
> bent way over.]

This segment returns to the synecdochal chain of the war sequence: the water and rocks are part of the illustration, which is
part of the book which the soldier opens, and so forth. The details of the description (rocks, seashore, cliff, waves) link it not

only to the two earlier seascapes, on pages 21 (water, rocks, waves) and 15 (waves, rocks), but also to the room in Part I, where the wallpaper is described in sea terms (waves, archipelago, islands, cliffs). If one works back up this metaphorical chain, a second trace can be established. In Part I, the sea terms are related to plaster and to the plants (*feuilles d'acanthe* [Acanthus leaves]) of the wallpaper design: "Au-dessous du minuscule et immobile déferlement de vagues végétales qui se poursuivent sans fin sur le galon de papier fané, l'archipel crayeux des morceaux de plâtre se répartit en îlots d'inégales grandeurs comme les pans détachés d'une falaise" (10) [Beneath the tiny, immobile cresting of vegetal waves which chase each other endlessly on the band of faded paper, the chalky archipelago of pieces of plaster is divided into small islands of unequal size like the detached walls of a cliff]. In the first seascape "elle [l'image de l'immobile tempête] est punaisée à côté de la fenêtre dont l'embrasure encadre un paysage champêtr" (15) [it (the picture of the motionless storm) is pinned next to the window whose embrasure frames a country scene]. Associated here with a rustic field, the seascape in its second appearance is linked to stone, which later is transformed back into plants (algae): the rocks of the seascape "s'étendent en un champ chaotique comme les ruines des temples, des palais et des portiques d'une ville engloutie où l'on croit deviner des fragments de frontons, de chapiteaux et de corniches sur lesquels ont pris racine des mousses verdâtres" (22) [stretch out in a chaotic field like the ruins of the temples, palaces, and porticos of a buried city where one thinks he recognizes fragments of pediments, capitals, and cornices in which greenish moss has taken root]. One can discover in these passages two series, one, vegetable in nature; the other, associated with buildings (to which can be added the "haute falaise aux parois [walls] noires" of the illustration). These two series can be opposed one to the other: animate versus inanimate. Such an opposition can then be expanded to include the problem of the walk sequence—"live" (animate) or a calendar picture (inanimate)—as well as the machine gunner's book, *Leçons de choses*, a book designed to familiarize children with basic natural phenomena (animate) and everyday objects (inanimate).

Abandonnant la béquille, mais la main droite toujours sur le pon-
tet de l'arme, le tireur feuillette le livre à l'envers et tombe sur une
autre illustration: Fig. 12. Ouvriers étendant le plâtre sur le plafond et sur les murs. Armés de truelles, des hommes vêtus de
blouses et juchés sur des planches supportées par des tréteaux sont
dessinés dans les diverses attitudes correspondant à ces travaux. Ils
sont coiffés de casquettes. L'un d'eux porte sur sa tête une auge à
plâtre de forme rectangulaire. Les parties du mur et du plafond
non encore recouvertes de plâtre laissent voir les briques et la claie
de roseaux. (24)

[Letting go of the stand, but with his right hand on the trigger-
guard, the machine gunner leafs backwards through the book and
comes upon another illustration: Fig. 12. Workmen spreading plaster
on the ceiling and walls. Armed with trowels, men dressed in
overalls and perched on boards supported by trestles are shown in
the various positions that correspond to these jobs. They are wearing caps. One of them has on his head a rectangular-shaped hod.
The parts of the wall and ceiling not yet covered with plaster reveal the bricks and the reed grid-work.]

This segment contains another part of the synecdochal chain belonging to the war sequence. The description of the illustration
(workmen, plaster, ceiling, walls, trowels, hods, bricks) form a
link to the work sequence, whose first segment, four pages earlier, deals with workmen, hammer, brick, mortar, pieces of plaster. This metaphorical association gives rise also to an opposition: in the illustration, the workmen are *constructing* a wall and
ceiling; in the earlier scene, the workmen are knocking down
(*destroying*) a wall. The link between the war and work sequences is reinforced phonetically and graphically by the similarity between *claie* [grid-work] and *haie* [hedge] (from the window in the farmhouse the machine gunner sees a hedge [16]). To
this trace can be added *baie* [berry], which has already linked the
war and walk sequences. Thus, the metaphorical link between
signifiers as well as the opposition in content provide continuity
between the three narratives.

Sans avertissement, sans le moindre écho préalable de bataille, proche
ou lointain, un sifflement se fait entendre qui grandit rapidement.
Un soldat se précipite dans la pièce par la porte ouverte et au moment où l'obus éclate il se trouve debout dans l'encadrement de

celle-ci, les deux bras levés, les deux pieds à quelques centimètres
du sol, comme suspendu en l'air. Un instant, la lueur de l'explosion (ou celle du soleil qui décline) projette son ombre distendue
et échassière sur le carrelage où il s'abat au milieu d'une pluie d'é-
clats de pierres, de morceaux de briques et de tuiles. (24)

[Without warning, without the slightest previous sound of battle,
near or far, a whistling noise is heard, which gets rapidly louder.
A soldier rushes into the room, and at the moment when the shell
bursts, he is standing in the frame of the open door, his hands
raised, both feet several centimeters above the ground, as if he
were suspended in air. For an instant, the glow of the explosion
(or of the setting sun) projects his overextended and storklike
shadow on the floor where he collapses in the midst of a rain of
stone chips, of pieces of brick and tile.]

The transitional phrases ("Without warning, without the slightest previous sound of battle") indicate the absence of metonymical links between this segment of the war sequence and the preceding one. But the apparent discontinuity is compensated for
by the relationships which can be established between the two
segments. The "rain of stone chips, of pieces of brick and tile,"
links the room in the farmhouse to the room in the illustration
and continues the opposition of animate versus inanimate. The
artillery shell knocks down the ceiling and wall; the workers in
the illustration are building a ceiling and wall: destruction versus
construction. The collapse of the wall in the farmhouse also links
the war sequence to the previously discussed scene in the work
sequence (p. 20). In addition, the description of the soldier ("debout dans l'encadrement de [la porte], . . . son ombre distendue
et échassière") intersects metaphorically the final paragraph of
Part I: "ombres portées très opaques (presque noires) qui s'allon-
gent sur le carrelage et peut-être aussi celle, échassière et
distendue, d'un personnage qui tient debout dans l'encadrement
de la porte" (11) [shadows thrown very opaquely (almost black)
which stretch out along the floor . . . and perhaps also the shadow,
storklike and overextended, of a person (character) who is standing
in the frame of the door].

En fait, c'est le plus jeune des deux ouvriers qui frappe les coups à
la cadence la plus lente, retentissant sourdement. Alors que son

compagnon abat peu à peu la cloison, il est occupé à pratiquer une saignée horizontale dans le mur de refend, à peu près à une hauteur de deux mètres, sans doute pour faire place au linteau d'une nouvelle porte. Il a commencé par arracher les deux couches de papier peint superposées dont une longue bande déchirée pend maintenant sur le côté, montrant son envers jaunâtre. Lorsque son outil rencontre une pierre, il fait tomber le plâtre qui la revêt de quelques coups de masse et enfonce ensuite l'outil dans le mortier qui la sertit. (24–25)

[In fact, the younger of the two workmen is the one who is striking blows in the slower cadence, creating a dull reverberation. While his companion slowly knocks down the partition, he is busy making a horizontal groove in the heavy dividing wall, approximately at the two-meter level, probably in order to make room for the lintel of a new door. He has begun by pulling off the two layers of wallpaper pasted one on top of the other, a long torn band of which is now hanging along the side, showing its yellowish back. When his tool strikes a stone, he knocks off the plaster covering it with several hits of the hammer and then sticks the tool into the mortar which holds the stone in place.]

Once again there appears to be a break. However, the two sequences (the previous war segment and the present work segment) can be integrated metaphorically and by opposition. The two passages share certain features: (*a*) youth—"the younger of the two workmen" and the "soldier," it having been established on page 20 that the soldiers are "very young"); (*b*) blows—the workman's hammer, the shell's explosion; (*c*) the knocking down of a wall; (*d*) the signifier 2—*deux mètres, Fig. 12, Fig. 20.* Polysemia adds to the relationship. The signifier *saignée* has two signifieds—*crack* or *groove* (the wall of the work segment) and *enormous loss of men or materiel during wartime.* The signifier *mortier* carries the signified *cement* and also the signified *mortar* (a kind of gun or cannon), which leads metonymically to *shell* (*obus*). Finally, the graphic and phonetic similarity between *abat* and *s'abat* sets up the link between *abat la cloison* [knocks down the partition] and *le soldat s'abat* [the soldier collapses]. What might appear to be a relationship of similarity can also be read as an opposition: construction (the workmen are knocking down the wall in order to install a door) versus destruction.

This word-by-word working out of the text so as to interweave the segments of various narrative sequences is paralleled on the diegetic level by the interweaving of narrative elements. The passage just analyzed reveals two such instances: the illustrations in the book the machine gunner is reading (war sequence) intersect the work sequence (the workmen and their equipment) and walk sequence (the walkers go along a cliff overlooking the sea). Such metaphorical links are not limited to the illustrations, however, nor to the plaster bits and bricks falling in the farmhouse and the room where the masons are at work. Sounds, objects, places, actions—all circulate to assure the continuity of the text. The following list offers only a few of the many possible examples:

—the croaking of frogs and the hooting of owls are heard by the soldiers in the farmhouse and by the lovers in the woods;
—the drunken soldier has finished his bottle of wine while the workmen drink their bottles of beer and Orangina;
—the younger workman eats sardines, the principal catch of the fisherman whom the walkers observe from the top of the cliff;
—the machine gunner uses a newspaper to clean his gun, the workman spreads a newspaper out as a tablecloth, and the man carries a rolled-up newspaper during the walk;
—the soldiers see a dead cow lying in the field, a cow comes to observe the love-making near the fence, and the older workman eats some cheese whose package has a picture of a cow;
—a cast-iron fireplace plate decorated with a scene (a woman in a long dress standing in a garden) is found both in the farmhouse and in the house with the workmen;
—at the end of their walk, the man, the woman, and the little girl stop at a house to examine the progress of the remodeling, a house which two workmen have just left;
—the young woman peels an orange for her daughter, and the younger workman peels an egg;
—one of the soldiers offers a twelve-page nonstop, unpunctuated monologue about his war experiences (World War II?), while the older workman delivers a similar monologue about his war experiences (World War I?);
—the young woman bursts into tears when she realizes that her

lover has not withdrawn (*se retirer*) before ejaculating; one of
the soldiers sobs that there's nowhere to retreat to (*se tirer*).

In like fashion, the oppositions (animate versus inanimate,
construction versus destruction) are continued, also providing
links between disparate segments. To these are added other oppositions: movement versus stasis, up versus down, human versus natural, voluntary versus involuntary, light versus darkness.[7]
Thus, the continuity sought for and yet frustrated on the level
of the story is discovered in the discourse itself.

If similarity and opposition therefore replace inclusion and
causality as the central first-level reading processes in *Leçon de
choses*, there also occurs, simultaneously, a second rhetorical displacement. Metonymy, subverted (along with synecdoche) in its
usual task of linking various elements of the story, reappears in
a new role. It is possible to read metonymical relationships as
functioning, on a second level of reading, to *explain* the relationships of similarity and opposition which form the connecting
traces of the discourse. Metonymy, in this sense, is generativity,
the production of the text by the text which reveals itself as the
reader, working back up the traces and examining the connections, reconstructs the activity of the writer-producer. The first
part of the text is entitled "Générique." The noun *générique* refers
to the list of actors, collaborators, writers, and technicians involved in the production of a film—the "material" (agents and
instruments) with which the film is made. By phonetic and
graphic similarity, the word also suggests its etymological source
genus and the family *générer* [to generate], *générateur* [generator].
These two terms propose, in turn, synecdochal (genus-species)
and metonymical (producer-produced) relationships. Part I can
then be read synecdochally (as the whole of which the rest of the
book develops the parts) and/or metonymically (as the generative source of the rest of the text). Such a reading is underlined
by the title of Part II, "Expansion": as has been pointed out, "the
plot has come out of the wall fragments of 'Générique,' *ex-pans*"
(from Latin *ex* [out of], *pans* [wall]),[8] another suggestion of the
generative or productive role of Part I.

From this perspective, the metaphorical link between the

book the machine gunner reads and the book the reader reads (intermediary = similar titles) serves to reinforce the generative role of *Leçons de choses*. This book of illustrations, an actual text used in France to teach children, can be read metonymically as a producer (or generator) of which the Simon novel, *Leçon de choses*, is the product. Generativity is not limited, however, to the role of this book as "source." The great majority of the work of generation takes place on the level of the word-by-word working out of the text, the play with signifiers as well as signifieds in the form of repetitions, synonyms and antonyms, polysemia, anagrams, and so on.

RHETORICAL "LESSONS"

Texts such as *Leçon de choses* have a "revolutionary" goal: they aim to undermine the way the reader has been reading and, ultimately perhaps, to change the reader's notion of literature. Whereas the traditional reader spends considerable time trying, by various sorts of mental gymnastics, to establish sequences that can be related in some coherent fashion to a basic story, the reader familiar with the New Novel (and particularly with Simon) concentrates on the generative traces that run through the text. Thus, what becomes important is not the sequence, but the apparent "breaks" between sequences—discontinuities which function as markers of an incompatibility to be resolved, not on the level of the story, but on that of the discourse. Their resolution consists, therefore, in discovering, or more exactly rediscovering, the processes of production of the text, those generative techniques used by the writer to produce the discourse. Herein lies perhaps the fundamental paradox of this kind of New Novel. On the level of production, the generative theory of writing frees the writer from the constraints of expression, representation, *a priori* meaning; on the level of reception (reading), however, it tends to control and to channel the reader, pushing him into identifying the generative operations of the writer, limiting his reading to a "reproduction" of the text. The theorists of the New Novel do try to resolve this paradox; for them, the reader does have the possibility of exerting his freedom—not in reading, but in writing. The reading of a New Novel can serve as a catalyst for the act of writing; the ultimate act of the reader, from this point of view, becomes the act of producing, of generating, inspired by the operations discovered in reading New Novels, his own text.

This notion of the reader as writer represents a theoretically possible, yet practically quite idealistic defense of the New Novel. Short of such radical reversing of the roles of reader and writer, we would suggest another value inherent in the rhetorical subversion and displacement imposed on the reader by texts such as *Leçon de choses*. In an effort to retrace the work of the writer, the reader extends his use of rhetorical processes to the level of the signifier, where he begins to play with the multiple possibilities available on this level as well as those possibilities involved in the exchange between signifiers and signifieds. This playfulness, specifically encouraged by the texts (and the theoretical pronouncements) of the New Novelists, provides a stimulus to apply such reading techniques to the signifiers of all texts. In this manner, New Novels contribute to the retroactive "liberation" of the reading process.

At the same time, one should recognize that *Leçon de choses*, despite its "revolutionary" aspects, does not manage, nor does it, undoubtedly, intend, to subvert completely the rhetoric of reading. Such an effort would require a much more radical tactic. The complete subversion of metaphor would involve replacing similarity by perfect identity: the endless repetition of exactly the same text.[9] To subvert metonymy totally, one would have to eliminate causal and generative links at all levels of the text. Total synecdochal subversion would require a series of entirely unrelated segments, the absence of any elements capable of suggesting a common whole. To subvert opposition completely would involve pure difference, a random selection of totally discontinuous elements. The most radical experiments with literature—Dadà, Expressionism, contemporary *écriture*—have not succeeded in pushing literature to this limit, in eliminating all possibilities of rhetorical relationships. One might wonder whether such an extreme is even realizable. Faced with a blank canvas or a poem of nonsense syllables, one can continue to "read," to find links (paradigmatic or syntagmatic), to establish rhetorical relationships. In short, rhetorical subversion ultimately reaffirms the force of the rhetorical.

Notes
Bibliography
Index

Notes

Introduction: Jakobson's New Rhetoric

1 Claude Lévi-Strauss, *La Pensée sauvage* (Paris: Librairie Plon, 1962), pp. 274–75, trans. as *The Savage Mind* (Chicago: University of Chicago Press: 1966), p. 207.

2 Jacques Lacan, *Ecrits* (Paris: Editions du Seuil, 1966), p. 511, trans. as "The Insistence of the Letter in the Unconscious," *Yale French Studies* 36–37 (1966): 129.

3 Roland Barthes, *Système de la mode* (Paris: Editions du Seuil, 1966), p. 249. Translations are ours unless otherwise indicated.

4 Parataxis involves syntactic contiguity. It represents the placing of clauses side by side without subordination or coordination.

5 Roman Jakobson, "Two Aspects of Language and Two Types of Aphasic Disturbance," in Roman Jakobson and M. Hall, *Fundamentals of Language* (The Hague: Mouton, 1956). Hereafter cited by page number in the text.

6 Roman Jakobson, "Linguistics and Poetics," in *Style and Language*, ed. T. Sebeok (Cambridge: M.I.T. Press, 1960), p. 350.

7 Roland Barthes, "Eléments de sémiologie," *Communications* 4 (1964): 115–16, trans. Annette Lavers and Colin Smith in *Elements of Semiology* (Boston: Beacon Press, 1970), pp. 60–61.

8 Anika Lemaire, *Jacques Lacan* (Brussels: Mardaga, 1977), p. 75.

9 Anthony Wilden, *System and Structure: Essays on Communication and Exchange* (London: Tavistock, 1972), p. 55.

10 David Lodge, *The Modes of Modern Writing: Metaphor, Metonymy, and the Typology of Literature* (Ithaca: Cornell University Press, 1977), p. 81.

11 Wilden, *System and Structure*, pp. 50, 62.

12 Lodge, *Modes of Modern Writing*, p. 11.

13 Wilden, *System and Structure*, p. 40.

14 Juan David Nasio, "Métaphore et phallus," in *Démasquer le réel*, ed. Serge Leclaire (Paris: Editions du Seuil, 1971), p. 101.

15 Paul de Man, "Semiology and Rhetoric," *Diacritics* 3 (1973): 33.

16 Albert Henry, *Métonymie et métaphore* (Paris: Klincksieck, 1971); Umberto Eco, "Sémantique de la métaphore," *Tel Quel* 55 (Autumn 1973); Gérard Genette, *Figures III* (Paris: Editions du Seuil, 1972); Jacques Dubois et al., *Rhétorique générale* (Paris: Editions Larousse, 1970); Tzvetan Todorov, "Synecdoques," *Communications* 16 (1970): 26–35.

17 Jakobson, "Linguistics and Poetics," p. 370.

18 In his "Eléments de sémiologie," Barthes also makes this sort of identification: "Jakobson, in a now famous text, has adapted this extension by applying opposition of the *metaphor* (of the systematic order) and the *metonymy* (of the syntagmatic order) to non-linguistic languages" (pp. 115–116, p. 60 in trans.). Barthes uses the term *systematic* to designate the paradigmatic order.

19 The discussion in this chapter has centered on Jakobson because it is his binary theory which has had the widest impact. Numerous other theoreticians have attempted to redefine tropes in light of modern linguistic theories, however. Among the more prominent are Michel Le Guern, Albert Henry, Umberto Eco, Tzvetan Todorov, and the Groupe de Liège. Le Guern follows Jakobson's lead, subsuming synecdoche within metonymy in opposition to metaphor; Henry and Eco subordinate metaphor to metonymy; Todorov and the Groupe de Liège treat synecdoche as the master trope. For a critical review of these major theories and definitions, see the first part of our article "Metaphor, Metonymy, and Synecdoche Revis(is)ited," *Semiotica* 21, nos. 1/2 (1977), as well as the article by Donald Rice "Catastrop(h)es: The Morphology of Metaphor, Metonymy, Synecdoche, and Irony," *Sub-Stance* 26 (1980).

20 The choice of four tropes has historical precedent. Both Vossius and Vico grouped a quadrumvirate of the same major tropes. See Genette, "La Rhétorique restreinte," in *Figures III* and Todorov, "Synecdoques."

CHAPTER 1: THE FOUR TROPES

1 We have selected the term *semantic feature* to avoid confusion with *sème* (as used by Greimas) and *component* or *marker* (as understood by semanticists such as Katz, Lounsbury, and Goodenough). The research of both Greimas and the Anglo-Saxons is oriented toward the discovery of universal minimal units of meaning. We are interested in units of meaning which, although components of the word, do not attain an abstract level of universality. Thus, the word *pail-*

lotte [straw hut] contains the semantic features "building," "to be lived in," "simple," "small," "made of straw," plus others which depend on the context and/or the speaker-reader; see Georges Mounin, *Clefs pour la sémantique* (Paris: Seghers, 1972), pp. 122 ff.

2 For Riffaterre, the microcontext includes not only the stylistic effect itself (of which our trope would be an example) but also that part of the signifying chain needed to show "context deviation." The macrocontext is that part of the literary message preceding the microcontext which contains other variations of the same effect—i.e., one of the "patterns" found in the text. See Michael Riffaterre, *Essais de stylistique structurale* (Paris: Editions Flammarion, 1971), pp. 64–94. Our concept of microcontext is thus more restrictive than Riffaterre's while our notion of macrocontext is more extensive, not being limited to variants of the trope in question. In this sense, we are closer to Max Black, who uses the terms *focus* and *frame* to designate the metaphorical word and the rest of the sentence (Max Black, *Metaphors and Models*, Ithaca: Cornell University Press, 1962, pp. 25–47).

3 We should recall, however, that Saussure recognized the existence of a referent. We accept the Saussurian principle that the primary bond is between the acoustical image and the concept, not the word and the thing. Yet just as signs do refer to other signs, they also refer, directly and indirectly, to a "reality."

4 Mounin, *Clefs*, p. 25.

5 Paul Ricoeur, *La Métaphore vive* (Paris: Editions du Seuil, 1975), p. 127.

6 For example, our nomenclature is basically parallel to that of Genette (S^1 = *comparé*, S^2 = *comparant*, I = *motif*) and to that of the Groupe de Liège (S^1 = *départ*, S^2 – *arrivée*, I = *intermédiaire*). It should be noted that our diagram of metaphor, modeled on that of the Groupe de Liège, differs radically because the group permits only one word as I, thus denying the multiplicity of possible meanings in metaphor.

7 Ricoeur, *Métaphore vive*, p. 217

8 Genette, *Figures III*, p 32. Genette, who in this discussion is showing the range from metaphor to comparison, also includes a fourth term, *modalisateur* (examples: *as, like, resembles*).

9 Pierre Fontanier, *Les Figures du discours* (Paris: Editions Flammarion, 1968), p. 213.

10 Friedrich Nietzsche, "Rhétorique et langage," trans. and ed. P. Lacoue-Labarthe and Jean-Luc Nancy, *Poétique* 5 (1971): 112–27.

11 Michel Le Guern, *Sémantique de la métaphore et de la métonymie* (Paris:

Editions Larousse, 1973), pp. 37–49; Ricoeur, *Métaphore vive*, pp. 228–38.

12 Genette, *Figures III*, p. 25; Todorov, "Synecdocques," p. 28.

CHAPTER 2: SYMBOLIZATION AND FIGURATION

1 Emile Benveniste, *Problèmes de linguistique générale*, 2 vols. (Paris: Editions Gallimard, 1966–74), pp. 86, 87.

2 Both Fontanier and Genette use the term *figure* in a much larger sense than we do. In *Les Figures du discours*, Fontanier defines *figures* as "the stylistic features, forms, turns of phrase . . . by which speech, in the expression of ideas, thoughts, or feelings, moves more or less away from what would have been the simple or usual expression" (64). *Figure* thus functions as a broad category encompassing both tropes (subdivided into *tropes en un mot* and *tropes en plusieurs mots*) and nontropes (*figures de construction, d'élocution, de style*, etc.). Genette uses Fontanier as the basis of his own definition: "The figure as a gap between the sign and meaning, as the internal space of language" (Gérard Genette, *Figures*, Paris: Editions du Seuil, 1966, p. 209); he also accepts the classification of tropes as a subdivision of figures. In developing this opposition between *langage réel* and *langage virtuel*, between what the writer wrote and what he or she thought, Genette defines rhetoric as a purely paradigmatic operation: "Rhetorical form is a surface, that sets the boundaries between the *present* signifier and the *absent* signifier" (210; our italics). Having adopted the point of view of the reader, we prefer not to classify tropes and figures as part of a hierarchy. Rather, we see them as two different yet parallel kinds of rhetorical activity. Our distinction between tropes (paradigmatic) and figures (syntagmatic) seems to coincide with the position suggested, somewhat obliquely, by Todorov: "The confusion that [Freud] makes between, on the one hand, co-present elements and, on the other, absent ones is found again in the inability of rhetoricians to define clearly the difference between trope and figure" (Tzvetan Todorov, *Théories du symbole*, Paris: Editions du Seuil, 1977, p. 316).

3 It might seem that there is a bond between the two signs, but many rhetorical processes are coded into the language or the literary genre, thus permitting the reader to grasp immediately the meaning and to ignore the fact that he or she is unconsciously performing a transformation. The cross, for example, accepted as a symbol (a metonymy), remains a symbol even in the statement "The cross on

which Christ died was made of wood," where the symbolizing
process is spelled out.

4 Tzvetan Todorov, *Symbolisme et interprétation* (Paris: Editions du
Seuil, 1978), p. 18.

5 Todorov proposes as the necessary condition for the start of the
symbolic processes the principle of pertinence: "In order to account
for the starting up of the interpretative process, one must posit at
the beginning that the production and reception of utterances (speech
acts, not sentences) obey a very general rule of pertinence, according to which if an utterance exists, there must be a reason for it.
The result is that, when at first glance a particular utterance does
not obey the rule, the spontaneous reaction of the receiver is to see
if, by a particular manipulation (operation), the aforementioned utterance can reveal its pertinence. 'Interpretation' (still in the narrow
sense of the word) is the name we give to this operation" (Todorov, *Symbolisme*, p. 26). In other words, an initial incompatibility
(lack of pertinence) pushes the reader to perform operations (which
we will show to be rhetorical in nature) to resolve the incompatibility (to establish pertinence). By tying interpretation to the symbolic, Todorov ends up by limiting the effectiveness of his theori-
zations. For example, he quotes this passage from Flaubert's *La
Légende de saint Julien l'Hospitalier*

> On vivait en paix depuis si longtemps, que la herse ne s'abaissait plus;
> les fossés étaient pleins d'eau; des hirondelles faisaient leur nid dans la
> fente des créneaux; et l'archer, qui tout au long du jour se promenait
> sur la courtine, dès que le soleil brillait trop fort rentrait dans l'échau-
> guette, et s'endormait comme un moine.
>
> [They had been living in peace so long that the portcullis was not
> lowered anymore; the moat was full of water; swallows made their
> nests in the lookout slits; and the archer who all day walked along the
> battlements, as soon as the sun got too hot, went back into his watch-
> tower and fell asleep like a monk.]

which he analyzes as follows: "The landscape, the castle, its special
features are not described just to 'be there,' as Robbe-Grillet would
have said, but in order to illustrate an abstract idea, an idea which
in this case is explicitly stated and *therefore does not participate in the
symbolic*" (54; our italics). Thus, Todorov excludes from the symbolic a passage where there is not incompatibility; however, he has
no other category into which to put it, having linked interpretation
exclusively to the symbolic. At the same time, he must admit that

the passage contributes to the meaning of the text; therefore, he suggests a second step in the interpretive process which, since he can't call it symbolic, receives no name, "but whose relationship to what follows forces upon the reader *a kind of interpreting*" (54; our italics). Our notion of incompleteness and our heavy emphasis on figuration are designed, in a sense, to fill the theoretical gap created by Todorov's organizing his system around paradigmatic relationships characterized by incompatibility. We thus rejoin Roland Barthes' position that in a literary text "everything has a meaning or nothing has one" (Barthes, "Introduction à l'analyse structurale des récits," *Communications* 8 [1966]: 7). In order to *complete* each element of a text, the reader seeks to determine its function(s) by relating it to other intratextual (syntagmatic operations) and/or extratextual (paradigmatic operations) elements.

6 It can be argued that the rhetorical operation actually begins with a trope, the metonymy *ses mains*, which are the agents of Hippolyte's distracted mind.

7 François Mauriac, *Thérèse Desqueyroux* (Paris: Editions Bernard Grasset, 1927), p. 11.

8 Todorov, *Symbolisme*, pp. 35, 36.

9 Jacques Prévert, *Paroles* (Paris: Editions Gallimard, 1962), p. 184.

10 In one major study of the question of irony (Wayne Booth's *A Rhetoric of Irony*, Chicago: University of Chicago Press, 1974) the description of a reading process for irony begins rather close to our general notion of tropic reading. For Booth, the first step is the reader's recognition of "some incongruity among the words or between the words and something else he knows" (parallel to our notion of incompatibility). However, Booth then introduces the question of intentionality. He argues that it is only after having decided that the author has intentionally created the incongruity that one moves on to construct a new meaning, one which will be in harmony with these intentions. This new meaning, for Booth, will be different from, but not necessarily opposed to, the original meaning in the text (i.e., Booth does not use opposition as the basic characteristic of irony). We disagree with Booth's analysis on two grounds. First, although we do accept extratextual evidence (i.e., general referential knowledge) as part of the process involved in recognizing and overcoming incompatibility, we do not concern ourselves with writers' intentions. Second, we argue that opposition is the cornerstone of irony, even in the examples given by Booth. Thus, in the sentence "Think it'll rain?" (uttered as the rain

pours down outside), we maintain that there is an understood opposition between "It is not raining now" (the necessary condition for asking a nonironic question about whether it will rain shortly) and "It is raining now" (the actual fact).

11   Alain Robbe-Grillet, *Dans le labyrinthe* (Paris: Editions de Minuit, 1959), p. 9.

12   Wolfgang Iser, *The Act of Reading* (Baltimore: Johns Hopkins University Press, 1978), p. 16.

13   Roland Barthes, *S/Z* (Paris: Editions du Seuil, 1973), pp. 165–66.

14   Harold Bloom, "The Breaking of Form," in *Deconstruction and Criticism* (New York: Seabury Press, 1979), p. 5.

15   Umberto Eco's model reader would probably not encounter any initial confusion or chaos, but this is because Eco barely goes beyond the *fabula*, and the meanings he seeks are lexical and not rhetorical. To be convinced that chaos is a part of reading, one need merely ask students in an introductory literature course to look beyond the plot and see what is "underneath." For a study of student reaction to poetry and the inability to go beyond superficial readings, see Howard Wainer and Peter Schofer, "Measuring the Effects of a Liberal Arts Education on the Perception of Poetry," *American Educational Research Journal*, 14, no. 2 (Spring 1977): 125–35.

CHAPTER 3: THE RHETORIC OF THE SIGNIFIER

1   Christian Metz, *Le Signifiant imaginaire* (Paris: Union générale d'édition, 1977), p. 359.

2   Jean Ricardou, *Pour une théorie du nouveau roman* (Paris: Editions du Seuil, 1971); Jean Ricardou, *Le Nouveau Roman* (Paris: Editions du Seuil, 1973); Jean Ricardou, *Nouveaux Problèmes du roman* (Paris: Editions du Seuil, 1978); Julia Kristeva, *La Révolution du langage poétique* (Paris: Editions du Seuil, 1974); Lucette Finas, *Le Bruit d'Iris* (Paris: Editions Flammarion, 1978).

3   One could well argue that *absolute* synonymy is also impossible on the level of the signifier. Even if the two signs share graphemes, phonemes, typeface, and order, they cannot occupy the same place on the page: i.e., there is always (and necessarily) a typographical difference.

4   A fine line separates similarity (for example, [ʒur], [fur]), inclusion ([ʒur], [ʒurne]), and opposition ([ʒur], [ruʒ]. See the discussions of synecdoche and irony later in this chapter.

5   Ricardou, *Pour une théorie*, p. 223.
6   Ricardou, *Le Nouveau Roman*, p. 84.
7   All French excerpts are from Michel Butor, *Mobile* (Paris: Editions Gallimard, 1962). All English translations are from Michel Butor, *Mobile*, trans. Richard Howard (New York: Simon and Schuster, 1963).
8   Alain Robbe-Grillet, *Le Voyeur* (Paris: Editions de Minuit, 1955), p. 174.
9   Ricardou, *Le Nouveau Roman*, p. 86.
10 Verena Andermatt, "Rodomontages of *Le Ravissement de Lol V. Stein*," *Yale French Studies* 57 (1979): 35.
11 Jonathan Culler, *Ferdinand de Saussure* (New York: Penguin, 1977), p. 118.
12 Ricardou, *Nouveaux Problèmes*, pp. 293, 196.
13 Lynn Anthony Higgins, "Jean Ricardou's Poetics" (Ph.D. diss., University of Minnesota, 1976).
14 Ricardou, *Pour une théorie*, p. 132.
15 For a summary of various theories of sound symbolism and a bibliographic note, see T. Todorov, "Le sens des sons," *Poétique* 11 (1977).
16 Ricardou, *Nouveaux Problèmes*, p. 158.
17 Ibid., p. 157.
18 Stéphane Mallarmé, *Oeuvres complètes* (Paris: Pléiade, 1945), p. 364.

CHAPTER 4: THE RHETORIC OF DISPLACEMENT AND
CONDENSATION

1   Jakobson, *Fundamentals of Language*, p. 81.
2   Lacan, *Ecrits*, p. 511, as translated in *Yale French Studies*, 36–37: 129.
3   J.-F. Lyotard, *Discours, Figure* (Paris: Klincksieck, 1971), p. 256.
4   Metz, *Le Signifiant imaginaire*, p. 271.
5   See, for example, Wilden, *System and Structure*, p. 55.
6   Jean LaPlanche and J.-B. Pontalis, *Vocabulaire de la psychanalyse* (Paris: Presses Universitaires de France, 1973), pp. 117, 89, trans. Donald Nicholson Smith as *Language of Psychoanalysis* (New York: W. W. Norton, 1973), pp. 121–22, 82–83.
7   Sigmund Freud, *Jokes and Their Relation to the Unconscious*, vol. 8 of *The Standard Edition of the Complete Psychological Works of Sigmund Freud*, pp. 163–64. Hereafter cited by page number in the text.

8 Tzvetan Todorov, *Les Genres du discours* (Paris: Editions du Seuil, 1978), p. 290.

9 The idea of decondensation and replacement comes from observations by Jean Bellemin-Noël, *Vers l'inconscient du texte* (Paris: Presses Universitaires de France, 1979), p. 62. He points out that in Swann's dream a single signified "decomposes" into several signifiers. He asks, "Should we speak of decondensation?" and we reply affirmatively.

10 According to our definitions, the Hugo trope *His sheaves* is a metonymy, the product for the producer.

11 Norman Holland (*The Dynamics of Literary Response*, New York: Oxford University Press, 1968) would probably argue that the intellect and the form control the fantasy more than does the individual. There is a point where intellect and fantasy cannot be separated.

12 Antonin Artaud, *L'Ombilic des Limbes* (Paris: Editions Gallimard, 1968), p. 185.

13 Tzvetan Todorov, *Théories du symbole* (Paris: Editions du Seuil, 1977), p. 306.

14 For a striking contrast of the constructions from whole to part and part to whole, the reader need only recall the beginnings of Balzac's *Père Goriot* and Robbe-Grillet's *La Jalousie*. Although no reader could retain all the details of the descriptions, Robbe-Grillet's "house" can be mapped out into a whole; Balzac's description, if mapped out, remains fragmentary on paper, even though readers imagine a "whole."

15 There are fairly common sexual allusions condensed in the word *bijoux*, among them Diderot's "bijoux indiscrets" and the expression "bijoux de famille" [family jewels].

CHAPTER 5: RHETORICAL READING

1 Susan R. Suleiman and Inge Crossman, eds., *The Reader in the Text* (Princeton: Princeton University Press, 1980), p. 3. Hereafter cited by page number in the text.

2 Iser, *The Act of Reading*, p. 22.

3 For a detailed analysis of Barthes's use of rhetoric and of the paradoxes of *S/Z*, see our "Barthes's *S/Z*: Rhetoric and Open Reading," in *L'Esprit créateur* 22, no. 1 (Spring 1982).

4 Finas, *Le Bruit d'Iris*, p. 137.

5 Norman Holland, *The Dynamics of Literary Response* (New York: Oxford University Press, 1968), esp. pp. 3–159.

6 Roland Barthes, *Le Plaisir du texte* (Paris: Editions du Seuil, 1973), and Julia Kristeva, *Polylogue* (Paris: Editions du Seuil, 1977).

7 Kristeva, *Polylogue*, and Lyotard, *Discours, Figure*.

8 LaPlanche and Pontalis, *Vocabulaire de la psychanalyse*, trans. Smith as *The Language of Psychoanalysis*, p. 223.

CHAPTER 6: BALZAC'S DUCHESS

1 Honoré de Balzac, *La Duchesse de Langeais*, in *La Comédie humaine*, vol. 5, ed. Pierre-Georges Castex (Paris: Bibliothèque de la Pléiade, 1977), p. 923. Hereafter cited by page number in the text. English translations are based on Balzac, *History of the Thirteen*, trans. Herbert J. Hunt (London: Penguin, 1974). We have at times changed the wording of the Hunt translation to follow more closely the original French.

2 The original edition, published in 1834, is divided into four chapters: "La Soeur Thérèse" (p. 905 in the Pléiade edition), "L'Amour dans la paroisse de Saint-Thomas d'Aquin" (p. 923), "La Femme vraie" (p. 987), and "Dieu fait les dénouements" (p. 1031).

3 The metaphor of a parent-child relationship is explicit in the text. At one point during the early stages of the courtship, Montriveau acknowledges his role as a child:

> — Mon Dieu, s'écria-t-il, je suis comme un enfant.
> — Un enfant volontaire et bien gâté, dit-elle, en caressant l'épaisse chevelure de cette tête qu'elle garda sur ses genoux. . . .
> — Pour-quoi ne pas rester ainsi? pourquoi ne pas me sacrifier des désirs qui m'offensent? (978–79)

> ["My God!" he cried. "I am like a child."
> "A willing and spoiled child," she said, stroking the thick hair of his head which she kept on her lap. . . .
> "Why not keep things like this? Why not sacrifice to my desires which offend me?"].

The duchess thus wishes to continue playing the role of mother, as a protection against his sexual desires. After the kidnapping the roles reverse. The duchess exclaims: "Oui, je suis une enfant, ton enfant, tu viens de me créer" (999) [Yes, I'm a child, your child, you have just created me]. Montriveau now plays the role of the father (her creator), lecturing her and repressing his sexual attraction.

4 The rhetorical traces explored in this chapter all depend on the signifieds of the text. The homonymy in French between *hache* [axe] and the letter *H*—both are pronounced [aʃ]—suggests a possible play with the signifier. The letter *H* is characterized by its contradictory nature. No longer pronounced in spoken French, it is at once present as a grapheme and absent as a phoneme. As such, it can be metaphorically linked to the aristocracy, still present in France, yet absent from its rightful place in society. Another possible trace is suggested by the family name of the duchess, Antoinette de Navarreins. By synecdoche, one finds in Navarreins the word *Navarre*, which then leads to the *H* of Henri. Henri de Navarre, Henri IV, was one of the great kings of France, a powerful leader who succeeded in reestablishing the power of the monarchy. A similar play with the letter *H* leads to the *H* of Honoré de Balzac. For those who see in *La Duchesse de Langeais* a fictionalized account of Balzac's "affair" with the marquise de Castries, *ne touchez pas à l(a)'hache* suggests a vengeance and a warning to future objects of his attention: "Don't play around with Balzac!"

5 Montriveau's potential stems from the fact that he was a man whose life had been "une suite de poésies en action" (908) [a series of poems in action]. Cf. Balzac's *Père Goriot*, where Vautrin says to Rastignac: "Je suis un grand poète. Mes poésies, je ne les écris pas: elles consistent en actions et en sentiments" [I am a great poet. I do not write my poems: they consist of actions and feelings]. For Balzac, the word *poème* contrasts negatively with *poésies*. In *Goriot*, Vautrin is described as "un poème infernal" [a hellish poem] after his capture, i.e., when he has been at least temporarily rendered inactive. Similarly, in the first version of *La Duchesse de Langeais*, Montriveau, looking back on his failed adventure with the duchess, says: "Ça n'a été pour moi qu'un poème!" [That for me was only a poem!].

CHAPTER 7. BAUDELAIRE'S JEWELS

1 Stéphane Mallarmé, *Propos sur la poésie*, ed. Henri Mondor (Monaco: Editions de Roche, 1953), p. 47.

2 Judd Hubert, *L'Esthétique de "Fleurs du mal"* (Geneva: Pierre Cailler, 1953); Leo Bersani, *Baudelaire and Freud* (Berkeley and Los Angeles: University of California Press, 1977). Hereafter cited by page number in the text.

3 In order not to upset his storyline, Hubert attenuates the activity
   of the jewels in the opening stanzas by referring to them as "inanimate," even though, metonymically, they can be read very easily
   as the instruments of the woman, who activates them for the poet.
   Likewise, he attributes the words *air vainqueur* to the jewels (they
   attract and distract the poet), not to the woman. The verbs of vision and references to the eyes (*mes yeux clairvoyants, je croyais voir
   . . .*), when referring to the poet, are passive and detached. A key
   word in Hubert's interpretation is *pour* in *pour troubler le repos* and
   pour la déranger. He interprets the *pour* to mean "in order to," as
   part of the instrumentality of seduction. Finally, in the last stanza,
   Hubert does not, and cannot, establish a metonymic link between
   inondait de sang and the poet, since he insists on relating the resig-
   nation of the lamp to the poet's gaze.
   While Bersani also must make metonymic suppressions and transformations similar to those of Hubert, the most interesting one
   appears in his own text, when he states that "the loved one is 'broken up' into shifting, partial designs" (65). By whom is she broken
   up? Who is the agent of her disintegration? It is crucial to Bersani's
   interpretation that the apparently passive man-poet be the agent,
   the producer of the fragmentation. The man-poet produces fragmentation through the desires of hs vision-fantasy, which must be
   active. For Bersani, the *pour* of lines 21 and 23, rather than stating
   a cause ("in order to"), as in Hubert, is a consequence of the man-
   poet's own causal chains: the creation of his fantasy turns on him.
4 Martin Turnell, *Baudelaire: A Study of his Poetry* (New York: New
   Directions, 1972), p. 111.
5 One exception is Martin Turnell, who observes that, at the end of
   the poem, "the curtain is lowered after a splendid performance, but
   there is no connection" (111).
6 Roman Jakobson and M. Hall, *Fundamentals of Language*, and Hayden White, *Metahistory: The Historical Imagination in Nineteenth-
   Century Europe* (Baltimore: Johns Hopkins University Press, 1973).
7 Michael Riffaterre provides a reading complementary to ours in
   which he stresses the "metonymies" of part and whole. He argues
   that "l'expression est donc le mécanisme par lequel la phrase passe
   du narratif au descriptif, de l'énoncé non motivé à une représenta-
   tion vraisemblable, ou aussi capable de susciter des émotions que la
   chose représenté. . . . Baudelaire décrit une banale scène d'alcôve
   qu'on pourrait résumer un peu crûment ainsi: *elle essayait des poses
   érotiques pour m'exciter*. Cette phrase nucléaire, nous la trouvons

d'ailleurs, sous sa forme minimale, dans le texte même deux vers avant celles qui en sont dérivées: *elle essayait des poses* (v. 14)." By selecting as the "phrase nucléaire" the words *elle essayait des poses*, Riffaterre proves our point that all reading, even his, is partial and implies repressing parts of the text while valorizing others. By repressing line 7 and emphasizing line 14, Riffaterre underlines the poet's passivity at the expense of active violence. We may also infer that there is no absolute "phrase nucléaire" or matrix in texts and that different readers select different "key" parts.

For his full argument, see Michael Riffaterre, *La Production du texte* (Paris: Editions du Seuil, 1979), pp. 58–60, and *Semiotics of Poetry* (Bloomington: Indiana University Press, 1978), pp. 51–53.

CHAPTER 8: MALLARMÉ'S CLOWN

1 Robert Greer Cohen, *Toward the Poems of Mallarmé* (Berkeley and Los Angeles: University of California Press, 1965), p. 37.

2 Guy Michaud, *Mallarmé*, trans. Marie Collins and Bertha Humez (New York: New York University Press, 1964), pp. 25–27.

3 Barbara Johnson, *The Critical Difference: Essays in the Contemporary Rhetoric of Reading* (Baltimore: Johns Hopkins University Press, 1980), p. 65.

4 Finas, *Le Bruit d'Iris*, p. 138.

5 Reading of the graphic properties of the letter itself, although not common, is not without precedence: Lucette Finas, in her multifaceted reading of the *Le Pitre châtié*, projects the *Y* onto its side in a literal figuration of the one-legged, two-armed swimmer. For a more extensive reading of graphic signifiers, see Tom Conley, "Verbal Shape in the Poetry of Villon and Marot," *Visible Language* 9, no. 2 (Spring 1975): 101–22 and Jean-Claude Coquet, "La Lettre et les idéogrammes occidentaux," *Sémiotique littéraire* (Paris: Mame, 1973), pp. 131–45.

6 One might well object that such play with numbers is gratuitous. In this particular case, we argue that the numerical reading is doubly overdetermined: the 1 and 2, as will be seen, enter into traces with other elements of the text, and those familiar with Mallarmé's *Le Livre* will recognize the great interest he had in numbers.

7 *Mauvais* could also be read as *mot V*. On the one hand, such a reading fits the trace involving graphic signifiers, the interplay between *V* and *Y* and *A*. On the other hand, in this particular line, the reading of *mauvais V* is reinforced by the *A bon(s)*.

8 At the same time, however, if one listens only to the phonetic signifier, one hears a bilingual play between the French *C* ([se], *c'est*)
and the English *C* ([si], *si*), which might encourage us to search for
other bilingual plays. The first word in the poem, *yeux*, in English,
eyes, can thus produce the grapheme *I* (key trait in the graphic games
with *A* and *Y*). The phonetic value of this *I* in French ([i]) leads to
the English grapheme *E*. Continuing the paradigmatic chain, [e]
gives the English A, which in turn leads to the French [a]. The
reader can thus produce the three graphic vowels of the title (*EIA*)
as well as the three major vowel sounds of the poem ([i] [e] [a]).

9 Phonetically, the central consonant of this stanza (as well as of the
poem) is the [r]. According to the *théories pulsionnelles* of Fonagy,
the [r], by its articulation dependent on the position of the tongue
(metaphorically linked to the phallus), represents the investment of
the phallus. From the first line of the poem, however, the [r] has
been juxtaposed to consonants with opposed investments: *ivresse*
[r] + [v] (fricative produced by the lips) vs. *renaître* [r] + t] (occlu-
sive produced by the activity of the glottal sphincter). In the first
stanza, the anal-phallic [tr] dominated; in the second, the oral-phallic
[vr], [nr], and [rʒ] assert themselves more strongly. Thus, one has
the potential for a conflict between anal-phallic agressivity and oral-
phallic regression.

10 To the reader familiar with Mallarmé's *Crise de vers*, an extratextual
explanation for these metaphors can be found in Mallarmé's theory
of the "incompatibility" between the signifiers and the signifieds of
many words (ex., *jour* and *nuit*). It is as if he wished to compensate
for the "dullness" of soleil [sɔlɛj]—two opposing vowels slightly
open, one front, the other back, trapped between consonants and
semiconsonants—by accompanying the word with signifieds suggesting force, sound, brilliance, and activity. Such compensatory
work can be read also on the level of the signifier. The verse is
dominated by the vowels [i] and a], front spread vowels located at
the extremes of articulation ([i], very closed; [a], very open). The
consonants—[l], [r], [t], [b], [p]—can be inserted in traces stem-
ming from *Les Mots anglais* (where Mallarmé associates these sounds
with strength, activity, and domination) and in the trace coming
from Fonagy (anal-phallic investment).

11 Moreover, the oral-phallic investment of the [rf], in this final appearance of the [r] in the poem, is captured (surrounded) by the
anal-phallic investment of [p] and [d]: the castrating power of the
father triumphs.

12 Most of Mallarmé's commentators read the *pitre*, either directly or

indirectly, as a metaphor of the poet and propose as a central theme his quest for purity, the Ideal. See, for example, Pierre Beausire, *Mallarmé: Poésie et poétique* (Lausanne: Mermod, 1949); Michaud, *Mallarmé*; E. Noulet, *L'Oeuvre poétique de Stéphane Mallarmé* (Brussels: Jacques Antoine, 1940; reprint ed., 1974); Frederic C. St. Aubyn, *Stéphane Mallarmé* (New York: Twayne, 1969); Pierre-Olivier Walzer, *Mallarmé* (Paris: Seghers, 1963). Wallace Fowlie extends the meaning of the poem beyond the plight of the poet to that of any man in his relationship to a vocation (Wallace Fowlie, *Mallarmé*, Chicago: University of Chicago Press, 1953). For a reading which treats the *pitre* as a clown (rather than as a metaphor for something else), see Will McClendon, "A New Reading of Mallarmé's *Pitre châtié*," *Symposium* 24 no. 1 (1970): 36–45.

13 This reading was initially suggested to us by analysis of the signifiers, what we have called "the adventure of the [r]." Phonemically, the rhyme scheme is dominated by the phonemes [r], [e], [t], and [k]. The [r], carrying the phallic investment, finds itself between the [e], oral investment, and the [t] [k], anal investment. This situation suggests that of the *pitre-son*, torn between the orality associated with the mother (nursing at the breast, a stage in the regression to the womb) and the anality associated with the father (agressivity and control, a stage in the formation of the superego). This drama is played out as the [r], the phallic investment of the son, is combined throughout the poem with various other consonants. At the end, however, the oral-phallic investment which carried the son toward the mother finds itself surrounded by the anal-phallic investment of the father (*père*-fide). Simultaneously, the graphemes play out the same drama. The *R* of the title searches for the *O* (mother, womb) only to find, upon arriving at the final verse, the presence of the *I* (father, phallus). The result is the symbolic castration of the son in *glaciers*.

14 Barthes, *Le Plaisir du texte*, pp. 37–38.

CHAPTER 9: SIMON'S LESSON

1 Boris Tomashevsky indirectly underlines the principle of synecdochal continuity with his notion of *motivation*: "Not a single property may remain unused in the telling, and no episode may be without influence on the situation" (*Russian Formalist Criticism: Four Essays*, trans. Lee Lemon and Marian Reis, Lincoln: University of Nebraska Press, 1965, p. 79).

2 Even a novel with a chronology as complex as Michel Butor's *La*

Modification—which intermingles one present, two future, and six past narrative sequences—is ultimately reintegratable.

3 All page references are to Claude Simon, *Leçon de choses* (Paris: Editions de Minuit, 1975); the translations are ours.

4 The following reading of the novel takes as a starting point the perspective of a reader unfamiliar with the techniques of reading a "New Novel." Certainly, as numerous writers and critics have pointed out, every novel creates to some extent its own readers. The New Novel, in existence in France under various guises since the early 1950s, has formed a group of readers capable of dealing with it on its own terms—i.e., without trying to discover a coherent plot, true-to-life characters, a recognizable setting, etc. On the other hand, there remain a large number of readers who resist the changes required by the New Novel, who persist in reading metonymically and synecdochally. Moreover, to a certain degree, many New Novels need this initial "misreading," for they are written, so to speak, *against* the traditional narrative and its mode of being read. Thus, it is by frustrating attempts at reading traditionally that the New Novel attempts to undermine the very nature of its predecessor. Consequently, by adopting initially a "naïve" point of view for our reading, we can re-create the reading situation of someone confronting a New Novel for the first time and also underline what is "new" about this different kind of narrative.

5 A traditional narrative covers temporal gaps in the narration by the use of transitional phrases—"an hour passed," "the next day," "three months later," etc.

6 The term "capture" is used by Jean Ricardou in *Le Nouveau Roman*, Ecrivains de toujours (Paris: Editions du Seuil, 1973), p. 112. He distinguishes two kinds of mutations: supposedly real events being "captured" by an image, and images being "liberated" by their transformation into "real" scenes. The walk sequence illustrates the alternation of the two processes.

7 For a more complete discussion of these oppositions, see the following readings of *Leçon de choses*: Colette Gaudin, "Niveaux de lisibilité dans *Leçon de choses* de Claude Simon," *Romanic Review* 68, no. 3 (1977): 175–96; François Jost, "Les Aventures du lecteur," *Poétique* 29 (1977): 77–89; Thomas O'Donnell, "Claude Simon's *Leçon de choses*: Myth and Ritual Displaced," *International Fiction Review* 5, no. 2 (1978): 137–42; Stuart Sykes, *Les Romans de Claude Simon* (Paris: Editions de Minuit, 1979).

8 O'Donnell, "Simon's *Leçon de choses*," p. 136.

9 The final section of *Leçon de choses*, "Courts-circuits," appears at
first to be an exact repetition of the opening pages of the novel.
Slight changes in wording, however, signal a relationship of similarity rather than of identity.

Bibliography

Barthes, Roland. "Elements de sémiologie." *Communications* 4 (1964): 91–135.

Barthes, Roland. "Introduction à l'analyse structurale des récits." *Communications* 8 (1966): 1–27.

Barthes, Roland. *Le Plaisir du texte*. Paris: Editions du Seuil, 1973.

Barthes, Roland. *Système de la mode*. Paris: Editions du Seuil, 1967.

Barthes, Roland. *S/Z*. Paris: Editions du Seuil, 1970.

Bellemin-Noël, Jean. *Vers l'inconscient du texte*. Paris: Presses Universitaires de France, 1979.

Benveniste, Emile. *Problèmes de linguistique générale*. 2 vols. Paris: Editions Gallimard, 1966–74.

Bersani, Leo. *Baudelaire and Freud*. Berkeley and Los Angeles: University of California Press, 1977.

Black, Max. *Models and Metaphors*. Ithaca: Cornell University Press, 1962.

Bloom, Harold. *A Map of Misreading*. New York: Oxford University Press, 1975.

Bloom, Harold. *Poetry and Repression: Revisionism From Blake to Stevens*. New Haven: Yale University Press, 1976.

Bloom, Harold, et al. *Deconstruction and Criticism*. New York: Seabury Press, 1979.

Booth, Wayne. *The Rhetoric of Fiction*. Chicago: University of Chicago Press, 1961.

Booth, Wayne. *A Rhetoric of Irony*. Chicago: University of Chicago Press, 1974.

Burke, Kenneth. *A Grammar of Motives*. New York: Prentice-Hall, 1954.

Burke, Kenneth. *The Philosophy of Literary Form: Studies in Symbolic Action*. Berkeley and Los Angeles: University of California Press, 1974.

Cohen, Jean. *Structure du langage poétique*. Paris: Editions Flammarion, 1966.

Cohen, Robert Greer. *Toward the Poems of Mallarmé*. Berkeley and Los Angeles: University of California Press, 1965.

Culler, Jonathan. *Structuralist Poetics*. Ithaca: Cornell University Press, 1975.

Davidson, Donald. "What Metaphors Mean." In *On Metaphor*, edited by Sheldon Sacks. Chicago: University of Chicago Press, 1978.

Derrida, Jacques. *La Dissémination*. Paris: Editions du Seuil, 1972.

Derrida, Jacques. *L'Ecriture et la différence*. Paris: Editions du Seuil, 1967.

DuBois, Jacques, et al. *Rhétorique générale*. Paris: Editions Larousse, 1970.

Dumarsais, César. *Les Tropes*. Paris, 1730. Facsimile ed., Geneva: Slatkine, 1967.

Eco, Umberto. *The Role of the Reader*. Bloomington: Indiana University Press, 1979.

Eco, Umberto. *A Theory of Semiotics*. Bloomington: Indiana University Press, 1976.

Finas, Lucette. *Le Bruit d'Iris*. Paris: Editions Flammarion, 1978.

Fish, Stanley. *Is There a Text in This Classroom? The Authority of Interpretive Communities*. Cambridge: Harvard University Press, 1980.

Fontanier, Pierre. *Les Figures du discours*. Paris: Editions Flammarion, 1968.

Foucault, Michel. *Les Mots et les choses: une archéologie des sciences humaines*. Paris: Editions Gallimard, 1966.

Freud, Sigmund. *The Standard Edition of the Complete Psychological Works of Sigmund Freud*. Edited by James Strachey. 23 vols. London: Hogarth Press, 1953–66.

Genette, Gérard. *Figures*. Paris: Editions du Seuil, 1966.

Genette, Gérard. *Figures II*. Paris: Editions du Seuil, 1969.

Genette, Gérard. *Figures III*. Paris: Editions du Seuil, 1972.

Grammont, Maurice. *Le Vers français, ses moyens d'expression, son harmonie*. Paris: A. Picard et fils, 1904.

Grice, H. P. "Logic and Conversation." In *Syntax and Semantics*, edited by P. Cole and J. L. Morgan. New York: Academic Press, 1975.

Grice, H. P. "Meaning." *Philosophical Review* 66 (1954): 377–88.

Harari, Josué V., ed. *Textual Strategies: Perspectives in Post-Structuralist Criticism*. Ithaca: Cornell University Press, 1979.

Henry, Albert. *Métonymie et métaphore*. Paris: Klincksieck, 1971.

Hirsch, E. D. *The Aims of Interpretation*. Chicago: University of Chicago Press, 1976.

Hirsch, E. D. *Validity in Interpretation*. New Haven: Yale University Press, 1967.

Holland, Norman. *The Dynamics of Literary Response*. New York: Oxford University Press, 1968.

Bibliography

Hubert, J. D. *L'Esthétique des "Fleurs du mal"*. Geneva: Pierre Cailler, 1953.

Iser, Wolfgang. *The Act of Reading*. Baltimore: Johns Hopkins University Press, 1978.

Iser, Wolfgang. *The Implied Reader: Patterns of Communication in Prose Fiction from Bunyan to Beckett*. Baltimore: Johns Hopkins University Press, 1974.

Jakobson, Roman. *Essais de linguistique générale*. 2 vols. Paris: Editions de Minuit, 1963–73.

Jakobson, Roman, and M. Hall. *Fundamentals of Language*. The Hague: Mouton, 1956.

Johnson, Barbara. *The Critical Difference: Essays in the Contemporary Rhetoric of Reading*. Baltimore: Johns Hopkins University Press, 1980.

Kellner, Hans. "The Inflatable Trope as Narrative Theory: Structure or Allegory?" *Diacritics* 11 (Spring 1981): 14–28.

Kristeva, Julia. *Polylogue*. Paris: Editions du Seuil, 1977.

Kristeva, Julia. *La Révolution du langage poétique*. Paris: Editions du Seuil, 1974.

Lacan, Jacques. *Ecrits*. Paris: Editions du Seuil, 1966.

Lacan, Jacques. *The Language of the Self*. Translated by Anthony Wilden. Baltimore: Johns Hopkins University Press, 1968.

LaPlanche, Jean and J.-B. Pontalis. *The Language of Psycho-Analysis*. Translated by Donald Nicholson-Smith. New York: W. W. Norton and Co., 1973.

Le Guern, Michel. *Sémantique de la métaphore et de la métonymie*. Paris: Editions Larousse, 1973.

Lemaire, Anika. *Jacques Lacan*. Brussels: Mardaga, 1977.

Lévi-Strauss, Claude. *The Savage Mind*. Chicago: University of Chicago Press, 1966.

Lewis, Thomas. "Notes toward a Theory of the Referent." *PMLA* 94 (May 1979): 459–73.

Littérature 18 (May 1975). Entire issue devoted to rhetoric.

Lodge, David. *The Modes of Modern Writing: Metaphor, Metonymy, and the Typology of Literature*. Ithaca: Cornell University Press, 1977.

Lyotard, Jean-François. *Discours, Figure*. Paris: Klincksieck, 1971.

Man, Paul de. *Blindness and Insight: Essays in the Rhetoric of Contemporary Criticism*. New York: Oxford University Press, 1971.

Man, Paul de. "Semiology and Rhetoric." *Diacritics* 3 (1973): 27–33.

Mehlman, Jeffrey. "Entre psychanalyse et psychocritique." *Poétique* 3 (1970): 365–85.

Merrell, Floyd. "Of Metaphor and Metonymy." *Semiotica* 31, nos. 3/4 (1980): 289–307.

Metz, Christian. *Le Signifiant imaginaire*. Paris: Union générale d'édition, 1977.

Michaud, Guy. *Mallarmé*. Translated by Marie Collins and Bertha Humez. New York: New York University Press, 1964.

Morin, Edgar. *La Méthode: la nature de la nature*. Paris: Editions du Seuil, 1977.

Mounin, Georges. *Clefs pour la sémantique*. Paris: Seghers, 1972.

Nasio, Juan David. "Métaphore et phallus." In Serge Leclaire, *Démasquer le réel*. Paris: Editions du Seuil, 1971.

New Literary History 9, no. 3 (Spring 1978). Entire issue devoted to rhetorical analysis.

Nietzsche, Friederich. "Rhétorique et langage." Translated and edited by Philippe Lacoue-Labarthe and Jean-Luc Nancy. *Poétique* 5 (1971): 99–142.

Perleman, Ch., and L. Olrechts-Tyteca. *La Nouvelle Rhétorique: traité de l'argumentation*. Paris: Presses universitaires de France, 1958.

Poétique 36 (November 1978). Entire issue devoted to irony.

Rhétoriques sémiologiques. Paris: Union générale d'édition, 1979.

Ricardou, Jean. *Le Nouveau Roman*. Paris: Editions du Seuil, 1973.

Ricardou, Jean. *Nouveaux Problèmes du roman*. Paris: Editions du Seuil, 1978.

Ricardou, Jean. *Pour une théorie du nouveau roman*. Paris: Editions du Seuil, 1971.

Richards, I. A. *The Philosophy of Rhetoric*. New York: Oxford University Press, 1936.

Ricoeur, Paul. *La Métaphore vive*. Paris: Editions du Seuil, 1975.

Riffaterre, Michael. *Essais de stylistique structurale*. Paris: Editions Flammarion, 1971.

Riffaterre, Michael. *La Production du texte*. Paris: Editions du Seuil, 1979.

Riffaterre, Michael. *Semiotics of Poetry*. Bloomington: Indiana University Press, 1978.

Rosalato, Guy. *Essais sur le symbolique*. Paris: Editions Gallimard, 1969.

Rosalato, Guy. "Symbol Formation." *International Journal of Psycho-Analysis* 59 (1978): 303–13.

Ruegg, Maria. "Metaphor and Metonymy: The Logic of Structuralist Rhetoric." *Glyph* 6 (Baltimore: The Johns Hopkins University Press, 1979): 141–57.

Ruwet, Nicolas. "Synecdoques et métonymies." *Poétique* 23 (1975): 371–88.

Schofer, Peter, and Donald Rice. "Metaphor, Metonymy, and Synecdoche Revis(it)ed." *Semiotica* 21, nos. 1/2 (1977): 122–49.

Schofer, Peter, and Donald Rice. "Tropes and Figures: Symbolization and Figuration." *Semiotica* 35, nos. 1/2 (1981): 93–124.

Serres, Michel. *L'Interférence*. Paris: Editions de Minuit, 1972.

Shapiro, Michael, and Mariane Shapiro. *Hierarchy and the Structure of Tropes*. Bloomington and Lisse: Research Center for Language and Semiotic Studies, with the Peter de Ridder Press, 1976.

Suleiman, Susan R., and Inge Crossman, eds. *The Reader in the Text*. Princeton: Princeton University Press, 1980.

Todorov, Tzvetan. *Les Genres du discours*. Paris: Editions du Seuil, 1978.

Todorov, Tzvetan. *Symbolisme et interprétation*. Paris: Editions du Seuil, 1978.

Todorov, Tzvetan. "Synecdoques." *Communications* 16 (1970): 26–35.

Todorov, Tzvetan. *Théories du symbole*. Paris: Editions du Seuil, 1977.

Tompkins, Jane. ed. *Reader-Response Criticism: From Formalism to Post-Structuralism*. Baltimore: Johns Hopkins University Press, 1980.

Turnell, Martin. *Baudelaire: A Study of His Poetry*. New York: New Directions, 1972.

Vico, Giambattista. *The New Science*. Translated by Thomas Goddard Bergin and Max Harold Fisch. Ithaca: Cornell University Press, 1948.

Wainer, Howard, and Peter Schofer. "Measuring the Effects of a Liberal Arts Education on the Perception of Poetry." *American Educational Research Journal* 14, no. 2 (Spring 1977): 125–35.

White, Eugene E., ed. *Rhetoric in Transition: Studies in the Nature and Uses of Rhetoric*. University Park, Pa.: University of Pennsylvania Press, 1980.

White, Hayden. *Metahistory: The Historical Imagination in Nineteenth-Century Europe*. Baltimore: Johns Hopkins University Press, 1973.

White, Hayden. *Tropics of Discourse: Essays in Cultural Criticism*. Baltimore: Johns Hopkins University Press, 1978.

Wilden, Anthony. *System and Structure: Essays on Communication and Exchange*. London: Tavistock, 1972.

Williams, Linda. "Hiroshima and Marienbad: Metaphor and Metonymy." *Screen* 17, no. 1 (1976): 34–39.

Yale French Studies 55/56 (1977). Entire issue devoted to literature and psychoanalysis.

Index

JACKET DESIGNED BY QUENTIN FIORE
COMPOSED BY GRAPHIC COMPOSITION, INC., ATHENS, GEORGIA
MANUFACTURED BY THOMSON-SHORE, INC., DEXTER, MICHIGAN
TEXT AND DISPLAY LINES ARE SET IN BEMBO

Library of Congress Cataloging in Publication Data
Rice, Donald.
Rhetorical poetics.
Bibliography: p.
Includes index.
1. French literature—History and criticism.
2. Rhetoric.   3. French language—Style.   I. Schofer,
Peter, 1941–   .   II. Title.
PQ226.R52   1983   840'.9   83–47768
ISBN 0–299–09440–5